Global Research Strategy
and
International Competitiveness

Global Research Strategy
and
International Competitiveness

Edited by Mark Casson

Basil Blackwell

Copyright © Basil Blackwell Limited 1991

First published 1991

Basil Blackwell Ltd
108 Cowley Road, Oxford, OX4 1JF, UK

Basil Blackwell, Inc.
3 Cambridge Center
Cambridge, Massachusetts 02142, USA

British Library Cataloguing in Publication Data
A CIP catalogue record for this book is available from the British Library.

Library of Congress Cataloging in Publication Data
Global research strategy and international competitiveness/edited by
Mark Casson.
    p. cm. – (ESRC competitiveness series)
    'This book reports the results of a two-year project carried out
at the Department of Economics, University of Reading, 1988–9'-Pref.
    Includes bibliographical references (p. 297) and index.
    ISBN 0–631–18023–0:
    1. Research–Methodology. I. Casson, Mark, 1945–xxxx.
II. Series.
Q180.55.M4G46 1991
338.9'26–dc20
90–23083 CIP

Typeset in 10 on 12pt Sabon
by Mathematical Composition Setters Ltd, Salisbury
Printed in Great Britain by T.J. Press (Padstow) Ltd, Padstow, Cornwall

Contents

Preface and Acknowledgements

This book reports the results of a two-year project carried out at the Department of Economics, University of Reading 1988–9. It is a pleasure to thank the Economic and Social Research Council (ESRC) for their financial support under Phase Two of their Competitiveness Initiative. The programme was coordinated by Arthur Francis, Imperial College, London, and we are grateful to him for his advice and support. Other research groups participating in the initiative supplied useful suggestions at various stages of the work. Discussions with Peter Buckley, V.N. Balasubramanyam and T. Nguyen were particularly useful. The work of the other groups will be published separately in this series. Thanks are also due to our colleagues Colin Ash, Peter Hart, Geoff Jones and Allan Webster, and to François Chesnais and Monty Graham, for comments on various drafts of the report. A preliminary version of chapter 4 was presented at a Conference of the Industrial Economics Study Group, and early versions of chapters 4, 6 and 8 were presented to the Conference on Technology Management and International Business in Stockholm, June, 1990. In each case valuable comments were received from the participants.

The project benefited greatly from a cooperative arrangement with the Science Policy Research Unit (SPRU), University of Sussex, for the exchange of data. In return for access to the International Business database at Reading, SPRU made available their comprehensive patent database, which proved invaluable to our research. Thanks are due to Keith Pavitt and Pari Patel for transferring the data (and their know-how) so readily.

A special acknowledgement must be made to the research directors who gave up their time to be interviewed. We were treated most hospitably by the interviewees, and were often given a tour of the laboratory too. This was true even in cases where the laboratory was being closed down and when the company was up for sale! We are also grateful to the directors who attended the mini-conference we organized at Reading in January 1990, and who provided us with very useful feedback on an early draft of this work. Some of the directors were kind enough to comment on the finished report as well.

The management of the project involved a significant division of labour. John Cantwell liaised with the ESRC and SPRU and also assumed responsibility for analysing the patent data with the assistance of Christian Hodson. Bob Pearce was responsible for the design of the questionnaire, in conjunction with Satwinder Singh, who took primary responsibility for the statistical analysis of the responses. Satwinder Singh also conducted most of the interviews. John Dunning provided advice on policy issues in the early stage of the research. Mark Casson assumed responsibility for the production of the report.

Finally, we would like to thank Linda Graves for acting as secretary to the project, and putting up with our varied idiosyncrasies in so cheerful a manner. A final version of the report was typed by Jill Turner to a very tight deadline, and we would like to thank her for producing such an immaculate typescript from our untidy drafts.

1

Introduction

1.1 KEY ISSUES

Can a country's international competitiveness be improved by better management of research and development (R&D)? If so, what are the appropriate policies for firms and for government? These questions are difficult to answer without a thorough understanding of international business practice. Much of the privately funded research in high-technology industries is undertaken by multinational enterprises (MNEs). Technology developed in the firm's laboratories can be simultaneously exploited in several different producing countries. The firm's 'internal market' in know-how facilitates international technology transfer and promotes the spatial disassociation of production and R&D (Buckley and Casson, 1976; Dunning, 1977).

It is often assumed that MNEs are structured as spatial hierarchies, in which key functions are centralized and only routine activities are dispersed. There is certainly a tendency towards centralization in areas such as finance and personnel (Brooke, 1984) but in other respects the hierarchical view is misleading. This is certainly the case with R&D. In large firms R&D is not necessarily concentrated in a single headquarters laboratory. Some major firms decentralize research activities, creating a network of laboratories in different countries. Overseas laboratories may enjoy considerable autonomy – they are not necessarily subordinated to a single central facility. The decentralization of R&D effects a further separation of activities. A firm headquartered in one country may carry out research in a second country and produce the resulting product in a third country. The fact that a firm is headquartered in a country is no longer a guarantee that it will carry out its research there. It may be attracted to another country which offers a better research environment. This country will then be the one most likely to benefit from the initial export of the product.

Should foreign-owned research facilities be welcomed? Do they create useful employment, or merely crowd out indigenous research activity by taking scientists away from local firms? Are they merely listening posts trying to steal ideas from indigenous firms or are they instead carrying out basic research from which local firms can benefit? Does foreign-owned R&D attract foreign-owned production, and is such production desirable in order to enhance export performance?

Now consider the same questions the other way round. Should indigenous firms be encouraged to set up research laboratories overseas? Will this strengthen the core research of the indigenous firm by allowing it to tap into centres of excellence in overseas universities and research institutes? Or does it merely export jobs and erode the science base of the home economy? Will overseas R&D strengthen exports by helping the firm to adapt its products better to the overseas market, or will such refinement simply encourage the shifting of all its activities abroad? In other words, is overseas R&D a key factor in global competitive strategy, or just 'the thin end of the wedge' in splitting the firm completely away from its national base?

The present study aims to provide an informed assessment of how far the internationalization of corporate R&D should be encouraged. It suggests that the economic forces promoting internationalization are virtually unstoppable. The economic factors are similar to those that have promoted the internationalization of production in the past – although in the case of R&D they manifest themselves in a somewhat different way. The policies of both individual firms and nation states will be crucial in determining how the costs and benefits of this development are distributed. The coordination of intra-corporate networks of R&D requires considerable management skill (Bartlett and Ghoshal, 1990;

Håkanson, 1990) – successful coordination of R&D, it is argued, depends crucially on the quality of corporate culture. Corporate R&D is likely to agglomerate around major international centres of excellence, and national governments have considerable power to influence whether such a centre of excellence develops (or is sustainable) in their country.

The arguments supporting these conclusions are developed step-wise through the book. This introductory chapter aims to clarify the key concepts of 'competitiveness' and 'R&D', and to elaborate the policy issues outlined above. It also presents a range of historical and statistical material which helps to set the specific issue of global R&D within a wider context.

1.2   THE CONCEPT OF R&D

R&D is closely allied to innovation, but it is important to realize that many scientists and engineers in R&D departments carry out relatively routine work. Mundane activities such as quality control often provide the 'bread and butter' work of a laboratory. Sometimes innovative work may be stimulated only as a response to a crisis. This is exemplified by the 'reverse engineering' of a competitor's newly launched product, or the search for alternative inputs when material supplies are disrupted by strike or war.

Today, however, most large firms gear at least part of their R&D to a programme of continuous innovation. The research manager has a portfolio of projects at various stages of completion. Sometimes projects may make competing demands on the specialists at the manger's disposal, and the allocation of priorities then becomes crucial. In this context the management of research becomes first and foremost a variant of human resource management.

It is conventional to distinguish between basic and applied research, and sometimes between applied research and development too. The exact nature of these distinctions is somewhat controversial, however. Academics tend to regard any research directed at understanding fundamental natural processes as basic, whereas industrialists tend to regard such research as applied if it is undertaken with a view to some specific application; basic research signifies to the industrialist research undertaken for unspecified long-term benefits, independently of how 'academic' it is. It should not be forgotten, either, that in addition to development costs the actual launch of a product involves a very large commitment of resources – even though most of this is incurred through advertising and the build up of production and retail inventory. After launch, researchers still need to be 'on their toes' to advise on unforeseen side-effects of product use (or misuse), excessive warranty claims, and so on.

Most research managers claim to do very little basic research, but what qualifies as 'basic' tends to vary greatly between industries. To an academic researcher, for example, most of the R&D in the food industry would qualify as development, whereas in the pharmaceutical industry a great deal of what is called development could well be described as basic research.

In food processing, for example, it is possible to 'cook up' new products without understanding all of the chemistry involved. A typical product might involve the development of a new fast-food by extruding novel shapes of pasta, or potato crisps. It is often a trial and error process, conducted using full-scale plant and equipment, and marketing imperatives may require development to be completed in less than a year.

In pharmaceuticals, by contrast, resources are concentrated more on what an academic would consider to be basic research. Because the research is typically targeted on curing a particular medical condition, however, research directors tend to regard it as applied. In any case, some very sophisticated biochemistry is required to discover the body's own mechanisms and how they govern the progression of the illness. Exhaustive laboratory work, involving the systematic investigation of many possibilities, is needed to discover some active compound which can modify the mechanism. The compound is administered within some formulation which is tested out through animal experiments and clinical trials. The process can take up to 15 years to complete – and even more if serious problems arise. Very often compounds have a capability to modify the body's mechanisms in a manner calculated to do much more than cure the specific disease. The negative aspect of this is that further research is needed to inhibit adverse side-effects. The positive aspect is that the compound may be modified to tackle other illnesses as well. In this way spin-offs from one project can lead to other projects that follow on.

R&D activities in different industries reveal strong complementarities. For example, agricultural research may improve the natural ingredients available to the pharmaceutical industry. The pharmaceutical industry draws on knowledge originally developed in connection with synthetic dyestuffs. The chemical building blocks used in synthetic dyestuffs are common to those used in fertilizers, which are in turn applied in agriculture. These chemical building blocks are derived from petroleum cracking which establishes a link to the oil industry. Oil is a process industry that is heavily dependent on scientific instrumentation, and so on. . . .

These interdependencies suggest a concept of 'core technologies' such as chemical synthesis, electronic circuitry, controlled combustion, and so on, which can be applied in many different industries. Individual firms may well build their own operations around a concept of core competence which determines the range of activities they can successfully diversify into. The need to synthesize the core competencies of different firms for a particular range of applications can motivate mergers and joint ventures. Likewise, the spinning-off of peripheral ideas generated in the course of research directed to other goals leads to intra-corporate entrepreneurship and buy-outs.

1.3 THE CONCEPT OF COMPETITIVENESS

R&D is one of the key factors in maintaining and enhancing international competitiveness (Sterlacchini, 1989). National industrial policies and regional development policies all reflect this belief to some extent. Yet the concept of competitiveness is by no means straightforward, and in consequence the link between R&D and competitiveness is an ambiguous one (Buckley, Pass and Prescott, 1988; House of Lords, 1985).

It seems obvious that during the 1980s western industrial

countries lost competitiveness relative to Japan (Baumol and McLennan, 1985; Dertouzos, Lester and Solow, 1989; Lawrence, 1984). The rising penetration of Japanese imports of high-technology products certainly suggests this. Trade performance would seem to be the natural indicator of international competitiveness, but exactly what performance measure is appropriate is difficult to say.

A crude merchantilist measure of competitiveness is the *surplus of exports over imports* (a positive balance of trade). Since, however, the overall balance of payments must balance, this surplus is associated with the net acquisition of assets from foreigners. There is a crucial question here concerning the direction of causation (Fröhlich, 1989). Does a balance of trade surplus cause international capital exports, or is it the other way round? If trade flows accommodate capital movements then merchantilist competitiveness may reflect little more than international differences in savings rates.

A country with a high saving rate, and limited investment opportunities at home, may run a trade surplus to finance its foreign investment. The exports are necessary to pay (in real terms) for the foreign assets acquired. This was the situation in late nineteenth-century England, and is part of the story of late twentieth-century Japan where, because of the shortage of housing, the lack of state social security benefits and specific cultural attitudes, the savings rate is particularly high. This leads to the rather ironic conclusion that a favourable balance of trade may reflect a perceived lack of economic potential at home and a consequent desire to invest abroad instead. In the case of Japan, the desire to gain control of overseas mineral supplies is an important motive too.

However, a country cannot run a trade surplus, whatever the motives, if the real labour costs of tradeable goods are higher than in rival nations. When domestic money wages are indexed to domestic money prices, real wages may be fixed at a level out of line with productivity. Whatever the exchange rate, unit labour costs will be higher than the international level. This cost premium provides an alternative measure of competitiveness. The higher the premium, the less competitive the country.

Employment adjustments will tend to eliminate this premium, however. Employment in the tradeables sector will contract until average productivity has risen to a level which restores unit costs to their international level. Although the premium disappears, however, the unemployment will remain for as long as real wages remain inflexible. Thus unemployment in the tradeables sector may be a more reasonable measure of competitiveness.

Job losses will be concentrated in the tradeables sector because non-tradeables are immune to international competition. Although unemployment in the tradeables sector could have a knock-on effect on demand for non-tradeables, much of this demand is either price-inelastic – for example, transport and communication – or financed out of taxation – health and education, for example. This does not mean that the non-tradeables sector is irrelevant to competitiveness, though. Low productivity in publicly funded services can lead to higher taxation, while low competitiveness in essential services can lead to higher prices, both of which may lead to higher wage demands in the tradeables sector.

Unemployment itself can impact on competitiveness. By reducing domestic demand it can encourage the development of export markets. On the other hand, if the domestic market is large, and scale economies are important, then domestic demand and foreign demand may be complements rather than substitutes and, as the total market shrinks average costs rise and competitiveness is further undermined.

The extent of job losses in the tradeable sector will depend on the elasticity of the demand for labour. This demand is a derived demand which depends upon both technology and the price-elasticity of product demand. With rapidly diminishing marginal returns to labour, a small reduction in employment may raise average productivity sufficiently to restore competitiveness.

With constant marginal returns, however, the influence of price-elasticity is crucial (Fagerberg, 1988). A low price-elasticity reduces the amount of job loss required to restore productivity because a small contraction in employment significantly increases the value of the goods produced. The greater the extent to which the tradeable sector is concentrated on the production of differentiated products, the lower the elasticity of demand is likely to be.

Innovation is an important source of product differentiation. New products are perceived by customers as different from old products. What is more, innovation is a potential source of monopoly rents. New products of improved design (or higher fashion) can command a premium which enhances profitability. Products can, of course, be imitated, or their market eroded by the proliferation of other varieties. Sustained innovation is thus required to retain a monopoly position in the long run. This suggests that the trade performance of an economy in innovative industries is a key indicator of long-run competitiveness. On this view, competitiveness is essentially a structural phenomenon (Chesnais, 1986).

Table 1.1 examines the trade performance of 10 leading industrialized countries in 12 innovative industries. The trade performance of a national industry is measured by an index of revealed comparative advantage. The index is a modification of the original Balassa (1965) index employed by UNIDO (1986). It is the ratio of the trade surplus of the national industry to the average value of the country's trade, normalized by the world industry's share of total world trade in manufacturing. Equivalently, it is the net exports of the national industry normalized both with respect to the country's trade and the share of the product in world trade. A positive value indicates a comparative advantage and a negative value a comparative disadvantage. It can be seen that the UK enjoys a strong comparative advantage in cosmetics, pharmaceuticals, dyestuffs and aircraft, and a strong comparative disadvantage in domestic electrical equipment.

Among the other countries, the US has a strong comparative advantage in aircraft and office machines, West Germany in dyestuffs and motor vehicles, France in cosmetics, Italy in domestic electrical equipment, Netherlands in plastics, Switzerland in dyestuffs and pharmaceuticals, Sweden in tools and Japan in domestic electrical equipment, motor vehicles, instruments and photographic equipment. It is worth noting that in several cases (West German motor vehicles, Dutch plastics and Swedish tools) it is the activities of a handful of large firms rather than a legion of small and medium-sized firms that is crucial. This exemplifies the general proposition that in the high-technology area the competitive advantage of a nation often reflects the competitive advantages of a few leading firms (Porter, 1990).

Table 1.1 Revealed comparative advantage in innovative manufacturing industries of ten industrialized countries, 1981–1983

Country	512 Organic chemicals	531 Dyestuffs	541 Pharmaceuticals	553 Cosmetics	581 Plastics	695 Tools	714 Office machines	725 Domestic electrical equipment	732 Motor vehicles	734 Aircraft	861 Instruments	862 Photographic equipment	Average value of index	Rank
North America														
United States	0.34	−0.17	0.68	0.36	0.73	0.13	1.26	0.38	0.98	2.85	0.05	0.83	0.47	4
Canada	0.11	...	−0.43	−0.48	−0.54	0.94	−1.01	−0.94	0.24	−0.07	−1.23	−0.87	−0.56	10
Europe – EC														
United Kingdom	0.36	0.97	1.15	1.24	−0.13	0.23	−0.55	−1.04	−0.29	0.85	0.07	0.02	0.24	6
West Germany	0.56	2.51	0.58	0.13	0.75	0.95	−0.06	0.60	1.35	−0.27	0.53	−0.05	0.63	3
France	0.17	−0.75	0.70	4.56	0.04	−0.08	−0.44	−0.39	0.33	0.76	−0.33	−0.20	0.30	5
Italy	−0.45	−0.82	0.01	−0.50	−0.17	0.03	−0.13	2.41	−0.14	0.22	−0.25	−0.60	0.03	8
Netherlands	1.14	−0.23	0.14	−0.50	1.59	−0.19	−0.30	−0.17	−0.27	0.02	−0.02	0.21	0.12	7
Europe – Non-EC														
Switzerland	0.81	7.64	4.02	−0.10	−0.47	0.91	−0.66	−0.55	−0.76	−0.73	0.67	−0.43	0.86	2
Sweden	−0.18	−0.47	0.09	−0.84	−0.36	2.47	−0.25	0.27	0.69	−0.12	−0.29	−0.82	0.02	9
Japan	0.08	0.26	−0.79	−0.09	0.59	1.10	1.04	1.87	3.07	−0.54	2.62	1.54	0.90	1

Source: UNIDO (1986), pp. 75–197.

A country with a strong minerals sector is unlikely to perform as well as others, on this criterion, because mineral exports will strengthen the exchange rate and tend to make manufacturing uncompetitive. At a more fundamental level, the mineral sector's demand for labour will 'crowd out' manufacturing in a fully employed economy and so raise real factor costs (Neary and van Wijnbergen, 1986). This is reflected in the case of Canada, whose comparative advantage in minerals results in a comparative disadvantage in manufacturing. The argument applies in reverse to Japan. A key factor in Japan's manufacturing competitiveness is the relative absence of an indigenous minerals sector – Japan must export manufacturers to pay for the mineral imports she needs. This is another reason, besides her high saving rate, why Japan's manufacturing trade performance may not be entirely the miracle it seems.

Services can crowd out manufacturing too. The strength of financial services and tourism bids away labour from manufacturing. Autonomous growth in these invisible exports can reduce the visible trade balance. Considering the size of its service sector, the UK's trade performance in innovative manufacturing industries is therefore not quite so bad as it is sometimes made out to be.

International competitiveness, as reflected in trade performance, reflects competitiveness in production and is, to some extent, independent of where the technology comes from. The separation of production and R&D is difficult for novel products, though. In the early stages of the product life cycle it is useful for production to remain close to the R&D facility so that teething problems can be rectified. Indeed, in some cases the final stage of development may involve experimenting with a full-scale production facility, which leaves it already tooled up to commence mass production.

With mature products, however, it may be feasible to relocate production away from R&D (Vernon, 1966, 1979). The firm may then obtain monopoly rents from another country. If the firm internalizes the market for know-how, then the generation of these rents will be associated with foreign direct investment. It follows that a trade-based measure of international competitiveness may understate the overall competitiveness of a national industry because it ignores the fact that overseas production can substitute for exports. The understatement is potentially large when there is a global market for the product, and transport costs and tariffs are sufficiently high to encourage local production in the overseas market. Understatement can also arise in internationally rationalized production when mature products are produced offshore in cheap-labour countries.

Cantwell (1987a) has made the necessary corrections using data on overseas production by the world's leading MNEs – 792 firms which are estimated to account for 85 per cent of international production in the world. Cantwell's index of revealed comparative advantage in trade is based on *gross* exports rather than net exports (which were used in table 1.1) and employs a different industrial classification because of the limitations of the international production statistics. He also excludes the exports of foreign-owned firms from his trade measurements. When allowing for overseas production, Cantwell adds overseas production to indigenous firm exports in all the terms which appear in the index.

The results are shown in table 1.2. An index greater than unity indicates a comparative advantage and an index less than unity a comparative disadvantage. It appears that UK-owned firms are much stronger than the UK production sector in foods, rubber and non-metallic minerals, but weaker in chemicals, mechanical engineering, electrical equipment, motor vehicles, other transport equipment and other manufacturing. The gain in competitiveness in rubber and non-metallic minerals may well reflect backward integration into sources of supply, and the same may be true, to some extent, of the food industry with its backward linkages into agriculture. On the other hand the reduction in revealed competitiveness in the other industries is almost certainly due to the superior performance of foreign-owned firms in these industries. The export performance of foreign-owned firms in the UK is superior to the production performance of UK-owned firms overseas.

Given that national comparative advantage often reflects large-firm corporate competitive advantage, this suggests that UK comparative advantage is unusually dependent on the transfer to the UK of the competitive advantages of foreign-owned firms. This is

Table 1.2 Effect of international production on revealed comparative advantage in the UK, 1982

Industry	International production (world)		International production plus indigenous exports (world)		UK Comparative advantage	
	Value ($000 m)	Percentage	Value ($000 m)	Percentage	All exports	International production plus indigenous exports
Food products	132	15.7	281	14.9	0.66	1.62
Chemicals	119	14.2	219	11.6	1.46	1.05
Metals	57	6.8	176	9.3	0.87	0.76
Mechanical engineering	60	7.1	200	10.6	1.52	0.74
Electrical equipment	97	11.6	203	10.7	1.02	0.77
Motor vehicles	86	10.2	184	9.8	0.70	0.49
Other transport	9	1.1	56	3.0	1.22	0.77
Textiles	15	1.7	108	5.7	0.74	0.84
Rubber products	21	2.5	38	2.0	1.19	1.33
Non-metallic minerals	23	2.7	39	2.1	0.94	1.39
Coal and petroleum products	188	22.3	226	12.0	0.62	1.53
Other manufacturing	35	4.2	158	8.4	1.19	0.57
Total	842	100.0	1888	100.0	—	—

Source: Cantwell (1987a), tables, 3, 4, 6, 7.

because the trade performance of the UK in innovative industries is heavily dependent on foreign-owned technology used in the UK. The merits of the UK as a production site in innovative industries are not reflected in indigenous ownership of the technologies in these industries. In terms of owning technology, the UK seems to be more backward than its trade performance suggests.

1.4   A HISTORICAL PERSPECTIVE

In historical terms the decentralization of corporate R&D is a quite recent phenomenon. Until the turn of the century there was very little corporate R&D of any kind. Branch plant research laboratories began to emerge in the inter-war period, but it was really only in the period of consolidation that followed the early post-war multinational expansion that a coherent strategy of decentralization was evolved.

Going further back, it is only since the mid-eighteenth century that the application of the scientific method in industry has been a significant force. One of the key aspects of the industrial revolution in England was the use of systematic experimentation to generate improvements in industrial processes – notably in metal manufacture and the textile industry. The initiative frequently rested with one individual, who funded his research out of retained profits from his family business, or relied on a wealthy patron who was anxious to get a higher return than that available from his landed estates.

These experiments were guided by intuition, and by pragmatic judgement distilled from analysing the deficiencies of existing methods. They did not derive from any great theoretical insights into the fundamental nature of the physical and chemical processes involved. Nor did the conduct of the experiments normally call for very sophisticated equipment.

The discovery of the periodic table, the development of spectral analysis and the study of the laws of electromagnetism, together with other theoretical advances, changed all this. The methodical craftsman–innovator gave way to the educated scientist analysing

experimental measurements generated by increasingly sophisticated laboratory equipment.

In the early companies that were geared to R&D the influence
of a single individual was often paramount. This individual was
usually a member of the family that owned the firm – sometimes
the founder's son who was enthused by the progressive scientific
spirit of the Victorian age. Thus young William Siemens was the
driving force in Siemens's London telecommunications laboratory
(established in the 1860s), while Tom Vickers was largely responsible, from the age of 22, for the transition of Vickers from a steel
firm to the world's leading armament manufacturer by 1900
(Scott, 1962; Trebilcock, 1977; von Weiher, 1980).

These individuals did not usually run the entire company single-
handed, however. They were part of an informal intra-family
division of labour, vividly illustrated in the Vickers case, where
Tom's brother Eric had a quite different personality and concentrated almost entirely on the commercial side of the firm's operations. This entrepreneurial partnership between the introverted
scientist and the extrovert market opportunist proved highly successful.

The reform and extension of the patent system in the 1870s and
1880s encouraged speculative financing of patent-driven research
– particularly in the US, where the most notable example was
Edison's Menlo Park laboratory. Patents, however, proved costly
to enforce, for reasons which transaction cost theory makes very
clear – namely the ease of 'inventing around' a patent and the
difficulty of monitoring covert use. The initiative in innovative
industries gradually passed to firms which integrated forward into
the production activities which utilized their ideas.

The scientific approach was well adapted to factories which
were making the transition from small-scale batch production to
large-scale continuous flow. As the division of labour within the
factory increased, individual tasks became sufficiently simple that
they could be mechanized, and carried out routinely by machine
tools powered from a common source. The capital goods industries played a crucial role in these innovations, with the capital
good producer designing the machinery in close collaboration
with the users.

The scientific approach was important not only in innovation but in the routine aspects of production too. In the Sheffield steel industry, for example, the mystique of the melter's eye for colour and texture was replaced (at least partially) by optical measurement (Tweedale, 1988). Quality control was important in wholesaling too. One of the earliest roles for scientists in the UK pharmaceutical industry was in checking the purity of natural ingredients. The firms which later dominated pharmaceuticals through their mastery of synthetic chemicals often began as wholesalers employing chemists to maintain the reputation of the natural medicines in their range (Liebenau, 1987, 1988).

Nowhere was the harnessing of basic science to commercial innovation so systematically applied as in Germany. The Prussian élite, bent on modernizing Germany through rapid industrialization and the expansion of the internal market, financed the development of polytechnics in which some brilliant chemists were employed. These chemists addressed themselves to practical issues, such as recycling waste products to reduce pollution, increasing thermal efficiency, and expanding the supply of useful intermediate inputs to other industries. The strong emphasis on practical study at the laboratory bench generated a stream of highly professional inventors (Wrigley, 1986).

The rest of the world benefited enormously from this. Foreigners came to Germany to be trained in the polytechnics. Young Germans left for England and the United States – to set up plants to work their patents, to gain access to new sources of funds, to avoid conscription and, in some cases, to escape anti-Semitism (Cohen, 1956).

The first fully fledged industrial research laboratory was established by the German pharmaceutical company Bayer in 1886 to develop new synthetic dyestuffs from a coal tar base (Kaku, 1980). The Bayer example was followed in the US by General Electric (Edison's successor) in 1900 and Du Pont in 1902. The German influence was very strong, with many recent immigrants being employed in the new chemical research laboratories (Wilkins, 1989).

Two main factors gave the impetus to the formal organization of research. The first was the need to synthesize knowledge from different scientific disciplines by adopting a team approach. The photographic industry affords an excellent example (Edgerton, 1988). The optical properties of lenses needed to be understood for camera design. The properties of synthetic dyes were crucial in the formulation of the film emulsion. Precision machine tools were required to produce reliable cameras on a sufficient scale to make photography an affordable hobby for the masses. The ability of the Eastman Kodak laboratory to synthesize the relevant skills was crucial to the company's enduring success in this field.

The need for team research meant that it was no longer possible to rely solely on contacts with individual inventors. Some firms, like Elliott Brothers of London, seem to have addressed this issue by establishing a laboratory for the use of inventors (Williams, 1988). But modern experience with 'small-firm incubator' centres suggests that lone inventors do not work well together, even when they share a facility. Scientists had been employed in industry since the 1860s, and it was therefore natural to extend the employment relation to the members of a team (Neumeyer and Stedman, 1971).

The second factor was the trust movement, which was particularly influential in the two newly-dominant industrial powers of the time – Germany and the US. Although horizontal combination was usually the principal aim of a trust, the outcome was often a rather diversified group of activities under common ownership and control (Chandler, 1977). There was particular reason for this in the US – political reaction led to antitrust legislation which obliged many firms to divest in their major industry, and so pushed them into diversification elsewhere.

The search for a rational method of managing diversified operations led to the idea of a general laboratory that could support more applied projects within the various production divisions. In time this would evolve into the idea that the general laboratory could carry out technical appraisals of potential new diversifications. In some cases this might involve simply a 'technological audit' of a potential acquisition, while in others it could involve investigating a spin-off from existing research.

The trust movement is also a landmark in the development of

managerial control in place of family control. The financial requirements of a trust could rarely be satisfied by a single family. A single family could not easily staff all the key management positions either. Nevertheless, some wealthy families with large numbers of children managed to maintain control even in rationalized organizations – a family member still controlled R&D policy in Du Pont at the time the general laboratory was established in 1902 (Hounshell and Smith, 1988).

In the long run, however, the increasing availability of academic specialists with a practical orientation in the land-grant universities provided an important source of salaried research managers which US industry could not ignore (Lazonick, 1986). General Electric was one of the first US companies to appoint an 'outsider' to head its research department – Willis R. Whitney, recruited from MIT (Reich, 1985).

Britain lagged behind Germany and the US in these developments (Mowery, 1986). The small family firm remained influential, and a formally organized research department was practically unknown. This was part of a general lack of sophistication in management. Scientific input came from academic consultants, an educated member of the family, or a lone specialist employee. When photographic and chemical supplies from Germany were interrupted during World War I, the government intervened to promote domestic production, but firms were often reluctant to respond. They expected the war to finish quickly, they thought that post-war tariff protection was unlikely, and they feared infringing the patents of German firms on whom they would be dependent for intermediate inputs after the war was over (Robson, 1988).

After the war the government promoted collaborative research through industry trade associations, and there was some rationalization through merger and acquisitions, prompted, in part, by government concern to develop a national champion in strategic industries. One of the most successful mergers led to the creation of ICI. Branch R&D facilities began to appear as early US investors increased their commitment to the European market. Kodak established what was probably the first major US-owned overseas laboratory in Harrow, near London, in 1928. Kodak's

British subsidiary had a wide-ranging mandate for supplying markets as far afield as South Africa and Singapore (Wilkins, 1974).

On the whole, however, international exploitation of technology in the inter-war period was mainly effected through cartel agreements which involved cross-licensing of patents and the division of the world market into European and American spheres of influence. Major industrial markets for a product were normally reserved for one of the members, with *ad hoc* arrangements being made in the smaller less significant ones (Reader, 1975). Cartel agreements tended to inhibit radical innovation as they were costly to renegotiate in the light of new developments.

In the post-war period, foreign direct investment replaced the international cartel as the main contractual arrangement through which technology was transferred. There was a growing perception of the need to adapt products to the local market environment. Small laboratories were created for quality testing and for the reverse engineering of competitor's products, and these gradually evolved a capacity for adaptive work, often under the influence of an enterprising indigenous manager who was sensitive to local requirements (see chapter 6).

Dependence on a headquarters laboratory often remained significant, however. In the motor industry, for example, Ford and General Motors subsidiaries depended heavily on US technical support for the design and engineering of vehicles for the European market (Maxcy and Silberston, 1959). It was only when the larger multinationals began to rationalize their international operations in the 1960s that the idea of devolving major research responsibilities to an overseas laboratory gained momentum. Until then only a few firms, such as the Anglo-Dutch food firm Unilever, had employed this approach (Fieldhouse, 1978; Wilson, 1954, 1968). In a typical case some small laboratories attached to local plants were relegated purely to technical support, and their other activities transferred to a new or expanded laboratory at a regional or continental centre. Some of these new laboratories were designated as centres of excellence for research of a particular kind within the group as a whole. In this way the spatial division of labour that began with production was systematically applied to R&D as well.

A major advantage of rationalization is that it avoids unnecessary replication, and so reduces the fixed costs of R&D required to sustain a given market share in an innovative industry. Intra-firm rationalization may not go far enough, however. Costs of research have recently escalated quite significantly in many industries. It has been estimated by a large UK MNE that R&D costs have risen consistently at a few percentage points above the retail price index during the 1980s. Rationalization *between* firms is required to cope with this. Unless the proliferation of products is reduced, no product will have sufficient market share (on average) to reimburse its costs of development.

This has provoked a variety of responses. A merger can completely rationalize the product lines of the firms involved. A less radical strategy is to delegate the more basic research to a joint venture established by the leading firms. The overheads of basic research are spread over a larger volume of output, but the firms remain free to compete with different variants of the same basic technology. For a firm that already enjoys a large market share, and is concerned about its competitors' drive to increase theirs, protection of the domestic market may be useful. The dominant firms in some US industries have lobbied for protection – both through tariffs and through the limitation of inward direct investments that have been designed to 'jump the tariff wall'.

The escalation of research costs is due to a mixture of factors. Higher safety standards and increasingly strict environmental health constraints have been imposed by government regulation in certain industries. Consumers demand increasingly high standards of performance and reliability as their incomes rise. The exhaustion of technological potential – as reflected in a declining pace of fundamental innovation – may be a factor in some cases too. In some industries the escalation of costs may lead to a premature 'maturing' of the product – further innovation ceases to be worthwhile. In other cases demand may be sufficiently buoyant that research will continue. In the pharmaceutical industry, for example, the ageing of the population (particularly in wealthy countries) promises a boom in demand. While the increasing length of the post-patent development process threatens monopoly rents, the potential for harnessing advances in genetic engineering to commercial innovation is enormous. While further rationalization may occur in this and other growth industries – perhaps through inter-company specialization agreements as well as more conventional means – there seems little doubt that the management of R&D in such industries will remain a crucial determinant of corporate performance well into the next century.

1.5 RECENT INTERNATIONAL TRENDS IN R&D: A STATISTICAL SUMMARY

This section presents further evidence on recent trends and establishes a few benchmarks from which the magnitude of the resources involved in international R&D can be assessed.

Table 1.3 presents data on the percentage of Gross Domestic Product (GDP) allocated to R&D in some of the leading industrialized countries over the period 1975–87. The data show that although the UK scores quite highly over the period as a whole, its relative position declined quite significantly. The leading R&D investor – the US – increased its percentage from 2.3 in 1975 to 2.8 in 1987, while the UK increased its proportion only marginally from 2.2 to 2.3. As a result, it was 'overtaken' by three countries – Sweden, which rose dramatically from 1.7 to 3.0, Japan which rose from 2.0 to 2.8, and France, which rose from 1.8 to 2.4.

The percentage of R&D funded by business rather than government remained disappointingly low for the UK, 46 per cent – as compared to 77 per cent in Switzerland and 69 per cent in Japan. Even the US, with its huge defence commitments, managed to fund a higher proportion of its R&D from business sources. One reason for this relatively low proportion of private funding may be that government funding is overstated. Kennedy (1989) claims that defence-related R&D expenditures are deliberately inflated by the UK Ministry of Defence in order to disguise the UK's poor overall performance in R&D: they include 'VAT, nuclear

Table 1.3 National R&D expenditures 1975–1987 in selected OECD countries

Country	Gross R&D expenditure as percentage of GDP				Percentage of gross R&D funded by business			
	1975	1979	1983	1987	1975	1979	1983	1987
US	2.3	2.3	2.7	2.8	43	46	49	47
Switzerland	2.4	2.4	2.3	2.5[c]	72	75	77	n.a.
West Germany	2.2	2.4	2.5	2.7[b]	50	55	60	63
UK	2.2	n.a.	2.3	2.3[b]	38	n.a.	42	46[b]
Netherlands	2.0	1.9	2.0	2.1[b]	50	47	46	52[b]
France	1.8	1.8	2.1	2.4	39	43	42	41[b]
Sweden	1.7	1.9	2.5	3.0	57	60	61	63[b]
Japan	2.0	2.1	2.6	2.8[b]	58	59	65	69[b]
Canada	1.1	1.1	1.3	1.3[b]	31	36	39	42
Italy	0.8	0.7	1.0	1.3	51	55	45	45[b]

Note: [b] Indicates 1985 statistic.
[c] Indicates 1986 statistic.
n.a. Indicates not available.

Source: OECD (1989), tables 4, 12.

weapons production, and a large proportion of work that is not in fact R&D at all'.

Recent experience is even more depressing, as table 1.4 shows. Carrying the story forward from 1979 to 1986 and beyond shows the UK bottom of the league table in terms of the annual average rate of growth of R&D expenditure, despite the manipulation of the statistics designed to counter this. Within the OECD countries as a whole, only Ireland, Greece and Portugal have turned in a worse performance.

Expenditure on R&D is an input rather than an output measure, as Soete and Wyatt (1983) and others have noted. Table 1.5 reports the results of Archibugi and Pianta (1989) on the productivity of R&D expenditure in terms of external patents granted for selected OECD countries 1979–86. Although the UK is ranked fourth in the world, behind US, Japan and West Germany, in terms of cumulative R&D expenditure (notwithstanding the adverse trend over this period noted above), it ranks only fifth in terms of external patents granted (that is, the number of patents granted outside the country of origin). This is because of the superior productivity of France in converting R&D into patents. The UK in fact ranks seventh in terms of productivity

Table 1.4 Average annual compound rates of growth of R&D expenditures in selected OECD countries 1979–1988

Country	Period	Percentage growth
Japan	1979–86	11.8
Switzerland	1979–88	5.9
Netherlands	1979–86	5.5
West Germany	1979–87	5.0
Canada	1979–88	4.5
Sweden	1979–87	4.5
US	1979–88	4.4
Italy	1979–88	2.3
France	1979–88	2.2
UK	1981–86	1.1

Source: Archibugi and Pianta (1989), table 1.5.

Table 1.5 R&D expenditure and external patenting in selected OECD countries 1979–1986

Country	Cumulative R&D expenditure 1979–86 (million US dollars 1980 prices)	Number of external patents 1979–85	Ratio of patents to R&D expenditure	Ranking by Expenditure	Ranking by Patents	Ranking by Ratio
US	589,761	904,324	1.53	1	1	9
Japan	223,756	381,995	1.71	2	3	8
West Germany	118,652	577,223	4.86	3	2	3
UK	81,263	226,114	2.78	4	5	7
France	72,519	234,044	3.23	5	4	6
Canada	28,439	37,817	1.33	6	10	10
Italy	27,807	97,760	3.52	7	7	5
Netherlands	20,749	87,669	4.23	8	9	4
Switzerland	14,060	156,839	11.16	9	6	1
Sweden	13,874	90,141	6.50	10	8	2

Source: Archibugi and Pianta (1989), tables 1.10, 1.11.

within this 'top ten' of R&D-spending countries. This result must be interpreted with caution, however, because two apparently successful countries – the US and Japan – are ranked even lower. There may well be a country-size effect in the data which gives a spuriously high productivity to small countries because of their greater propensity to patent outside rather than inside the country. This is consistent with the fact that Switzerland and Sweden are the two countries with the highest measures of productivity. The UK performance still gives cause for concern, however, because large countries like West Germany, France and Italy also do better than the UK.

Another reason why measured productivity may differ is that different countries may allocate R&D differently between sectors, with some countries concentrating on sectors in which the propensity to patent is particularly high. National patterns of specialization in research are not only of intrinsic interest, but are of particular importance for the globalization of R&D. Patterns of specialization should, in theory, reflect national comparative advantage, not just in manufacturing operations but in R&D too. Countries which are advantaged, relative to others, in certain fields of research, should tend to concentrate their research efforts in those fields, and to generate a higher than average proportion of their external patents in these fields as a result. The tendency for a country to have a high proportion of its patents clustering in a certain field, relative to an average for the world as a whole, is captured by an index of revealed technological advantage, which is the ratio of the percentage of national patents in a particular industrial category to the percentage of all patents in the same category.

Archibugi and Pianta have calculated, for each OECD country, the rankings of industries according to this index. Table 1.6 reports the top five industries in this ranking for the ten OECD countries listed above. So far as the UK is concerned, the pattern of technological comparative advantage revealed by the index is fairly satisfactory, in the sense that high-technology industries with growth potential – notably pharmaceuticals and aircraft – are represented, rather than low-technology ones with less growth potential – such as metals and metal working, which figure in the

Table 1.6 Revealed technological advantages of selected OECD countries, calculated from US patents granted 1982–1988

Countries	First	Second	Third	Fourth	Fifth
			Rank		
US	Oil extraction	Missiles	Other	Farm Machinery	Lighting
Switzerland	Agricultural chemicals	Organic chemicals	Textiles	Industrial machinery	Ordnance
West Germany	Industrial machinery	Ordnance	Railways	Organic chemicals	Metal working
UK	Detergents	Missiles	Agricultural chemicals	Pharmaceuticals	Aircraft
Netherlands	Radio, TV	Food	Computers	Detergents	Farm machinery
France	Missiles	Railways	Detergents	Aircraft	Pharmaceuticals
Sweden	Shipbuilding	Ordnance	Railways	Ferrous metals	Missiles
Japan	Radio, TV	Office computing	Motorcycles	Motor vehicles	Engines
Canada	Shipbuilding	Farm machinery	Miscellaneous transport	Other	Non-ferrous metals
Italy	Household appliances	Agricultural chemicals	Industrial machinery	Pharmaceuticals	Railways

Source: Archibugi and Pianta (1989), pp. 97–112.

rankings for West Germany, Sweden and Canada. Unfortunately, however, a good deal of UK aircraft (and missile) expertise is defence-related, and attempts to apply it to purely civilian products have had only limited success. Possibly UK defence spending cuts may encourage the diversion of this expertise to civilian use in the future, though.

Stoneman (1989) has recently articulated concern that UK R&D may be peculiarly dependent on foreign sources of funds. This concern is corroborated by table 1.7 which presents OECD data relating to 1983. Stoneman notes that overseas funding, as defined for these statistics, comprises a number of elements including contract R&D undertaken for foreign customers and funds made available from Brussels under EC incentive schemes such as ESPRIT. But the major element is likely to be funds made available by a parent MNE for R&D carried out in a UK subsidiary (R&D funded out of the subsidiaries' retained earnings is not included in these figures).

The industrial breakdown of overseas funding is shown in table 1.8. It can be seen that the industrial breakdown of overseas funding is remarkably similar in the UK and the two 'control' countries France and Italy. Four industries dominate – aerospace, chemicals, electronics and computers – and in three of the four industries the proportion of overseas funding is highest in the UK.

Further information on overseas R&D in the UK is provided by the UK Department of Trade and Industry, whose statistics relate

Table 1.7 Overseas funding of business enterprise R&D (natural sciences and engineering) in 1983

Source	Funds (million US dollars at 1980 prices)	Percentage of total UK funding
US	687	7.0
France	271	4.6
West Germany	137	1.4
Italy	107	4.3
Japan	23	0.1
Sweden	22	1.8

Source: Stoneman (1989), tables 2, 3.

Table 1.8 Industrial distribution of overseas funding of business enterprise R&D in manufacturing in UK, France and Italy, 1985

Industry	Percentage of total funds from abroad			Overseas funds as a percentage of total funds in the industry		
	UK	France	Italy	UK	France	Italy
Aerospace	13.6	40.9	46.2	8.4	14.9	23.8
Chemicals	28.0	9.6	18.7	14.5	3.4	5.2
Construction	0.1	0.0	0.0	3.3	0.5	0.6
Electrical equipment	21.0	11.8	15.9	7.8	3.8	6.7
Electrical machinery	1.1	0.0	0.5	4.3	0.1	0.4
Food, drink and tobacco	1.8	2.2	0.0	7.4	11.3	0.4
Ferrous metals	0.6	0.0	0.0	7.2	0.3	0.0
Machinery n.e.s.	3.5	2.4	0.0	7.0	4.6	0.1
Motor vehicles	3.6	0.4	0.0	5.0	0.3	0.0
Office machinery and computers	24.8	24.1	7.7	35.9	32.8	6.2
Not allocated	1.9	8.5	11.0	—	—	—
Total	100.0	100.0	100.0	10.9	7.4	6.5

n.e.s. = Not elsewhere specified.
Source: Stoneman (1989), tables 4, 5, plus author's calculations.

Table 1.9 Percentage of UK-based R&D carried out by overseas-controlled enterprises, 1985

Industry	Self-financed expenditure	Employment
Chemicals and allied products	21	18
Mechanical engineering	9	12
Electronics	26	20
Electrical engineering	6	6
Vehicles	44	41
Aerospace	1	1
Others	9	8
Total	18	15

Source: UK Department of Trade and Industry (1988), table 9.

to foreign *control* of R&D rather than the source of funding. Table 1.9 shows that overseas control is very significant in vehicles, because both Ford and General Motors (but especially Ford) have major design and engineering facilities. Most of this R&D is financed out of local retained earnings. Electronics and chemicals R&D is also foreign controlled to a significant extent – and as noted earlier much of this is foreign-funded too.

The US is the dominant overseas direct investor in UK R&D. Even so, the UK is not the major European destination for US overseas R&D. Table 1.10 shows that, according to the US Benchmark Survey of 1982, West Germany is ahead of the UK with 28.3 per cent of US overseas R&D expenditure, compared to 21.0 per cent for the UK. Other major recipients of US R&D expenditure are Canada (13.9 per cent) and – perhaps rather surprisingly, in view of its nationalist stance on technology policy – France (6.4 per cent). France has been particularly successful in attracting US R&D in the chemical and pharmaceutical industry, partly because it has stipulated for local 'R&D content' in return for market access.

The industrial breakdown of US overseas R&D in table 1.11 highlights the importance of five industries – pharmaceuticals, machinery, electrical and electronic equipment, scientific instruments and – above all – motor vehicles (which almost certainly accounts for most of the expenditure recorded under transportation equipment).

Detailed information on the geography of US overseas R&D expenditures is not available after 1982 because the results of the next Benchmark Survey (for 1987) are not yet published. Summary statistics from the *Survey of Current Business 1986*, however, are sufficient to show that there has been a significant change in the geographical distribution between the date of the first Benchmark Survey (1977) and 1986. Table 1.12 shows that the importance of Europe as a location for US-controlled R&D has declined. Europe accounted for nearly three-quarters of US overseas R&D expenditure in 1977 but for only about four-sevenths in 1986. Within Europe there was a remarkable shift away from the UK, West Germany and France towards Switzerland and Netherlands, and to some extent towards

Table 1.10 R&D expenditure by US overseas affiliates, 1982, by host country (million US dollars)

Country	By affiliates for themselves		By affiliates for others		For affiliates by others	
	Amount	Percentage	Amount	Percentage	Amount	Percentage
Europe	2,215	72.1	677	87.0	376	65.5
UK	645	21.0	179	23.0	160	27.9
West Germany	869	28.3	210	27.0	24	4.2
France	197	6.4	135	17.4	66	11.5
Belgium	168	5.5	54	6.9	13	2.3
Italy	117	3.8	33	4.2	19	3.3
Netherlands	57	1.9	8	1.0	45	7.8
Sweden	22	0.7	6	0.8	7	1.2
Switzerland	48	1.6	12	1.5	3	0.5
Other European	92	3.0	40	5.1	39	6.8
Japan	95	3.1	17	2.2	9	1.6
Canada	426	13.9	79	10.2	119	20.7
Australia	113	3.7	1	0.1	7	1.2
New Zealand	3	0.1	n.a.	n.a.	3	0.5
South Africa	23	0.7	0	0.0	n.a.	n.a.
Developing countries	198	6.4	4	0.5	63	11.0
Other	11	0.4	n.a.	n.a.	3	0.5
Total	3,073	100.0	778	100.0	574	100.0

n.a. = Not available.
Source: US Department of Commerce (1985), table III, H.1.

Table 1.11 R&D expenditures by US overseas affiliates, 1982, by industry (million US dollars)

Industry	By affiliates for themselves		By affiliates for others		For affiliates by others	
	Amount	Percentage	Amount	Percentage	Amount	Percentage
Petroleum	120	3.9	31	4.0	106	18.5
Food	103	3.3	5	0.6	16	2.8
Chemicals	615	20.0	43	5.5	102	17.8
Industrial chemicals	139	4.5	25	3.2	55	9.6
Pharmaceuticals	347	11.3	15	1.9	21	3.7
Detergents etc.	60	2.0	n.a.	n.a.	25	4.4
Agricultural chemicals	12	0.4	0	0.0	n.a.	n.a.
Other	57	1.9	4	0.5	2	0.3
Metals	46	1.5	n.a.	n.a.	3	0.5
Non-electrical machinery	218	7.9	355	45.6	42	7.3
Farm machinery	44	1.4	0	0.0	n.a.	n.a.
Construction machinery	42	1.4	1	0.1	n.a.	n.a.
Office and computing machines	46	1.5	348	44.7	38	6.6
Other	86	2.8	6	0.8	3	0.5
Electrical and electronic equipment	477	15.5	66	8.5	42	7.3
Transport equipment	889	28.9	27	3.5	72	12.5
Instruments	184	6.0	25	3.2	125	21.8
Other manufacturing (exc. instruments)	158	5.1	36	4.6	32	5.6
Wholesale trade	205	6.7	8	1.0	31	5.4
Non-banking financial services	1	0.0	n.a.	n.a.	1	0.2
Services	45	1.5	181	23.3	1	0.2
Other industries	14	0.4	1	0.1	2	0.3
Total	3,073	100.0	778	100.0	574	100.0

n.a. = Not available.

Source: US Department of Commerce (1985), table III, H.2.

Table 1.12 Geographical distribution of US overseas
R&D expenditures by affiliates, 1977–1986

| | *Percentage* | |
Location	*1977*	*1986*
Europe	73.0	58.9
UK	18.9	13.3
West Germany	22.3	11.3
France	14.0	6.0
Belgium	4.4	0.4
Italy	4.1	0.6
Netherlands	2.7	9.4
Sweden	1.0	2.3
Switzerland	2.3	13.5
Other Europe	3.4	0.4
Japan	1.7	5.9
Canada	12.3	27.8
Australia, New Zealand and South Africa	5.3	0.6
Other countries	7.7	8.6
Total	100.0	100.0

Source: US Department of Commerce (1985, 1990).

Sweden too. Europe's losses have provided major gains for
Canada (up from 12.3 per cent to 27.8 per cent) and Japan (up
from 1.7 per cent to 5.9 per cent). It is interesting to note that the
developing countries have increased their share of overseas R&D,
despite their continuing economic difficulties, although much of
this R&D seems to be concentrated in just a few countries. The
data are consistent with the view that US overseas R&D is now
driven less by the need to adapt products to the local market and
more by the advantages of utilizing cheap scientific labour (in
Canada, and certain developing countries, for instance) or by
accessing special localized expertise (Japanese electronics know-
how and Swiss pharmaceutical know-how). The results reported
later in this book tend to support this view.

It seems likely that Japan will play an increasing role as a source
of ownership and control in UK-based R&D. Figure 1.1 shows

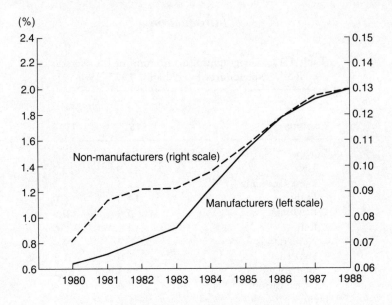

Ratio of R & D expenses to sales

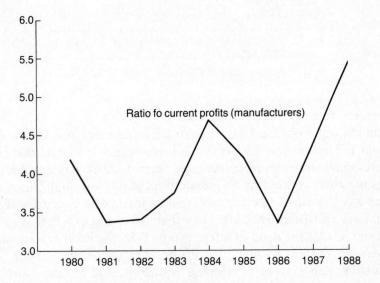

Ratio of current profits to sales (manufacturers)

Figure 1.1 R&D expenditure, profit and sales of principal enterprises in Japan, 1980–1988

Source: Bank of Japan Research Statistics Department (1990).

that R&D has been increasing steadily as a proportion of sales among leading Japanese enterprises, and has maintained its upward trend in spite of a temporary reversal of profit growth in the period 1984–6. Information on Japanese global R&D strategy is provided by a recent survey of 437 Japanese firms with more than three overseas affiliates carried out in September and October 1989 (Export-Import Bank of Japan, 1990). Ninety per cent of the 247 respondents had a globalization strategy, and 84 per cent had concrete plans for foreign direct investment either through new ventures or expansion of existing facilities for the period 1989–91. The R&D strategies of the 218 globalizing respondents are summarized in table 1.13. The different objectives are not mutually exclusive. It can be seen that the differentiation of products to local tastes is the major motivation for overseas R&D; 57 per cent of the companies plan to undertake overseas R&D for this purpose. This is linked to plans to decentralize the marketing function within many Japanese MNEs.

Differentiation is also planned to cope with the problem of local content requirements, which are perceived as an important constraint on the competitiveness of Japanese products manufactured overseas. Local redesign of motor vehicle components, for example, is expected to improve backward linkages between

Table 1.13 R&D Policies of Japanese enterprises with a globalization strategy, 1989

| | Firms with such objective | |
Objectives	Number	Percentage
Developing products tailored to local needs	124	57
Designing parts to increase the level of local content at the overseas site	24	11
Strengthening overseas basic research	22	10
Employing competent researchers in the region	14	6
Other objective	10	5
Total	218	100

Source: Export-Import Bank of Japan (1990), exhibit 5.2(d).

Japanese car assembly plants and indigenous suppliers who are often dependent on a different type or grade of raw material from that available in Japan.

Strengthening overseas basic research and employing local researchers also figure in Japanese globalization plans, but only to a modest extent. The fact that more firms plan to strengthen basic research than to employ local researchers suggests that collaboration with local research institutions may be mainly what the Japanese have in mind. Independent evidence from our own survey corroborates this interpretation of the evidence.

1.6 NATIONAL TECHNOLOGY POLICY

Technology gap models of economic growth demonstrate, both theoretically and statistically, that the pace of innovation in a country, whether measured by patent output or R&D input, is a significant determinant of its overall rate of growth. This is particularly true of the leading industrialized countries, and of newly industrializing countries too (Fagerberg, 1987). National technology policy, by influencing the propensity to innovate, clearly has the potential to significantly influence the national growth rate.

Ergas (1987) distinguishes between 'mission-oriented' technology policies and 'diffusion-oriented' ones. Following Weinberg (1967), mission-oriented research is identified as 'big science deployed to meet big problems'. Diffusion-oriented policy, on the other hand, seeks a 'broadly based capacity for adjusting to technological change throughout the industrial structure'. Its major manifestation is heavy investment in vocational training in export-oriented industries. The administration of mission-oriented research in typically centralized, whereas that of diffusion-oriented research is decentralized, he claims.

In the 1960s mission-oriented research was most conspicuous in France, the UK and the US. Both France and the UK were heavily involved in aerospace and nuclear power, and the US in the space programme. Big science seems to have worked most effectively in France, where a tightly knit élite spanning the public and private sectors shared a common educational background with a strong mathematical and scientific bias. It was least successful in the UK, where poor communication between scientists and administrators led to major cost overruns caused by a failure to kill off uneconomic projects. Lack of continuity in political attitudes to state planning, and overemphasis on the importance of 'buying British', also played a part in UK failure.

It might be thought that mission-oriented research would cause national technological activity to become highly concentrated in certain areas. This may be true of France, but it is certainly not true of the UK. Figure 1.2 shows that, given the size of its technological base (as measured by R&D expenditure), the UK is fairly well diversified compared to most other countries. One explanation is that UK missions have not related to natural areas of strength, such as food, chemicals and textiles, but to areas of conspicuously advanced technology in which UK competence was

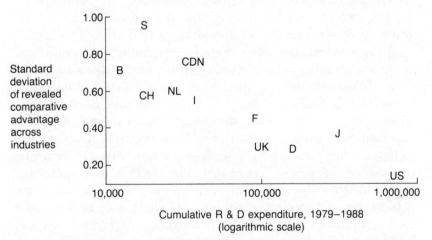

Figure 1.2 Technological specialization between countries, based on patents granted in the US, 1981–1987

Key: B = Belgium, CDN = Canada, CH = Switzerland, F = France, UK = United Kingdom, D = West Germany, I = Italy, J = Japan, NL = Netherlands, S = Sweden, US = United States.

Source: Archibugi and Pianta (1989), figure 4.1, p. 116.

unproven. Even where the academic expertise existed, the ability of UK firms to manage 'big science' projects seems to have been weak. This bias towards championing technological novelty may have directed scientific efforts from commercially more rewarding areas.

The commercial failure of UK mission-oriented research is exemplified by the high operating costs of its advanced gas-cooled reactor. Such failures have left the UK without a credible scientific mission, although it continues to collaborate in European fusion research. Attempts to win leadership in aspects of electronics and computing have been half-hearted under-funded affairs.

The loss of mission has led to a renewal of interest in diffusion-oriented policies. Diffusion-orientation was a feature of nine-teenth-century UK industry, when mechanics institutes, City and Guilds Colleges and numerous clubs for the self-improvement of 'working people' were set up. In late-Victorian Britain many phil-anthropic entrepreneurs and paternalistic employers invested in the education and training of their employees. Today, however, the UK looks to West Germany and Switzerland for models on which to reconstruct its vocational training system.

At the moment, therefore, there appears to be no mission, and not much diffusion either, in policy terms. One mission suggested in this book is to develop the UK as a centre for basic industrial research. Our findings indicate that large multinationals in high-technology industries have developed organizational networks that facilitate the decentralization of basic research. In an attempt to reduce their overheads, basic research has ceased to be a pre-rogative of the parent laboratory. The UK has been quite suc-cessful in attracting such work, even in the absence of any major policies directed specifically to this end. There is no evidence that such laboratories have actually crowded out UK firms. It is clear, however, that competition between locations to host such research is intensifying, and so more positive policy-intervention may be required, if only to match what is being done at rival locations.

By maintaining a critical mass of basic research, diffusion-oriented policies are rendered more viable too. For example, aided by strategic subsidies, firms establishing basic research in the UK would find it a good base at which to collaborate with other firms. Such collaborative projects would not only yield the usual measurable economic benefits, such as greater employment opportunities, but also improve the quality of social and intellectual life.

This policy invites the objection that it does not encompass the high-risk, high-return product development stage of R&D. This is true – but our findings suggest that product development is best carried out close to major high-income markets where the most sophisticated consumers are found. The relatively low standard of living in the UK relative to other leading industrialized countries, coupled with conservatism of UK buyers (Parkinson, 1984) makes it difficult for the UK to compete in the long run with the US, West Germany and Japan in the global product development stakes. By attracting basic research, however, some product development work may also be gained because of the costs of shifting projects between laboratories at the pre-development stage.

1.7 PLAN OF THE BOOK

Chapters 2 and 3 develop a theory of globalized R&D, the first chapter concentrating on microeconomic issues at the firm level, and the second on macroeconomic issues of concern to the nation as a whole. The next five chapters present empirical results. Chapters 4 and 5 analyse data on patents granted in the US between 1963 and 1986. Through cooperation with researchers at the SPRU of the University of Sussex it proved possible to establish the ultimate ownership of patents where they were granted to affiliates of multinationals. In addition to identifying the firm to which a patent was granted, in each case the location of the research facility originally responsible for the innovation, and an industrial classification of the technological activity with which the patent is associated were obtained. A consolidation of the US patenting records of international corporate groups was successfully carried out for 727 of the world's largest 792 industrial firms. Together, they account for nearly 43 per cent of all patents granted in the US between 1969 and 1986.

Chapters 6 and 7 analyse the results of a questionnaire sent to 1,028 R&D establishments all over the world. After one reminder, the total response was 296, comprising 163 from headquarters laboratories and 133 from subsidiary ones. The questionnaire asked a comprehensive range of questions, with particular emphasis on the desirability of the location, relation with other laboratories in the firm and the evolution of the laboratory from its early beginnings to its present state.

Chapter 8 draws on the third source of evidence – interviews with senior R&D personnel – to elaborate on the findings of the earlier chapters. Altogether 27 interviews were carried out – 14 in the UK, 6 elsewhere in Europe, 4 in the US and 3 in Canada. The interviews were open-ended discussions in which research managers were invited to discuss the strategic problems which were of greatest importance to them. Interviewees placed particular stress on the management of human resources within R&D and the quality of personal relations between senior staff in R&D and other functional areas of the firm. This is reflected in the subjects addressed in the chapter.

Chapter 9 summarizes the main findings and evaluates possible policy responses to the issues identified at the outset. A major issue that emerges is the competitiveness of the UK as a location for R&D. It is evident that over the last decade the UK has lost some of the significant advantages it previously enjoyed – partly because of self-inflicted damage caused by government financial policies and partly because of the emergence of attractive alternative sites – both within the European Community (EC) and further afield. New supply-side policies are advocated to maintain and, indeed, enhance, the UK's position. It is argued that the UK stands to gain significantly from increasing its share of the global provision of both UK-owned and foreign-owned R&D facilities. But positive steps need to be taken by government if this is to be achieved.

2

A Systems View of R&D

2.1 INTRODUCTION

This chapter analyses corporate strategies towards international R&D from the standpoint of the economic theory of the MNE (as set out, for example, in Buckley and Casson, 1985). Although important empirical work has been done on the subject (see for example Behrman and Fischer, 1980; Hewitt, 1980, 1983; Pearce, 1989; Ronstadt, 1977) there has been no systematic attempt to analyse global R&D strategies from the economic efficiency point of view. Hirschey and Caves (1981) identify a number of important influences on strategy – such as scale economies in research – but are more concerned with their additive effect than with their interactions.

To emphasize the interactions, this paper builds on the systems view of international business outlined in Casson (1990). This approach is concerned with the way in which a progressive division of labour splits economic processes into an increasing number of more specialized activities. These activities are linked by flows of intermediate products. The functional scope of a firm's operations is determined by how many of these linkages are internalized around its core activity. The geographical scope of the firm's operations – including R&D – is determined by where the internalized activities are located. Thus the interaction of internalization and location factors within a systems view can be used to analyse the determinants of international corporate R&D.

The chapter is organized in three main parts. Sections 2.2 to

2.5 introduce the systems approach, focusing on the division of labour within the firm between production, marketing and R&D. The core of the paper in sections 2.6 to 2.8 examines the division of labour within R&D, and considers which activities will be carried on inside the firm and which will be devolved to others. The interaction between internalization and location is discussed. The final part examines some special topics, such as inter-firm collaboration, and concludes by summarizing the forces fashioning global R&D strategy.

2.2 INFORMATION LINKAGES BETWEEN ACTIVITIES

Information flows are of crucial importance in a system involving R&D. Figure 2.1 derives from Buckley and Casson (1976), chapter 2, and shows schematically the close interaction between production, marketing and R&D within a profit-maximizing firm. The thin lines indicate information flows and the thick line

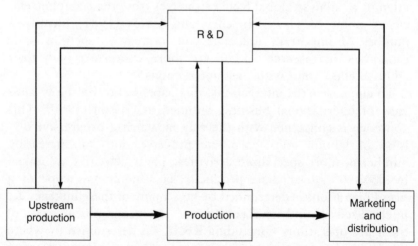

Figure 2.1 Elementary view of interactions between production, marketing and R&D

Source: Buckley and Casson (1976), chapter 2.

the flows of physical product moving downstream. Note that each activity is linked to two or more other activities. Although the physical linkages are rather sparse, they are supplemented by the dense network of information linkages. While the physical linkages are one-directional, the information linkages are all two-way.

When all activities are owned by the same firm, all the linkages are internal to it. But if just one of the activities is independently owned, then *several* linkages are externalized, because the activity has been separated from all the other activities within the ownership unit. Conversely the reintegration of a single activity simultaneously internalizes several linkages. Because of the complex web of interdependencies, therefore, changes in ownership structure cannot be analysed in terms of the internalization of a single linkage. It is the simultaneous internalization of several linkages that is involved.

2.3   RELATIONS BETWEEN MARKETING AND R&D

In figure 2.1 all innovative activities are subsumed under R&D. This approach is consistent with the view that all innovative activities differ from routine activities in the same fundamental respect, namely that they require a high degree of judgement in decision making, and a high tolerance of risk as well. Because people differ significantly in their quality of judgement, it is advantageous to effect a division of labour in which those with good judgement team up to take responsibility for innovation.

Further consideration, however, suggests that a division of labour between the technical and market-oriented aspects of innovation may also be desirable. In technical work the role of judgement is to tie up the loose ends and fill in the missing data within a rigorous analytical framework which must first be mastered. The sensitivity of theoretical predictions to practical applications must also be appreciated. In market-oriented work, on the other hand, the analytical framework is much less sophisticated and the scope for hunch and guesswork correspondingly greater. Marketing-oriented judgement requires much less formal education, but correspondingly more untutored imagination, than do judgements of a technical nature.

Figure 2.2 adapts figure 2.1 so that R&D now refers only to technical innovation. This reflects the most usual interpretation of R&D in the corporate context. Market-oriented innovation is of two kinds – *marketing*, which is the innovative aspect of downstream distribution, and *supply development*, which is the innovative aspect of upstream production. In most industries marketing dominates supply development, and so the two activities have been consolidated in the figure for visual simplification. (In some industries, however, such as oil, supply development is just as important as marketing.) This leaves *distribution*

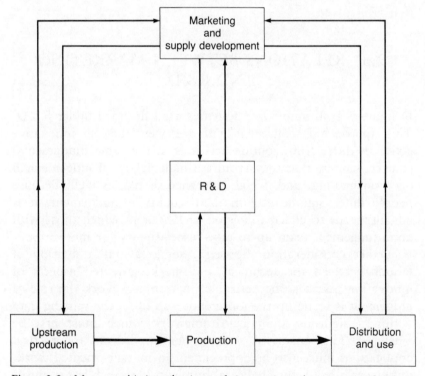

Figure 2.2 More sophisticated view of interactions between production, marketing and R&D

and use representing the routine aspects of downstream activity, and *upstream production* now representing only the routine aspects of upstream operations.

The configuration in figure 2.2 shows R&D having two channels of two-way information flow with the rest of the corporate system (flows from outside the corporate system are considered later). Technical information flows directly to and from production, while market information from both upstream and downstream sources is mediated through marketing and supply development.

2.4   THE DIVISION OF LABOUR WITHIN R&D – PRELIMINARY CONSIDERATIONS

Within R&D, a further division of labour may be implemented, typically producing a sequential flow of ideas as indicated in figure 2.3. These stages have not been differentiated by whether they are *research* or *development*, to avoid the rather sterile controversy over where research ends and development begins. Instead, we distinguish between *generic* and *adaptive* R&D. Generic R&D develops a new product or process concept, such as a medicinal drug, or power-generating unit. Within generic R&D a further division could be made, although for reasons of simplicity this will not figure prominently in the subsequent analysis – it is the distinction between the core concept and the major functional applications. The typical concept can be embodied in various forms, all of which are of potentially global application. Thus a drug may be incorporated into a tablet, a bottled liquid, an injection, and so on, while a new power unit may be configured either for vehicular or stationary use, and among stationary uses for pumping, compressing air, generating electricity, and so on.

Adaptive R&D modifies the applications with a specific local environment in mind. Like generic R&D, both products and processes are included in it. Tablets, for example, may be given tastes or colours according to local preferences, and power units may be adapted to run under different climatic conditions, or to cope with local impurities in fuels. In some cases local conditions may turn out to be less idiosyncratic than first thought, so that what commences as adaptive R&D may turn into application-centred generic R&D. Generic and adaptive R&D are linked by a two-way flow of information, as indicated in the figure. Global applications flow from generic to adaptive R&D, while information on local opportunities for new types of application flows in the opposite direction.

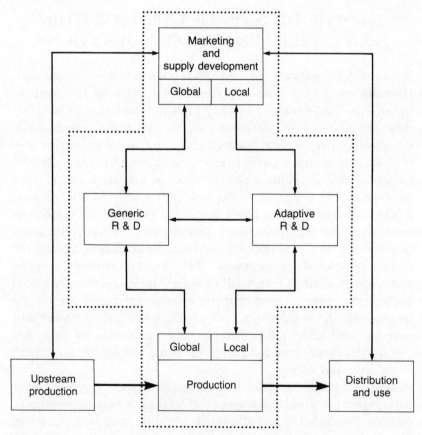

Figure 2.3 A division of labour within R&D which distinguishes generic and adaptive R&D

2.5   INTERNALIZATION AND LOCATION – PRELIMINARY CONSIDERATIONS

A typical pattern of internalization is illustrated by the dotted line in figure 2.3. All activities within the perimeter of the dotted line are owned and controlled by the same firm, while those outside it are independent of it.

The case illustrated is one commonly discussed in the MNE literature. Production, marketing and R&D are integrated, internalizing the dense network of information flows between them. Upstream production, however, is conducted by independent suppliers, while downstream distribution relies on independent wholesalers and retailers, though in both cases the marketing and purchasing departments will maintain a staff to monitor these activities, as far as they are able, by visits to the independents' premises. Notice that the two stages of R&D are vertically integrated whereas the three stages of the production sequence are not. This reflects the importance attached by conventional theory to the internalization of proprietary information flow.

When considering the locational dimension, it is important to distinguish between activities and facilities. Production, marketing and R&D are each activities which may be carried out in several different facilities. A facility is a plant or office at a specific location, and sometimes forms part of a larger multi-purpose site. Because of the public good nature of knowledge, it is unusual for a firm to replicate the same kind of R&D activity in different facilities. Transport costs and barriers to trade, however, frequently make it economic to replicate production (though not normally when there are major economies of scale). The highly specific nature of information in local markets often encourages firms to replicate marketing facilities too.

When activities are replicated, some of the facilities may be owned by the firm and others not. This makes it difficult to talk of the integration of activities; it is more precise to talk of the integration of facilities instead. Facilities of the same type may be treated differently because when linkages become spatially specific, internalization may be contingent on location factors which vary from one facility to another.

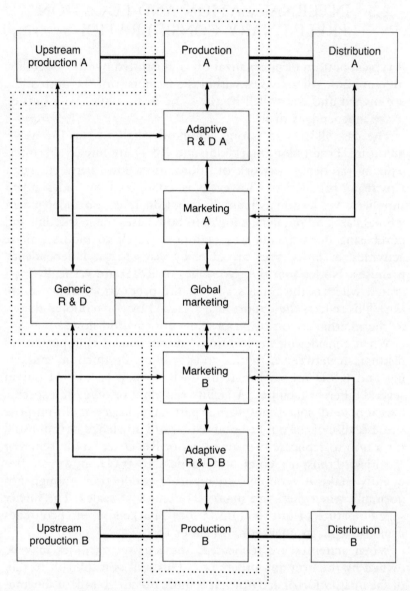

Figure 2.4 A possible structure of facilities for a firm serving two autarkic markets

Conventional theory, for example, suggests a variety of reasons – risk of expropriation, cultural obstacles to communication, and so on – why the costs of internalization may be higher for international linkages than for domestic linkages of the same kind. Thus a firm exploiting a certain generic technology may find it economic to internalize linkages within its home country, but to externalize linkages between home and overseas facilities. This distinction is illustrated in figure 2.4, which represents the spatially specific linkages – including both home and foreign facilities – which are generated when an innovative firm produces and sells in two distinct autarkic markets A and B.

The outer perimeter of dotted lines encloses all the facilities owned by the firm when the foreign market B is serviced through foreign direct investment. The inner perimeter indicates the ownership structure when foreign licensing is used instead. In the latter case facilities at home (in country A) remain integrated into the firm, but facilities abroad are integrated into a separate firm (the licensee), whose boundaries are indicated by the inner perimeter in the lower half of the figure. The licensing arrangement externalizes three two-way linkages: the flows of marketing information between the global marketing facility and the local marketing facility, the analogous flows of production information and, most importantly, the flow of technical information between generic R&D on the one hand and local adaptive R&D on the other.

2.6   THE SYSTEM STRUCTURE OF R&D

The preceding analysis has utilized the systems view to examine the context in which R&D is carried out. It has not looked at R&D itself in system terms, except for the simple distinction between generic and adaptive R&D. It is now time to go further 'inside the black box' and look at the structure of R&D itself. Two main perspectives on the R&D system can be discerned in the literature. One is the linear view, which sees R&D progressing in a sequence of stages from basic science through to product and process innovation. The other is the cyclic view which emphasizes

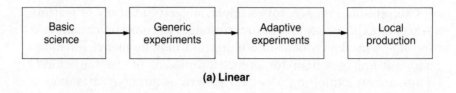

(a) Linear

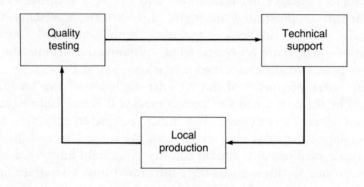

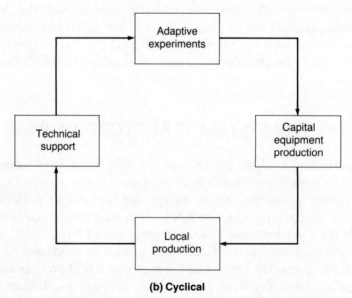

(b) Cyclical

Figure 2.5 Linear and cyclical perspectives on R&D

the feedback of information from later stages of the process. The linear view encourages the perception of innovation as a discrete and lumpy process, while the cyclic view emphasizes incremental and continuous aspects instead.

The linear view is illustrated in the top half of figure 2.5, while the cyclical view is illustrated by the two closed loops shown in the bottom half of the figure. Figures 2.6 and 2.7 elaborate upon this structure. The first half of the linear sequence constitutes the core of generic R&D. The picture has been amplified in figure 2.6 by recognition of the role of *global scanning* and *reverse engineering* in generating information inputs to generic R&D. Global

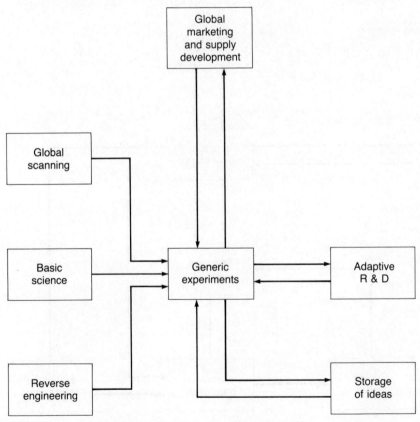

Figure 2.6 Structure of generic R&D

scanning includes monitoring public opinion and government policies on matters such as health and safety, conservation, strategic self-sufficiency and so on. Reverse engineering is particularly important in non-collusive differentiated-product oligopolies, where it not only helps to prevent rivals from gaining a major technical lead, but also supports the development of low-cost 'me-too' products, which can starve rivals of monopoly profits on their recent innovations (and thereby reduce their internal sources of finance for future R&D).

Figure 2.6 also recognizes the role of marketing in guiding generic R&D, and the role of corporate memory in storing ideas

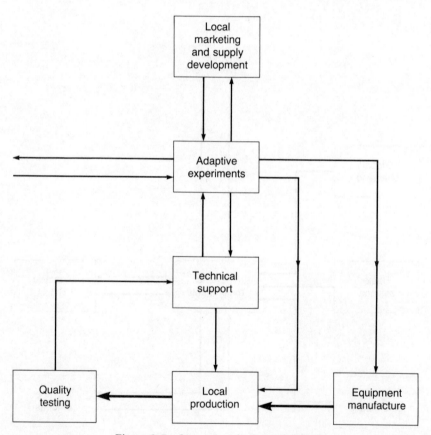

Figure 2.7   Structure of adaptive R&D

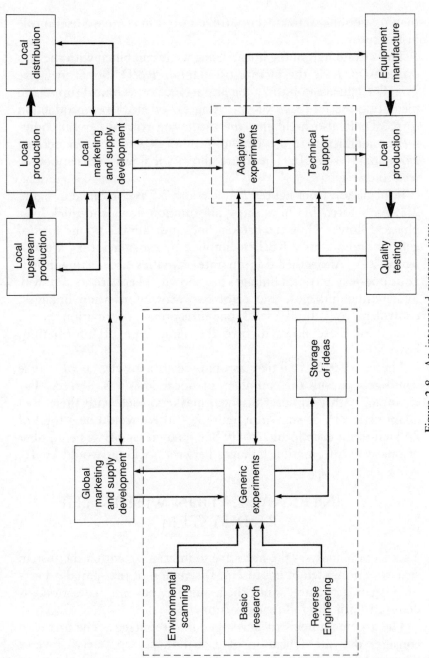

Figure 2.8 An integrated systems view

that are peripheral to current problems but may have a useful role in the future.

The second half of the linear sequence is combined with the two cycles to provide the picture of adaptive R&D shown in figure 2.7. The figure emphasizes the importance of technical support in mediating the feedback of operating experience from production to R&D. It also highlights the mediating role of capital equipment manufacture in the 'embodiment' of new technology derived from adaptive R&D. The figure allows for flows of disembodied technology too.

Information from figures 2.4, 2.6 and 2.7 is combined in figure 2.8. As before, thin lines show information flows and thick lines physical flows, while the broken lines indicate the boundaries of generic and adaptive R&D as implied by the 'black box' view of figure 2.4. Altogether 15 separate activities are distinguished. Four one-way physical linkages are shown. There are six one-way information linkages, and eight two-way information linkages, equivalent to a total of 22 one-directional information flows. Several of these flows involve the same type of information, however.

The number of facilities, as opposed to activities, is of course contingent upon the number of local markets served. For example, with two autarkic local markets, each with their own adaptive R&D, as shown in figure 2.4, there would be a total of 24 facilities if each local activity had its own facility. The number of one-way information linkages between facilities would be 41.

2.7   INTERNALIZATION WITHIN THE R&D SYSTEM

This section analyses the incentive to internalize within the system structure presented in figure 2.8. Discussion of the spatial aspects of system structure, and their impact on internalization, is deferred until the following section.

The argument below is developed in three stages. The first is to consider the internalization of each linkage separately. Twelve types of information linkage and four types of physical linkage are identified, according to the nature of the product flow involved. Some types of information are involved in as many as four separate linkages – through several are involved in only one. The relation between the product, the linkages and the activities is indicated in tables 2.1 and 2.2.

Table 2.1 Information flows catalogued from figure 2.8

	Linkages	
Market	*Source activity*	*Destination activity*
General knowledge	Environmental scanning	Generic experiments
Basic scientific results	Basic science	Generic experiments
Intelligence on rivals' products	Reverse engineering	Generic experiments
Previous ideas	Storage of ideas	Generic experiments
Global marketing requirements	Global marketing	Generic experiments Local marketing
Local marketing requirements	Local marketing	Adaptive experiments Local distribution Local upstream production Global marketing
New concept	Generic experiments	Adaptive experiments Storage of ideas Global marketing
Adapted designs	Adaptive experiments	Local production Equipment manufacture Technical support Local marketing
Quality measurements	Quality testing	Technical support
Solutions to day-to-day production problems	Technical support	Local production Adaptive experiments
Local customer intelligence	Local distribution	Local marketing
Local supply intelligence	Local upstream production	Local marketing

Each type of product is rated according to its degree of quality assurance. A suggested rating of the various information flows is presented in table 2.3, and a corresponding rating for physical flows in table 2.4. Low quality assurance implies a high propensity to internalize, and vice versa. This is because if quality cannot be assured then the user's risks are high, and need to be reduced by gaining the additional information and power of control that internalization provides.

Table 2.2   Physical flows catalogued from figure 2.8

| | Linkages | |
Market	*Source activity*	*Destination activity*
Intermediate inputs	Local upstream production	Local production
Product	Local production	Local distribution
Product samples	Local production	Quality testing
Capital equipment	Equipment manufacture	Local production

Table 2.3   Internalization strategies for information markets

Market	*Degree of quality assurance*	*Economies of scope and scale*	*Strategy*	*Comment*
General knowledge	Moderate	High	Externalize	Sometimes non-proprietary
Basic scientific results	Moderate	High	Externalize	Sometimes non-proprietary
Intelligence on rival products	Moderate	Low	Internalize	
Global marketing requirements	Low	High	Marginal	
Local marketing requirements	Moderate	Low	Internalize	
New concept	Low	Moderate	Internalize	
Adapted design	Low	Low	Internalize	
Quality measurements	Moderate	Moderate	Marginal	
Local customer intelligence	Low	Low	Internalize	
Local supply intelligence	Low	Low	Internalize	

Table 2.4 Internalization strategies for physical flows

Market	Degree of quality assurance	Economies of scope and scale	Strategy
Intermediate inputs	Moderate	Moderate	Marginal
Product	Moderate	High	Externalize
Product samples	Low	Low	Internalize
Capital equipment	Moderate	High	Externalize

The second stage places the system structure within the context of surrounding systems – including systems belonging to other industries. Economies of scope and scale within a facility give it a capacity to meet the requirements of other users as well. Thus information from generic experiments may be spun-off to peripheral applications. Specialized equipment used for quality measurement may be used to analyse samples from many different production units. The fixed plant and the skilled labour force of a capital equipment producer may be used to produce equipment for other industries as well – and so on.

The owner of a facility which affords significant economies of scope has a strong incentive to invest in promoting arm's length arrangements with different users because the costs of internalizing different uses will escalate beyond a certain point as diseconomies of bureaucracy set in. Although arm's length marketing for one use does not preclude internalization through forward integration for some other use, it reduces the owner's dependence on internalization strategy because of the experience gained in arm's length sales. On balance, therefore, economies of scale and scope promote the externalization of the relevant product market. Typical externalization policies include licensing concepts to other firms for application, licensing other firm's concepts for in-house application, renting out quality control facilities to other firms or doing subcontracted research for them, renting other people's facilities or getting them to act as subcontractors, and so on.

Overall estimates of economies of scale and scope are presented in the second column of tables 2.3 and 2.4. A combination of low

economies of scope and low quality assurance favours internalization. Conversely, a combination of large economies of scope and
high quality assurance favours externalization.

The third stage of the argument reintroduces the concept of
system interdependence between internalization decisions noted in
the introduction – albeit in an intuitive way. When a facility is
involved in several linkages, some of which are best internalized
and others not, the integration of the facility into the firm is determined by a trade-off between the benefit to one linkage and the
cost to another. The probable results of such a trade-off are
indicated in table 2.5. Among the information-generating
activities, only global scanning and basic research are externalized. They have just a single linkage to the rest of the system, and
their economies of scope are quite high. Externalization is therefore appropriate, despite the problems of quality assurance
involved. These problems are typically overcome by reliance on
the reputation of the source and, where appropriate, on the use
of multiple sources to provide checks on each other.

Quality testing and technical support might well be externalized
too, if just a single linkage were involved. But because of the
importance of quality assurance in the information feedback from
technical support to adaptive experiments, internalization is
appropriate instead. The incentives to internalize the physical
flows in the system are somewhat weaker because quality assurance is normally less of a problem where a physical product rather

Table 2.5 Activities classified by whether they are
likely to be integrated with generic experiments

Integrated	Not integrated
Reverse engineering	Environmental scanning
Storage of ideas	Basic research
Adaptive experiments	Equipment manufacture
Technical support	Local upstream production
Quality testing	Local distribution
Global marketing	
Local marketing	
Local production	

than information is concerned. Thus the level of integration in the nexus of production, marketing and R&D is greater than within the production and distribution sequence, as indicated in the cases discussed in section 2.5.

2.8   THE SPATIAL DIVISION OF LABOUR WITHIN R&D AND ITS IMPLICATIONS FOR INTERNALIZATION

In principle each R&D activity can be located on a different site. Different activities require different types of immobile input, as indicated in table 2.6, and so there may be locational specialization according to comparative advantage within R&D.

The greater the distance between the sites, however, the greater are the difficulties of communication. This may prove a significant constraint on specialization because of the importance of face-to-face communication in R&D. Information of an ambiguous and controversial character is best communicated face-to-face.

Table 2.6   Availability of local inputs as an influence on the location of activities

Activity	Major factor
Environmental scanning	Information hub
Basic research	Access to academic labour
Reverse engineering	
Storage of ideas	
Generic experiments	Access to scientific labour
Adaptive experiments	
Technical support	
Quality testing	
Global marketing	Access to managerial labour
Local marketing	
Equipment manufacture	Access to skilled labour
Local production	Access to skilled and unskilled labour
Local upstream production	Access to raw material deposits and energy sources
Local distribution	Proximity to customers' residences

Ambiguities can be minimized by supplementing verbal comments with gestures. Doubts about reliability can be settled through conversational traps, and through cross-examination which elicits spontaneous corroborative (or conflicting) evidence. Emotional bonds can also be built up to encourage integrity in the first place. Some of these effects can also be achieved by 'ear-to-ear' telephone conversation, but this is by no means a perfect substitute.

Table 2.7 rates the information flows listed in table 2.1 by the importance of face-to-face communication and the frequency of contact required. The more frequently face-to-face meetings are needed, the stronger the incentive to locate the activities close together. Overall, the ratings suggest that generic experiments will be pulled towards universities and research institutions where basic science is going on, while adaptive research will be pulled towards local markets.

This could create locational tension by pulling apart generic

Table 2.7 Quality assurance and communication strategies

Market	Importance of face-to-face communication	Frequency	Strategy
General knowledge	Low	High	Frequent written reports
Basic scientific results	Moderate	Moderate	Regular meetings and reports
Intelligence on rivals' products	Moderate	Low	Occasional meetings and reports
Global marketing requirements	High	Low	Occasional meetings
Local marketing requirements	High	High	Frequent meetings
New concept	High	Low	Occasional meetings
Adapted designs	High	Moderate	Regular meetings
Quality measurements	Low	High	Frequent written reports
Solutions to day-to-day production problems	High	High	Frequent meetings
Local customer intelligence	High	High	Frequent meetings
Local supply intelligence	High	High	Frequent meetings

and adaptive research. The problem should not be exaggerated, however. Adaptive research is likely to be focused on the largest and wealthiest markets where product demand is strong at an early stage of the life-cycle. Such markets may well be based in metropolitan centres within industrialized countries where many basic research institutions can be found. The overall effect, therefore, may be to pull both stages of R&D toward major regional agglomerations of sophisticated activity.

These results need to be qualified in three ways, however. Firstly, the spatial division of labour must be efficient not only with respect to the communication of information but with respect to the transport of physical products as well. Thus difficulties in transporting product samples could pull adaptive R&D towards production sites which (because of access to raw materials) are remote from major markets. Similarly, difficulties in transporting bulky equipment may tie production, and hence adaptive R&D, to major agglomerations of capital goods industries. Neither of these cases is of major practical importance, though.

Secondly, the political risks associated with a multinational R&D system must be taken into account. An R&D facility is probably less vulnerable to expropriation than a production facility, however, since there is usually a smaller degree of irreversible commitment to the site: brains and software are more portable than factory equipment. On the other hand, the expropriation of an R&D facility could have serious consequences for the long run viability of the firm.

The third qualification – differential threats of espionage – is much more important than the other two. The threat may come from the host-country government – this is one reason why western firms do not carry out major R&D in the CMEA countries even though scientific labour is very cheap there. More significantly, the threat may come from the firm's own rivals – either through clandestine operations or the overt poaching of key personnel. In oligopolistic industries firms wishing to catch up on the leader's technology may wish to site their own R&D facilities close to his, while the leader may wish to locate well away, if he can, from his follower's facilities.

2.9   INTER-FIRM COOPERATION

The preceding analysis has assumed that the firm faces a stark contrast between the internalization and externalization of markets, although in practice intermediate forms, such as joint ventures, are very common. The preceding analysis may be likened to the output of a generic R&D programme, which needs to be further adapted in order to accommodate the 'local' conditions encountered in practical applications.

One important use of joint ventures is to organize inter-firm collusion (Buckley and Casson, 1988). Collusion can apply not only to the marketing of products, but also to the establishment of inter-firm specialization in R&D which avoids replication of effort and reduces the risk of patenting and innovation races. The scope for such collusion varies between industries, of course. It depends on the height of the barriers to entry – not only the barriers to small firms, which may be quite high, but the barriers to other large firms diversifying into the industry, which may well be lower. It also depends on the number of firms behind the entry barrier.

Collusion may be effected through an informal gentleman's agreement or more formally through a cartel. An exchange of shares between firms, or the organization of a joint venture R&D affiliate, however, provides greater incentive against cheating, because each firm is to some extent a hostage to the other.

The advantages of collusion are greater the wider is the scope of application of the R&D across different segments of the product market. This suggests that firms may club together through industry associations to undertake concept-generating R&D (see section 2.4) collectively, while leaving individual members of the club free to compete in developing applications. One of the difficulties with such arrangements, however, is that it is often difficult to exclude non-members from access to knowledge generated by the club. This is, of course, one of the classic arguments for public funding of the early stages of R&D.

Because of the dangers of espionage, noted earlier, firms may prefer to locate their R&D in countries with a strong cooperative culture. This may be an important consideration when choosing between alternative centres of scientific excellence as a location for generic R&D. The governments of such countries are likely to be sympathetic to cartelization and inter-firm specialization, and to be willing to enforce contractual penalties against former employees who infringe corporate secrecy. There was a significant change in the US policy stance on this issue in 1984 (Evan and Olk, 1990).

Joint ventures have other uses too – for example, in the vertical coordination of upstream and downstream activities. In general, joint ventures are very useful for the capital-constrained firm that wishes to extend its influence over peripheral activities without having to finance their acquisition outright. The dangers with joint ventures are connected mainly with the loss of confidentiality, and the relatively high actuarial risk of premature termination due to the dissatisfaction of the other partner.

2.10 ORGANIZATION STRUCTURE AND PERSONNEL POLICIES

People are crucial to the production, communication and use of information, so it is obvious that personnel policies have a major influence on the performance of the research-oriented firm. It is personnel policies that are largely responsible for making internal markets in information work.

The importance of face-to-face communication in achieving clarity and trust means that when there is an extensive spatial division of labour in R&D careful planning of people's movements is vital. People can move for either short periods or long ones, and either on out-and-back trips or open-ended itineraries (see table 2.8). Short out-and-back trips are much less disruptive of office routine and family life than are the others and, provided they are not repeated too often, are less exhausting as well. Like round trips, they carry fewer risks for the individual than do relocations through secondment or promotion.

Day trips for internal meetings are quite feasible when R&D facilities are located close to major hubs, such as airports, railway

Table 2.8 Examples of various types of intra-firm personnel mobility

Structure	Short term	Long term
Out and back	Day trip	Secondment
Round trip	Tour of plants, sales facilities, etc	Sequential secondments for future chief executive 'getting to know the business'
Open ended		Sequential relocations through career promotions

junctions and motorway intersections. Costs of inputs close to major hubs are often relatively high, however (reflecting, for example, the higher cost of living of personnel, which in turn reflects the scarcity of land). A satisfactory substitute may be to network the various facilities to a common hub whose hotels and conference centres provide neutral ground on which meetings can be held.

When the messages to be communicated are very complex, however, the long-period strategies may be the only viable ones. Relocation through secondment and promotion may be quite attractive to young unattached research workers, though resisted by older – and correspondingly more experienced – ones. Personnel strategies may therefore require younger researchers to visit older researchers, broadening the minds of the young through travel and providing the older workers with the time to exploit their accumulated firm-specific skills more intensively on the job in hand.

When R&D work is spatially decentralized there may be a problem in supervising small groups of workers in outlying facilities. It is certainly a problem in some other types of multinational service activity. There is reason to believe, however, that most scientific researchers are strongly self-motivated, so that the major problem is not one of slacking but of deviation from corporate objectives into personal lines of research. Such deviation can usually be checked quite easily by requiring regular submission of written reports rather than by supervisors making personal visits to the site.

Perhaps the major cause of demotivation is the threat that interesting work may either be ignored by senior managers or appropriated for development by other people – particularly those closer to headquarters. Promoting scientific 'intrapreneurship' may therefore require small groups to be allowed to win mandates for the development of promising ideas. Decentralization through mandating cannot be pursued too liberally, however. Unless the economic logic outlined in previous sections is respected, the chaotic proliferation of loosely coordinated projects may undermine the viability of R&D activity as a whole.

It is not only communication within the R&D that is crucial, but communication between R&D and other functional areas – notably marketing and production. Section 2.3 raised the general issue of the desirability of a division of labour between production, marketing and R&D. While these activities clearly require different skills, it is important that the senior managers in each area are sufficiently broad-minded to understand messages received from their opposite numbers. They must be able, for example, to allow for differences in the length of the typical planning horizon in each area – recognizing that requirements in production and marketing are more volatile and urgent and those in adaptive R&D, which in turn are more pressing that those in generic R&D.

Personnel policies face a difficult trade-off in giving senior managers sufficient specialized competence to manage their own subordinates while also providing the breadth of experience that allows them to coordinate their own function effectively with others. One solution is to create a managerial career stream, within R&D, which recruits from the qualified technical staff, and offers accelerated promotion in return for accepting a greater risk of relocation and exposure to more varied experience. Another strategy is for the chief executive to engender a sense of corporate mission which homogenizes the preferences of the managers in the different functional areas involved. An extreme policy would be to eliminate the division of labour, and operate with a fully integrated team. This option is certainly viable for small firms operating on a single site, and may be one reason for the continuing vitality of the small-firm sector in many industries. In a large firm the integrated team is likely to become unmanageable, however; the most probable outcome then is that managers trained in one functional area gain control and subordinate the other functional areas to them, generating damaging biases in decision-making.

2.11   FURTHER CONSIDERATIONS

One of the objections to the systems view is that it leads to considerable complexity in the analysis. Its advantage is that when the system is correctly specified the complexity provides much greater realism. It advances the theory closer to the situation confronted by the practitioner.

There are many other complications which the practitioner confronts, however, and some of these are itemized below.

1   *Site economies*   Any site requires infrastructure – roads for access, security, maintenance, salary administration, and so on. The cost of this infrastructure normally increases less than proportionately with the area and employment of people on the site. By locating several different facilities on the same site significant economies can be achieved. Although independently-owned facilities can share a site, internalization economies can be quite significant, and the agglomeration of different facilities under common ownership is often the best solution to efficient site use. Thus a multinational producer may choose, in each country of operation, to agglomerate the factory, the R&D unit and the local marketing headquarters on the same site.

The counter-argument is that some production plants require large amounts of space close to rivers, which can be used for the bulk transport of materials and for the disposal of pollutant byproducts. This uncongenial environment is unsuited to offices and laboratories which are much less space-intensive and for which access to international airports and desirable residential districts is much more important. Choice of site is an important and delicate decision, the results of which may vary considerably from one industry to another.

2 *Multiple projects* A successful firm will always follow one innovation with a stream of others in the pipeline, and as a result there may be not just one but several projects in hand at any stage of research. This is particularly true of firms with a diversified product range and of firms with multi-component products in which the different components are independently researched within the firm.

R&D management must reallocate each resource between different projects as they progress to maturity. Furthermore with any given set of projects in hand, priorities in the use of the resource may have to be reassigned – for example, set-backs in the development of one component may put research on this component onto the critical path, and warrant a temporary diversion of resources from research on other components until research on the backward component has caught up.

3 *Accommodating different types of customer and supplier* It has been implicitly assumed above that the information requirements of marketing, and the information feedback from it, are essentially the same whether the customer base comprises a large number of private individuals, a smaller number of firms, or one or two major state-owned entities (for example, a national health service). Differences between products purchased regularly and those purchased occasionally, and between those which are mass-produced and those which are customized, have also been ignored. Similarly, relations with different types of raw material supplier, and capital-good producer, have not been considered either. To some extent, of course, these problems can be dismissed as purely marketing problems, but this is not entirely accurate, for the systems view, with its emphasis on inter-dependencies, shows that the kind of customer and supplier will affect the type of information involved.

Given these and other complexities, it is not surprising that many R&D managers seem to rely upon a small number of rather intuitive concepts to guide their thinking. The system effects underlying the internalization decision are often handled using the concepts of 'synergy' and 'fit'. These concepts are employed to consider whether linked activities should be included within the firm because they are sufficiently complementary to some other 'core' activity. Another approach is to rely upon simple guidelines, such as 'externalize routine activities and internalize non-routine activities so as to maximize the intensity of learning'. Simple ideas of this kind contain much wisdom, though difficulties may be encountered if they are applied uncritically outside those areas where they have a proven track-record of success.

The more complex question of the interaction between internalization and location is not, however, an issue which many managers seem to consider in conceptual terms at all. The more sophisticated aspects of R&D decision-making seem to be governed entirely by pragmatism – each case is considered on its merits. The analysis in this paper may therefore be useful in analysing the reasons for the success or failure of pragmatic decisions in various cases, and could even, if found useful, lead in the long run to a modification of R&D decision making as a result.

2.12   SUMMARY AND CONCLUSIONS

This paper has used the systems approach to internalization and location to identify the factors governing the economic efficiency of R&D. The economic principles handle the key issues quite successfully, but the principles do not readily translate into rules because the optimal strategy in any given case is heavily contingent on the particularities.

The need for face-to-face communication pulls different components of R&D in different directions, and the obvious way to reconcile these tensions is to ensure that all facilities are within easy reach of major transport hubs. The precise direction in which adaptive R&D is pulled is strongly influenced by the final product market; and especially by regional idiosyncrasies in product specification. Government attitudes to property rights, and the culture of inter-firm cooperation will similarly influence the location of generic R&D.

Activities such as global scanning and basic research, which afford major economies of scope, will typically be delegated to independent specialists, some of which, such as universities, provide their output on a non-proprietary basis. Apart from capital-equipment production – which also affords economies of scope – most other research activities will be internalized because of the problem of maintaining both confidentiality and quality assurance where proprietary information is concerned.

There is, however, considerable scope for variability of practice, not only because economies of scope and quality assurance vary from case to case, but because system interdependencies lead to complex trade-offs where the integration of facilities with multiple linkages is concerned. Understanding more fully the determinants of this variability is itself a complex task, but is of sufficient importance to warrant much more attention in future research.

3

International Comparative Advantage and the Location of R&D

3.1 THE NATIONAL PERSPECTIVE

It is often suggested that the sources of innovation and competitiveness lie at the firm level rather than the national level. The emphasis on corporate strategy in chapter 2 is in line with this thinking. But it is true only up to a point. In the short run an economy possesses a given number of scientists and engineers, and more demands placed by one firm mean fewer resources available for others. With inelastic supply, one source of growth crowds out another. During the 1960s and 1970s the growth in the numbers of young people, and the expansion of higher education, led to a rising output of university graduates which tended to mitigate supply constraints. But the subsequent reversal of underlying demographic trends and the reduction in state funding of higher education has led to renewed concern over both the quantity and quality of the scientific labour supply.

In the long run, of course, the supply of scientists and other specialists is elastic. Increased demand will raise returns to a scientific career, and encourage young people to switch into science away from alternative employment. But the degree of elasticity can differ significantly between countries. Even in countries where the elasticity is high, moreover, young scientists may be expensive to recruit because young people in general are in short supply.

The natural abilities of the population are an important determinant of the elasticity of supply of scientists. Some people are more readily educated as scientists than others. Because R&D makes intensive use of scientists, a country in which the population is relatively more productive in scientific work than in other work has a comparative advantage in R&D (Findlay and Kierzkowski, 1983). Other things being equal, international relative prices will establish internal wage relativities in a comparatively advantaged country which encourage a high proportion of the population to undertake scientific work. The country will specialize in R&D-intensive activities such as innovation and, as a result, tend to export new products.

This natural comparative advantage may not be fully revealed, however. Capacity constraints in education may prevent the supply of scientists from increasing. Where education is state funded, market signals emanating from changing wage differentials may be ignored by state planners. This is an obvious example of a supply constraint that is independent of the abilities of the population.

A more subtle supply constraint can arise from national culture (Casson, 1991). Certain types of culture – associated with religious fundamentalism, for example – are antipathetic to Western scientific concepts. Other cultures simply hold scientists and engineers in low regard – their status is low compared with that of other professions. This reduces the non-pecuniary rewards to a scientific career and encourages intelligent young people to choose other occupations instead.

There is considerable anecdotal evidence suggesting that cultural factors are an important deterrent to the choice of a scientific career in industry in the UK. In the nineteenth century UK industrialists made significant efforts to promote popular scientific education as well as more specific vocational training, but the gulf between pure research on the one hand and industrial practice on the other was even then not satisfactorily bridged (Bud and Roberts, 1984; Roderick and Stephens, 1972). The 'anti-business' culture of the establishment (Hannah, 1989) seemed to rub off onto the scientific community, so that the integration of pure and applied work was much less effective than in Germany. Problems of low status seem particularly to afflict engineers – in contrast to the situation in West Germany, Sweden and Japan (Ahlström, 1982; Divall, 1990a,b). Chapter 8 presents additional empirical evidence in support of this view.

Low status may also be reflected in low pay. It is by no means obvious that wage relativities adjust to equate demand and supply for labour in the same way that they do for products. Scientists' wages may be held down because the senior managers to whom they report believe that scientists must be paid some fixed percentage less than they themselves receive.

Another problem may be that scientists are less heavily unionized than other workers. Production workers often use strike-threat power to bargain for higher wages whereas scientists normally do not. This asymmetry in bargaining tactics distorts relativities. It lowers the relative wage of scientists and reduces the rate of return on education. It encourages school leavers to seek production work instead of going on to higher education to take a scientific training.

Furthermore, wage push among production workers can reduce scientists' wages not only relatively, but also absolutely. If scientists and production workers have strictly complementary roles in a given industry and production workers insist on a higher wage, firms can maintain profitability with the existing product range only if they reduce costs elsewhere. One way of doing this is to reduce scientists' wages.

If one firm does it alone, of course, it will lose its scientists to other firms. But if they all do it together then in the short run production can continue. This type of situation is most likely to arise when a small number of domestic firms are producing for a highly competitive export market. Competition from other countries prevents the firms from passing on higher costs in the form of higher prices. On the other hand, the small number of firms involved in the domestic labour market makes monopsonistic collusion against local scientists relatively easy.

It is not, of course, the case that scientists are totally non-unionized. Rather, their principal allegiance is to professional bodies which are more concerned with peer group support, accreditation and quality control than they are with organizing industrial action. Independent critical judgement is an important aspect of research, and this ethos is incompatible with 'downing tools' in the middle of an experiment.

Evidence for supply constraints is mixed. The number of firms reporting skill shortages has been on a rising trend in the UK since 1983, although the shortages reported relate more to technicians and engineers than to graduate scientists (Hart, 1990). The interviews in the present study suggest, though, that many research managers – particularly in the UK – are anxious about the future supply of scientists. The problem does not, however, seem to be one of educational capacity – in the sense that many degree sources in science and engineering are undersubscribed. This is true even in disciplines like chemistry which are crucial for research in the high-growth pharmaceutical industry. Nor does lack of basic ability in the population seem to be a problem.

The most common complaint from UK interviewees related to the high wages paid to newly qualified entrants to the City – and, indeed, in the accounting and legal professions as a whole. It was claimed that, at the same time, the status of science among young people had declined owing to a negative image of industrial research connected with pollution, radiation risks to health, and even an aversion to messy 'hands on' work at the laboratory bench. There may also have been concern that universities themselves promoted a negative image of industrial employment, though this was not specifically alleged.

The crucial question here is why the R&D sector does not respond by raising wages to match competition from the service sector and compensate for deteriorating status. One reason may be that firms cannot cope with the internal adjustment of relative salaries what would ensue. Perhaps a strong commitment to traditional culture-specific differentials renders the firms incapable of responding except by raising everyone's salaries, and this is quite uneconomic to do. They prefer to continue understaffed rather than disturb internal equity or raise the entire salary level in the enterprise.

Another reason may concern the age profile of the scientific workforce. In disciplines such as chemistry there was a rapid expansion of graduate output in the 1960s which led to excessive supply (Creedy, 1975). Salaries fell significantly and there are now many middle-aged chemists who are accustomed to relatively low salary levels. Young doctoral chemists are potentially more valuable than some of the older generation because they have a more up-to-date training even if they lack experience. Under purely competitive conditions the most promising young chemists might be hired at salaries well above the industry average, but because of a commitment to traditional age-related differentials they may not be. Expectations of future career earnings in chemistry, it could be suggested, are therefore based on the depressed earnings of a middle-aged cohort, whereas to encourage entry they should reflect the shortage of qualified chemists which employers currently fear. If this is correct, then it is principally a passive corporate personnel policy which is allowing science to be crowded out by other more lucrative professional careers.

3.2   CROWDING OUT

The argument about alternative employment in the City raises the question of demand side rather than supply side effects. The argument presupposes an autonomous increase in the demand for qualified manpower from the service sector. It asserts the competition from the service sector crowds out industrial R&D in the labour market.

Crowding out can occur not only in the market for qualified manpower as a whole, but also within the scientific sector itself. Two main aspects of this can be distinguished: crowding out between the public and the private sector (Bacon and Eltis, 1976) and crowding out within the private sector between foreign and domestic firms.

The UK defence industry has long been accused of absorbing an excessive number of scientists that would have been more productively employed in the private sector (Kaldor, Sharp and Walker, 1986). Compared to competition from the service sector, this is a more serious problem in the sense that the short-run elasticity of substitution between the public and private sectors within

R&D is potentially greater than the elasticity of substitution between scientific employment and other professional employment. It is easier for a scientist to move between publicly and privately funded R&D than it is for a scientist to move into another profession. Of course, in the long run the difference becomes smaller because the substitution between science and other professions is made by school leavers before much specific training has been imparted.

There is one advantage to defence employment, however, and that is that by raising the equilibrium scientists' wage, and providing an easy alternative to private sector employment, it reduces the risks of choosing science as a career. If it had not been for UK defence research, a scientific career might have had an even less positive image than it already does.

Recent cut-backs in spending on defence research, coupled with stagnation and decline in university employment, should have reduced the extent of crowding out in the scientists' labour market (see chapter 9). While crowding out by the public sector may have been a problem in the past, it seems implausible to perceive it as an increasing problem in the future.

3.3   CRITICAL MASS AND AGGLOMERATION

It is possible that domestically owned firms are being crowded out within the private sector by foreign-owned firms. The potential dangers, in terms of the poaching of key staff, are not difficult to see. There may be benefits too, however. One of these benefits could be that the presence of foreign firms helps to create a 'critical mass' of researchers in the country which improves R&D productivity among all the firms. In other words, positive externalities between researchers increase as the number of researchers increases. As scientists' wages rise to draw more people into R&D, the productivity of each researcher rises faster than the increase in the wage.

Externalities are, of course, often claimed for defence R&D.

Technological spillovers between military and commercial applications are of a rather different kind, however. In any case, current opinion holds that the magnitude of such spillovers has been exaggerated in the past. One of the most telling points is that two countries with highly successful industrial R&D – West Germany and Japan – have very few official publicly funded military research projects at all. Conversely, countries such as the US and UK, which devote a high proportion of GDP to defence, seem to have enjoyed few commercial spin-offs outside the aerospace industry.

Externalities that depend upon critical mass may well operate only within the private sector. This is because the secrecy that surrounds defence R&D is even stricter than that surrounding commercial R&D.

Within the private sector head-on rivalry between firms is often less significant than complementarity between distinct but related lines of research. The larger the number of scientists within the private sector, the greater is likely to be the number of specialist niches covered by local expertise. The potential number of local cooperative linkages between researchers may therefore expand exponentially with the overall scale of research.

These externalities are not unlike those which apply to telephone systems or computer networks, in which the value of the network to any user depends upon the number of other users they can get in contact with. Externalities of this kind generate economies of scale. In the present instance, the scale economies will be governed by the number of scientists employed in the private sector of the economy.

Scale economies, in turn, lead to economies of agglomeration. From the global point of view, overall research productivity is maximized by concentrating research in just a few centres which enjoy critical mass (Cantwell, 1989). If research planning began with a 'clean sheet' then possibly all research would agglomerate around a single location. But in practice the exploitation of such a location would soon encounter diminishing returns because of the rising supply price of scientists. It is only if scientists were perfectly mobile that such extreme agglomeration could occur.

3.4   MOBILITY OF RESEARCH WORKERS

The question of mobility is an important one. It has been assumed so far that labour is geographically immobile. This may be a reasonable approximation so far as production workers are concerned, but not for scientists. Mobility is particularly crucial where agglomeration is concerned, but it is important in other contexts too. For example, when rigid relativities or union pressures keep the scientists' wage artificially depressed, outward migration of scientists is likely to occur, quite independently of agglomeration effects. The UK has experienced significant 'brain drains' – to the US and, to a lesser extent, Canada and Australia – in 1960s and again in the 1980s – although the precise magnitude of the problem is difficult to assess. Published statistics on the qualifications of migrants are incomplete and in any case the quality of manpower is often difficult to assess from recorded qualifications. Nevertheless, there is considerable evidence to suggest that the expectation of higher lifetime earnings was a significant factor in emigration. In some cases it may have operated through an initial decision to work abroad after taking a higher degree in the UK, but in others it seems to have resulted from a decision not to return to the UK after going abroad to undertake graduate study for different reasons.

3.5   PUBLIC FUNDING OF BASIC R&D

With mobile labour, constraints on the capacity of the education sector are of limited importance for domestic R&D (Ulph and Winters, 1989). Provided personnel policies are flexible, the existence of an attractive location will stimulate demand, bid up wages and encourage immigration.

The crucial question is what constitutes an attractive location. Clearly an able indigenous population will give a good start. Assuming that critical mass is important, a large indigenous supply of able scientists means that private incentives alone, without government intervention, may generate critical mass. Given that the agglomeration process, on a global level, remains incomplete, good communications with other major agglomerations is also crucial. This requires, in particular, a local airport hub on trunk networks, served with good feeder motorways. Local use of an international language, such as English, is important too. Access to supporting services must also be considered. So far as employees are concerned, a healthy climate, good schools, employment opportunities for spouses and cheap housing are all obviously important. So far as the employer is concerned, a proficient indigenous scientific instruments industry offering good after-sales service is important. A 'well found' range of financial and accounting services is valuable too. But perhaps of greatest significance is excellence in basic R&D.

The output of basic R&D is characterized by its versatility. It is difficult to appropriate rents from basic R&D through contractual arrangements such as patents because of the sheer diversity of potential applications and the difficulty of policing them all. Because proprietary rights in general scientific knowledge are so difficult to sustain, the development of such knowledge is often funded out of taxation, on the grounds that everyone potentially benefits but that without compulsion everyone would attempt to free ride on the financial contributions of others (Arrow, 1962).

Competitive advantage is typically secured by gaining access to the results of basic R&D before others do. At the early post-discovery stage the results are often little more than beliefs and conjectures. While the scientific community may require more experimentation to provide additional evidence before it is fully convinced, acquisition of a commercial first-mover advantage may depend on developing potential applications right at the outset. At this stage the knowledge is essentially tacit and needs to be communicated face-to-face. Privileged access to such face-to-face briefings is an important advantage for commercial laboratories located close to centres of basic research.

3.6   INTERNATIONAL SERVICE CENTRES

All of the above requirements are most likely to be found in an international service centre (Bairoch, 1988; Casson and Jones, 1989). Typically these centres developed initially as ports, around which wholesaling, banking, hotels etc. developed. People are attracted to these centres because they specialize in activities which require face-to-face meetings between the layperson and an expert, or between one expert and another. For this reason they are often chosen as the site for corporate headquarters, and sometimes become the centre of national government too.

Often one of the parties (normally an expert) resides in the centre and the other party (expert or layperson) continues to visit him or her. This pattern of behaviour is well suited to the international coordination of R&D. Different types of scientific expertise agglomerate around different international service centres, and the synthesis of new knowledge from these separate sources is effected by scientists travelling between them. With its wide range of expertise and extensive supporting services for the traveller, the international service centre therefore makes an ideal location for R&D.

3.7 CONCLUSION

A country's comparative advantage in R&D has significant dynamic elements. In the very long run the migration of scientists can have a major impact on the scientific capability of the labour force. The historical review in chapter 1, for example, emphasized the enormous intellectual contribution of German emigrants to US industrial R&D, and there can be no doubt whatsoever of the continuing contribution made by their descendents. In a country as large as the US, inter-regional migration can also be significant – as exemplified by the growth of electronics R&D in California, which has relied significantly on the migration of scientists from the East Coast.

The attractions of the US conform to those indicated earlier – a good lifestyle for R&D workers and their families, and an agglomeration of complementary expertise for their employers. Agglomeration economies also extend to providing greater job security through a wider choice of local employers for workers, and an extensive pool of potential recruits for employers.

Government can play a significant role in promoting agglomeration economies. It can 'prime the pump' of the agglomeration process by subsiding the 'first movers' to the location. It can promote indigenous labour supply through its policies on higher education. It can reduce housing costs by releasing land for property development (while conserving key areas of the natural environment to maintain quality of life). It can also set out a strategic plan for the development of infrastructure, ranging from the layout of the road system to the promotion of the local airport as a hub.

The local retention of economic rents from R&D will tend to be greater if the key employers are locally-headquartered firms. Subsidiaries of other firms can also contribute to the local economy, but because their profits are ultimately remitted elsewhere their contribution will not be so great. These firms may be able to transfer technology into the area which purely indigenous firms would find it difficult to obtain, however. They may also be able to access international markets better than indigenous firms. This is particularly important if the scientists are engaged in development work which is likely to transform the locality into an export platform for a newly innovated product.

Agglomeration economies can also influence the probability that development work as well as basic research is carried out in the locality. Evidence reported in the later chapters suggests that it is development work rather than basic research that tends to be concentrated close to major markets. This means that if agglomeration proceeds rapidly, and the locality achieves a high international ranking in terms of local market size, it is more likely to attract development work and to become an export base for novel products. As noted in chapter 1, it is the performance of net exports in novel products that is one of the hallmarks of the 'internationally competitive' location.

There is, of course, the risk that non-indigenous firms will merely crowd out indigenous firms, but this is unlikely to be a serious problem in the long run because migration flows will adjust accordingly. Roughly speaking, the attraction of new investors will induce a corresponding inflow of qualified migrants, leaving indigenous firms with access to the same net supply of labour as before. On balance, the indigenous firms are likely to benefit because they can tap in to the know-how of the new investors (who are likely, at least initially, to be more technologically sophisticated than their indigenous counterparts) and because they benefit generally from the growth of local factor and product markets, and from the other externalities that 'critical mass' affords.

APPENDIX TO CHAPTER 3

3A.1   *Modelling International Comparative Advantage in R&D*

This appendix presents a mathematical model which encapsulates many of the points raised in the preceding discussion. Its formal structure is summarized in table 3A.1. The working of the model is explained heuristically below. It is inspired by the work of Falvey (1981); Ulph and Winters (1989) and Webster (1987), although it is not specifically concerned with strategic trade policy as some of these papers are.

Consider an economy which has three possible production activities: (1) generic R&D (as defined in chapter 2), (2) 'mature product' production and (3) 'new product' production. Two types of labour are available: (1) scientists and (2) production workers. Generic R&D requires *only* scientists, while mature product production requires *only* production workers. New product production requires a combination of both: the scientists work on adaptive R&D in a laboratory close to the plant where production workers are employed. The two groups of workers are employed in fixed proportion. All production takes place under constant returns to scale.

The output of all three activities is tradeable. Both the new product and the mature product can be exported, and both activities are subject to import competition too. The output of generic R&D is proprietary know-how, which can be either licensed overseas or transferred abroad through the internal market of an MNE. It is assumed for simplicity that all applications of the know-how are overseas: this eliminates complications arising from the role of know-how as an intermediate public good within the domestic economy. For a similar reason the transaction costs discussed in chapter 2 are ignored; the analysis below does not, therefore, directly address the question of why some R&D is overseas-owned and other R&D is not.

Let $p_j > 0$ $(j = 1, 2, 3)$ be the price of the output of the jth activity, and $q_j \geqslant 0$ the scale of that activity. The input of labour of the ith type required per unit output of the jth activity is

$a_{ij} \geqslant 0$, where, in the light of earlier assumptions, $a_{12} = a_{21} = 0$. The total value of production

$$y = \sum_{j=1}^{3} p_j q_j$$

is maximized by choosing a suitable mixture of activities. Figure 3A.1 shows the combinations of scientists and production workers required to generate a unit of revenue from each activity. The ray OR_1 shows that a_{11}/p_1 scientists are required to generate unit revenue from generic R&D. The ray OR_2 shows that a_{22}/p_2 production workers are required to generate unit revenue from mature product production. The ray OR_3 shows that a_{13}/p_3 scientists and a_{23}/p_3 production workers are required to generate unit revenue from new product production.

The line R_1R_2 shows the various combinations of scientists and production workers which serve to generate unit revenue when generic R&D is combined in varying proportions with mature product production. It can be seen that this combination of activities requires more labour than does a combination of generic R&D and new product production (as indicated by the line R_1R_3) or a combination of the new product production and mature product production (as indicated by the line R_2R_3). This is not invariably the case, however. If the price of new products fell, for example, then the ray OR_3 might expand to OR_3' where R_3' lies to the north-east of R_1R_2 in which case new product production would become uneconomic relative to a combination of mature product production and generic R&D.

When new product production is economic, the relevant iso-revenue schedule $R_1R_3R_2$ has a kink at R_3, whereas when it is uneconomic the relevant iso-revenue schedule R_1R_2 is a straight line.

It is assumed that domestic social welfare can be represented by the utility function of a representative household. The household values both the new product and the mature product, but not the results of generic R&D. Because all outputs are tradeable, the maximization of social welfare implies maximising the value of domestic production. Domestic consumption and domestic production are matched up through trade flows.

Table 3A.1   Structure of the model

NOTATION

Parameters

a_{ij} input of ith labour service per unit output of jth activity

M working population

p_j price of the output of the jth activity

Variables

c_j domestic consumption of the jth output

m_i number of people performing ith labour service

n_i output of the ith labour service

q_j scale of operation of the jth activity

u social welfare of the domestic country

w_i wage rate for the ith labour service

x_j net exports of the jth output

y domestic income

π_j profit accruing from a unit output from the jth activity

Identification

$i = 1$ scientist

$i = 2$ production worker

$j = 1$ generic R&D

$j = 2$ 'mature product' production

$j = 3$ 'new product' production

MODEL

Objective   Maximize the quasi-concave social welfare function

$$u = u(c_2, c_3) \tag{3.1}$$

where

$$\partial u/\partial c_1, \; \partial u/\partial c_2 > 0, \; \partial^2 u/\partial c_1^2, \; \partial^2 u/\partial c_2^2 < 0 \tag{3.2}$$

$$(\partial^2 u/\partial c_1^2)(\partial^2 u/\partial c_2^2) - (\partial^2 u/\partial c_1 \partial c_2)^2 > 0$$

Budget constraint

$$y = c \tag{3.3}$$

where

$$y = \sum_{j=1}^{3} p_j q_j \tag{3.4}$$

$$c = \sum_{j=1}^{3} p_j c_j \tag{3.5}$$

and

$$p_j, \; c_j \geqslant 0, \; c_1 = 0 \tag{3.6}$$

Definition of net exports

$$x_j = q_j - c_j \quad (j = 1, 2, 3) \tag{3.7}$$

Production technology

$$n_{ij} = a_{ij}q_j \quad (i = 1, 2; \; j = 1, 2, 3) \tag{3.8}$$

where

$$a_{ij} \geqslant 0 \quad (i = 1, 2; \; j = 1, 2, 3), \; a_{12} = a_{21} = 0 \tag{3.9}$$

$$q_j \geqslant 0 \quad (j = 1, 2, 3) \tag{3.10}$$

Labour market constraint

$$n_i = \sum_{j=1}^{3} n_{ij} \quad (i = 1, 2) \tag{3.11}$$

Education constraint

$$n_1 = n_1(m_1) \tag{3.12.1}$$

$$n_2 = m_2 \tag{3.12.2}$$

where

$$\partial n_1/\partial m_1 > 0, \; \partial^2 n_1/\partial m_1^2 < 0 \tag{3.13}$$

Population constraint

$$M = m_1 + m_2 \tag{3.14}$$

Note: The zero-profit condition in the dual problem is

$$\pi_j = p_j - \sum_{i=1}^{2} a_{ij}w_i = 0 \tag{3.15}$$

METHOD OF SOLUTION

To maximize u subject to the budget constraint it is necessary to maximize y. To maximize y it is necessary to generate any given amount of sales revenue using an efficient combination of labour inputs. Since there are three activities and only two types of input, a weighted average (linear combination) of two of the activities will normally dominate a third. The production technology and the labour market constraint together identify the dominated activity for any given ratio of inputs and so determine the shape of the iso-revenue line in $n_1 - n_2$ space. Because of constant returns to scale, the unit iso-revenue line uniquely determines all other iso-revenue lines. The education constraint and the population constraint together determine the feasible combinations of n_1 and n_2. The efficient combinations constitute the labour services frontier. The iso-revenue map is convex to the origin and the labour services frontier strictly concave. There is thus a unique optimal combination of labour services which is normally (though not invariably) associated with a unique production plan.

By constructing the dual to this problem it can be seen that the elimination of the inefficient production activity is equivalent to a condition that only activities which break even can operate, and that no activity can make a profit. The optimum combination of labour services is associated with a unique relative wage.

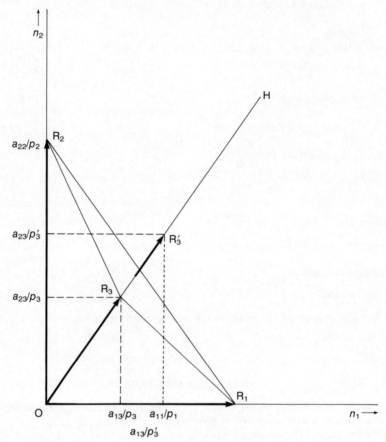

Figure 3A.1   Combining activities with differing degrees of R&D intensity

The constraints on the value of production stem ultimately from the supply of labour, measured by the length of the horizontal axis OM in figure 3A.2. It is assumed that there is a fixed working population. This means that changes in the supply of effort and of hours are ignored. International migration is ignored too; this simplifies the discussion of welfare since it eliminates the difficult question of how the welfare of migrants is to be treated.

It is assumed that scientists are products of the educational system and that their education is a continuing process. This means that changes in the provision of education will cause imme-

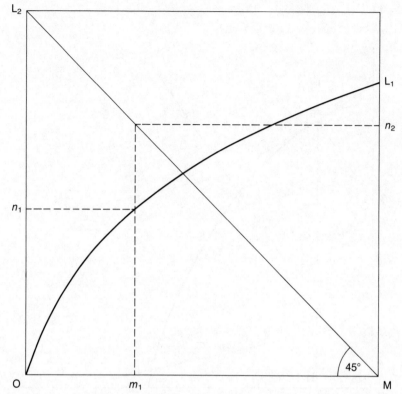

Figure 3A.2   Effect of education on the supply of scientists with a fixed overall supply of labour

diate adjustments to the relative stocks of scientists and production workers. If education is reduced, some scientists are demoted to production work. Perhaps more controversial is the converse case: if education is expanded, production workers become scientists without any lag on account of transitional full-time training.

People differ in their educability and are drawn into education in order according to their personal comparative advantage as scientists. This results in diminishing marginal returns to education. These diminishing returns are captured by the relation between the *number* of scientists m_1 and the *output of scientific services*, n_1, they generate. This relation is illustrated by the

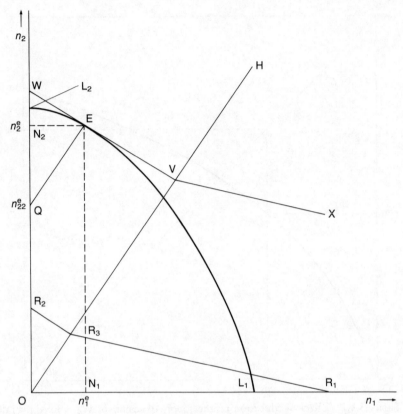

Figure 3A.3   Determination of optimal production strategy when there is low value productivity in generic R&D

schedule OL_1 in figure 3A.2. The corresponding relation in production work, between the number of workers m_2 and the output of production services n_2, is one-to-one, as indicated by the 45-degree line ML_2.

Moving along the horizontal axis OM from left to right, and reading off along the vertical axes, generates the labour services frontier L_1L_2 in figure 3A.3. This frontier is strictly concave to the origin O. This shows that as the supply of scientific services is increased, the opportunity cost of scientific services in terms of production services steadily increases.

The value of domestic output is maximized where the iso-revenue map is tangent to the labour services frontier. The iso-revenue map is weakly convex, so that there is a unique equilibrium point (but see later). Figure 3A.3 illustrates a special case in which the value productivity of scientists employed in generic R&D is very low. As a result the economy specializes in ordinary production. The unit iso-revenue line $R_1R_3R_2$ scales up to give the maximum attainable iso-revenue line WVX, which is tangent to L_1L_2 at E. This involves allocating ON_1 scientific services to new product production, together with QN_2 production services. The remaining OQ production services are allocated exclusively to mature product production.

The relative wage of scientists, compared to production workers, is measured by the slope of the tangent WEV. This may be deduced from the fact that in a competitive labour market producers of new and mature products will bid up the wage rates for both scientists and production workers until all supernormal profit is eliminated. Thus all revenue is imputed to labour income. The rate at which scientific services can be substituted for production services along the iso-revenue line thus determines the relative valuation of labour services so far as competitive producers are concerned.

Since the total supply of labour is fixed it is the relative wage and not the absolute wage that determines the supply of scientists. The concavity of the schedule L_1L_2 indicates that the supply of scientific services increases as the relative wage rises. The economy therefore adjusts towards the equilibrium E by changes in the scientists' relative wage.

The pattern of trade associated with this pattern of specialization is derived in figure 3A.4. To simplify the analysis the mature product is treated as a *numeraire* good. The units are selected so that one unit of production service generates one physical unit of the mature product. Since $a_{22} = 1$, production services, n_2, and output of the mature product, q_2, can thus be measured on the same vertical axis.

The north-east quadrant of figure 3A.4 reproduces the salient points of the equilibrium E in figure 3A.3. The north-west quadrant expresses the relative price of the new product in terms of the mature product by the slope of the line WY'. This line has the

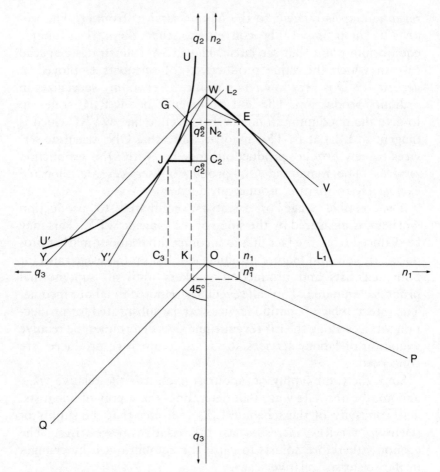

Figure 3A.4 Derivation of trade pattern in new and mature products

same intercept W on the vertical axis as does the maximum iso-revenue line. This indicates that all the revenue is available for consumption purposes. If the new product commanded no premium over the mature product then the budget constraint of the representative consumer would be represented by the 45-degree line WY. The steeper slope of the actual budget constraint WY' indicates that a premium is assumed to prevail.

The representative consumer's maximum attainable indifference curve UU' is tangent to the budget constraint at J. Under autarky, consumption would be constrained to G. G is derived by calculating the implications of the equilibrium employment of scientists ON_1 for the domestic output of the new product OK using the relevant input–output coefficient a_{13}, whose magnitude is represented in the south-east quadrant by the slope of the ray OP. Comparing G and J shows that the country exports C_2N_2 units of the mature product in return for C_3K unit of the new product. From the international point of view, therefore, the economy is specialized in mature product production.

3A.2 *Substitution Into New Product Production*

Suppose now that the international price of the mature product falls. This corresponds to the case where newly industrializing countries enter world markets using standardized products produced with unpatented technology. The natural response of a developed economy is to substitute towards new product production. This involves increasing the supply of scientists.

The adjustment is illustrated in figure 3A.5. The fall in the price of the mature product is illustrated by the outward shift in the ray OR_2 to OR_2'. This indicates that more production workers are now required to generate the same amount of revenue as before. The new unit iso-revenue schedule $R_2'R_3R_1$ scales up to give the relevant portion $W'E'V'$ of the maximum attainable iso-revenue schedule. Because of the concavity of L_1L_2, the new point of tangency E' lies to the right of the original point E. Output of the new product is increased. This is reflected in the greater supply of scientists' services to new product production, $ON_1' > ON_1$. Conversely, output of the mature product is reduced. This is reflected in the smaller allocation of production services to mature product production, $OQ' < OQ$. The total number of production workers does not fall by this amount, however, because some are diverted to the expanding new product production. Overall, the supply of production workers contracts by N_2N_2' and the supply of scientists' services increases by N_1N_1'. The supply adjustment is induced by a rise in the scientists' wage. This is reflected in the steeper slope of the iso-revenue line $W'E'V'$, compared with the original line WEV.

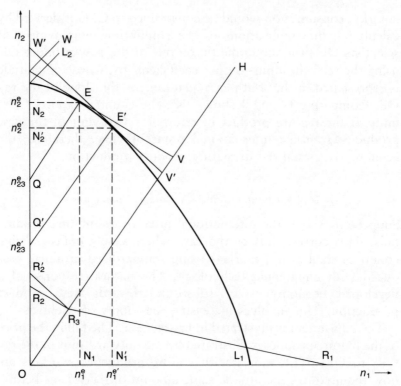

Figure 3A.5   Adjustment of production to a fall in the price of the mature product

Substitution could, however, be inhibited by an educational capacity constraint. Figure 3A.6 illustrates a situation in which a tight educational constraint, represented by the vertical line $N_1'D$, restricts the supply of scientists to ON_1'. Following a very sharp reduction in the world price of the mature product, labour market equilibrium in the absence of a constraint would be at E, where the iso-revenue line WV is tangent to L_1L_2. Employment of scientists would be ON_1. But with the constraint it is restricted to E', where the employment of scientists is only $ON_1' < ON_1$.

Wage relativities at E' are the same as at E because both new product production and mature product production are competing for labour in each case, and both therefore experience the same break-even constraints. But the marginal rate of substitution

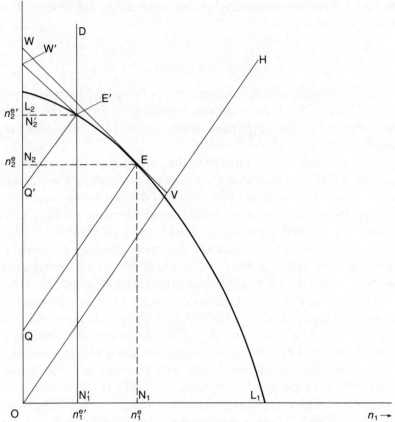

Figure 3A.6   Effect of a constraint on educational capacity

in supply, as represented by the slope of the labour services frontier L_1L_2 at E', no longer coincides with the relative wage. The premium on the scientists' wage is such that there is excess demand for education. The planners take no notice of this, and as a result the supply of scientific services falls by N_1N_1'. Frustrated potential scientists are forced to become production workers instead. The supply of production workers increases by N_2N_2'. To accommodate this 'forced' additional supply, mature product production is higher and new product production correspondingly lower than before. Mature product production, as measured by the input of production workers, increases from OQ to OQ'. Revenues, measured in the same units, fall from OW to OW' as a result.

3A.3   *Wage Rigidities*

A similar impediment to adjustment can be caused by wage rigidities. This has much more serious implications though. By way of introduction to this important issue, figure 3A.7 introduces the 'dual' to the production problem.

The schedule AA' indicates the break-even condition for generic R&D – namely that the scientists' wage should not exceed $\bar{w}_1 = p_1/a_{11}$. The schedule BB' indicates the break-even condition for mature production, namely that the production workers' wage should not exceed $\bar{w}_2 = p_2/a_{22}$. Finally, the schedule CC' illustrates the break-even condition for new product production, showing that the scientists' wage must fall as the production workers' wage rises if new product production is to remain viable.

Perfect competition in the markets for scientists and production workers implies that no production activity can do more than break even. The thick line $A'F_1F_2B'$ illustrates the zero-profit wage frontier. This line is predicated on given product prices.

Suppose that initially both the new product and the mature product are being produced. Generic R&D is uneconomic (as assumed earlier on). Competition for labour adjusts the wage rates to w_1^* and $\bar{w}_2$, as represented by the point F_2. Suppose that trade union pressure then increases the production workers' wage to $\bar{w}_2' > \bar{w}_2$, as indicated in the top quadrant of figure 3A.8. This renders mature product production uneconomic, but new product production is still potentially viable. The break-even condition on new product production implies, however, that the scientists' wage must fall to $w_1^{*\prime} < w_1^*$. This is indicated by the movement along the zero-profit frontier from F_2 to F'. The scientists' wage does not fall sufficiently, however, for generic R&D to become profitable.

The change in relative wages implies, in the lower quadrant, a divergence between the iso-revenue line WEV, which is predicated on break-even production in both activities and the wage line ZZ', which reflects the wage combination compatible with continued new product production.

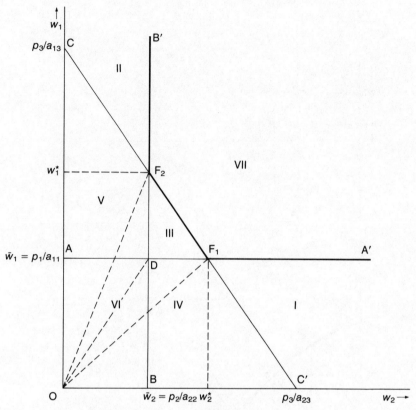

Figure 3A.7 The relation between wages and prices under competition, as illustrated by the dual problem

Key to regimes:

I Only generic R&D is profitable.
II Only mature product production is profitable.
III Only new product production is profitable.
IV Only generic R&D and new product production are profitable.
V Only new product production and mature product production are profitable.
VI All activities are profitable.
VII No activities are profitable.

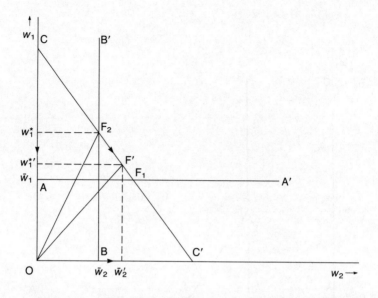

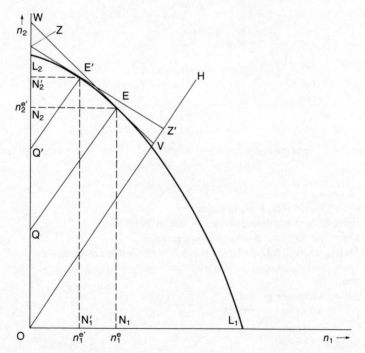

Figure 3A.8 Effect of an administered increase in the production workers' wage

Equilibrium shifts from E to E′, because of the supply constraint on scientific services. Fewer scientists, $ON_1' < ON_1$, are engaged in new product production, and fewer production workers, $N_2'Q' < N_2Q$. At the same time, the production workers that would have undertaken mature product production, OQ, become unemployed, together with those made redundant through the contraction of new production. These are augmented by N_2N_2' discouraged scientists who are seeking production work that no longer exists, making a total of OQ′ unemployed altogether. Thus to measure employment levels, E′ must be referred to an origin at Q′ rather than at O. Revenue from production, and hence social welfare, falls dramatically as a result. The combination of excess demand for scientists and excess supply of production workers represents, *par excellence*, the case of loss of competitiveness caused by excess wages for one kind of labour that are compensated for by too-low wages for another.

In the long run the high incidence of unemployment among production workers will reduce expected earnings to well below the union wage. This will induce production workers to switch into science, allowing new product production to expand and enabling those who remain production workers to gain additional employment too. The economy will still, however, remain in difficulty, so long as only new product production is viable. It is possible, though, that further downward pressure on the scientists' wage exerted by workers escaping unemployment may render generic R&D profitable. If so, then generic R&D can take up further scientific refugees from production work. This confirms the idea that in some economies the concern to promote R&D is a rational response to economic weakness – namely the excessive wages paid to production workers. But welfare is only maximized fully, in this kind of situation, by tackling the problem at its roots, and restoring competitiveness in production work.

3A.4   *Critical Mass and Generic R&D*

Critical mass can impact on R&D in several ways, and just two of them are considered here. In the first case critical mass pertains to the total supply of scientific services. Thus generic R&D

derives external benefits not only from other generic R&D but also from adaptive R&D, and *vice versa*. In the second case critical mass pertains solely to the impact of generic R&D on adaptive R&D. Generic R&D has negligible impact on adaptive R&D unless a critical mass of generic R&D is undertaken, at which point the productivity of adaptive R&D increases.

Case I   Let the critical mass of scientific services be n_1^c. Set

$$a_{ij} = \begin{cases} a'_{1j} & \text{if } n_1 < n_1^c \\ a''_{1j} & \text{if } n_1 \geqslant n_1^c \end{cases} \quad (j = 1, 3)$$

where $a'_{1j} > a''_{1j}$. Assume, furthermore, that the proportional impact of critical mass is the same on both generic and adaptive R&D, that is

$$a'_{11}/a''_{11} = a'_{13} a''_{13}$$

Suppose to begin with that new product production is ignored, and that the aim is to analyse the impact of critical mass on the allocation of activity between mature product production and generic R&D. In figure 3A.9 the effect of exceeding critical mass is to rotate the iso-revenue line $R_1 R_3$ about R_3 to give $R'_1 R_3$ instead. This is the result of a contraction in the length of the ray OR_1 to OR'_1. The rotated iso-revenue line applied only in the section of the figure to the right of the vertical line TT'. As a result, the iso-revenue map as a whole acquires a discontinuity where it crosses TT'. This is represented by the vertical distance UV in the iso-revenue line WUVX and the vertical distance $U'V'$ in the iso-revenue line $W'U'V'X'$.

It is possible for an economy to become trapped in an equilibrium where it fails to exploit economies of critical mass. This is illustrated by the equilibrium E where the lower of the two iso-revenues lies WUVX is tangent to the frontier $L_1 L_2$. Employment of scientific services is only ON_1, and the majority of people provide production services ON_2 to mature product production.

If, however, employment of scientists could somehow be raised to above the critical level the economy would then adjust to a new equilibrium E' where the higher iso-revenue line $W'U'V'X'$ is tangent to $L_1 L_2$. This affords a higher revenue, $OW' > OW$ in

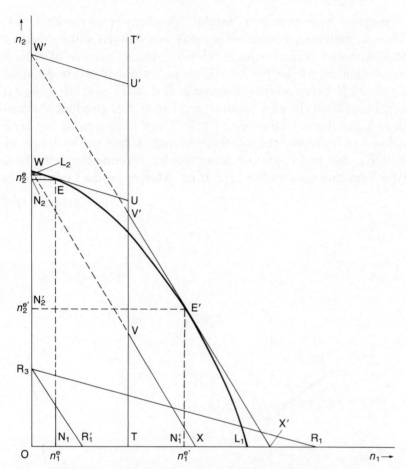

Figure 3A.9 Effect of critical mass on employment in generic R&D in the absence of new product production

terms of the mature product, resulting from a greater supply of scientific services $ON'_1 > ON_1$. Following the autonomous raising of the supply of scientific services to OT, a further supply N'_1T is attracted because with higher productivity in generic R&D employers bid up the scientists' wage. Overall, the additional supply of scientists results in a reduction in the supply of production services from ON_2 to ON'_2, which induces a corresponding contraction in mature product output.

Suppose now that new product production is possible too. Then in figure 3A.10 the iso-revenue line $R_1R_2R_3$ shifts down to $R_1'R_2'R_3$ when critical mass is achieved. In the absence of critical mass, that is, to the left of TT', equilibrium is at the point of tangency E between the iso-revenue line WU, parallel to R_2R_3, and L_1L_2. Both the new product and the mature product are produced, but there is no generic R&D. Once critical mass has been achieved, however, the iso-revenue map takes on the shape of $R_1'R_2'R_3$, and the maximum attainable iso-revenue line is $W'E'X$ which touches the frontier L_1L_2 at E'. Mature product production

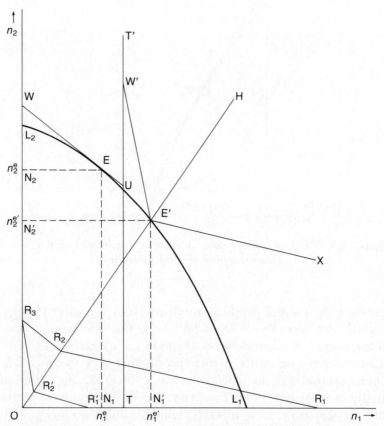

Figure 3A.10   Effect of critical mass with new product production

is eliminated. New product production expands, but generic R&D does not start up. The supply of production services contracts to $ON_2' < ON_2$ as the relative wage of scientists increases. The supply of scientists increases to $ON_1' > ON_1$, all of whom are employed in adaptive R&D.

Case II   The previous case illustrates that when critical mass affects both generic and adaptive R&D it need not stimulate basic R&D at all. This result seems somewhat counter-intuitive, and so it is appropriate to consider as well the case where critical mass affects adaptive R&D only through the scale of generic R&D. This is illustrated in figure 3A.11.

In the absence of critical mass, equilibrium is at E, as before. With critical mass, the iso-revenue map becomes parallel to

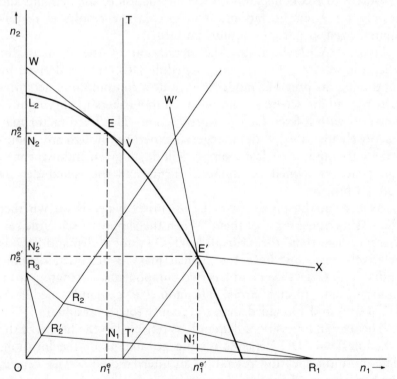

Figure 3A.11   Effect of critical mass on generic R&D on new product production

$R_1R_2'R_3$. The ray OR_2 has contracted to OR_2' as a result of spill-overs from generic R&D. Note that in the absence of the critical mass requirement generic R&D would be uneconomic, as before. The new equilibrium is at E' where the iso-revenue line $W'X$ touches the frontier L_1L_2. The supply of scientific services to generic R&D is equal to the critical amount OT', with the remaining scientific services $T'N_1'$ being allocated to adaptive R&D. A significant reduction in the supply of production services, due to the elimination of mature product production, releases people to train as scientists to go into generic R&D.

3A.5   Summary

The analysis demonstrates that the commitment of national resources to R&D depends on the interaction of the demand and supply for scientific labour. The gist of the results is readily summarized in partial equilibrium terms.

Figure 3A.12 illustrates the derivation of the demand for scientific services. The demand schedule $DGG'D'$ is derived by modifying the previous model to include a continuum of activities which combine scientists and production workers in varying proportions with a fixed factor of production. This fixed factor may be loosely identified with managerial expertise, though any complementary input in inelastic supply will do. A given endowment of the factor is owned by domestic firms and the remainder by foreign firms.

As before, the productivity of scientists depends on whether there is a critical mass of them. When the supply of scientific services is less than the critical level OT, total demand DG is relatively low, but once the critical mass is attained, demand shifts up to $G'D'$. Demand has two components, emanating from domestic and foreign firms. The domestic demand schedule is $DG_dG_d'D_d'$ and foreign demand accounts for the residual.

The overall intensity of demand, as reflected in the height of the schedule $DGG'D'$, depends on the attractions of the location. The more the location resembles an international service centre, the higher is the demand. The attractions influence both domestic and foreign demand; they prevent domestic demand being

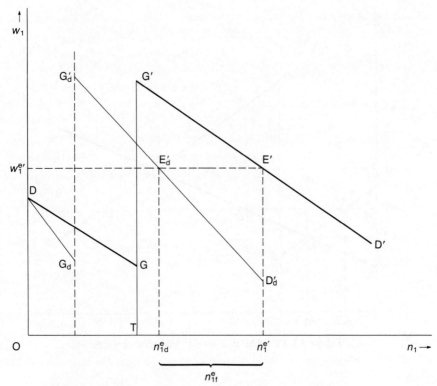

Figure 3A.12   Derivation of the demand for scientific services

diverted overseas, and help to bring foreign demand into the country. There is no particular reason to believe that a change in the ownership of a firm due to international take-over will necessarily alter its location strategy. In this case it is the total demand that is governed by the economic fundamentals and the split between foreign and domestic demand is of limited significance.

Figure 3A.13 illustrates the interaction of demand with supply. The supply schedule SS' is predicated on a given wage for production workers (which is endogenous in the general equilibrium model), and on international immobility of labour. With a perfectly competitive labour market two equilibria are possible. The equilibrium E, where SS' intersects the demand segment DG, fails

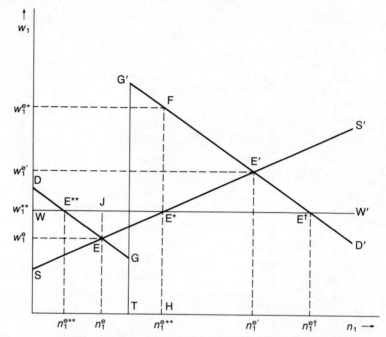

Figure 3A.13   The market for scientific services

to achieve critical mass. The supply of scientific services is only n_1^e and the scientists' wage only w_1^e. If the supply is somehow increased, though, then a new equilibrium can be achieved at E', where SS' intersects the segment G'D'. The supply of scientific services is $n_1^{e'} > n_1^e$ and the scientists' wage rises to $w_1^{e'} > w_1^e$. The division of employment between domestic and foreign firms n_{1d}^e, n_{1f}^e is indicated in figure 3A.12.

If there is a constraint on educational capacity the the equilibrium E' may no longer be feasible. For example, if capacity limitations restrict the supply of scientific services to OH then equilibrium will be constrained to E*. Competition between employers will bid up the scientists' wage to w_1^{e*}, corresponding to the point F. There will be substantial gains to becoming a scientist which will accrue to those fortunate enough to get a place in higher education.

A more plausible account of contemporary problems is

obtained by supposing that supply is restricted by the disincentive effect of a low wage. If the scientists' wage is forced down, say, to w_1^{**}, to compensate for higher production workers' wages, then supply may also be restricted to E^*. This time, however, the wage is not bid up to w_1^{e*}, and there is no excess demand for places in education.

The partial equilibrium approach can also be used to analyse migration. Suppose that scientists are in infinitely elastic supply at the world level at a wage w_1^{**}. Then constraints arising from domestic supply can be overcome through migration. Thus with perfect mobility of scientists employment can expand to $E\dagger$, where the new supply curve SE^*W' intersects $G'D'$. Thanks to immigration, employment of scientists, $n_1^e\dagger$, is higher than ever before.

Conversely, of course, if demand for scientists is less buoyant because of the absence of critical mass, emigration may reduce the supply. Thus if the economy is initially trapped in a domestic equilibrium at E, migration will lead to an exodus as the supply of scientific services contracts to n_1^{e**}, corresponding to an equilibrium E^{**}. The scientific services lost through emigration are $E^{**}J$. In addition, some production workers emigrate to become scientists, effecting a further loss of potential scientific services JE^*.

Overall, the analysis provides a coherent account of how demand – driven mainly by the attraction of the location, and the size of critical mass – interacts with supply – as determined by natural abilities, educational constraint and migration possibilities – to determine employment in R&D. It also highlights the role of wage distortions caused by both union wage-push in production services and the maintenance of traditional differentials.

4

The International Agglomeration
of R&D

4.1 INTRODUCTION

This chapter investigates the proposition that over the last 20
years or so there has been a tendency for technological activity to
agglomerate in international centres of excellence in research and
innovation. The proposition is examined through a statistical
analysis of US patent data. By distinguishing between the principal sectors to which each invention may be classified, the study
is conducted at the level of industries or common groups of technological activity. Since in some industries countervailing factors
may be more important, the trend towards the geographical concentration or dispersion of research is established in each case,
and its significance is assessed.

It has been argued in a variety of contexts that technological
development proceeds as a cumulative or path-dependent process
(Arthur, 1989; Cantwell, 1989; Dosi, 1989; Pavitt, 1987a;
Rosenberg, 1982; Usher, 1954). In the present connection, if the
probability of locating a research facility in a given centre is
increased by other such decisions taken previously, then centres of
excellence will tend to maintain their position over time. They are
subject to economies of agglomeration, as explained in chapter 3.
In the present context it is important to emphasize that agglomeration economies may follow from the role of user–producer
interaction in the development of technology. In a location
characterized by a high rate of innovation, sophisticated users
have complex requirements and they may draw in and support the

research facilities of the producers of the technology. Technology is systematically improved through more regular and diverse customer feedbacks, and through the establishment of joint testing procedures. For their part, a network of users gains benefits from the provision of a greater availability and variety of technological inputs in a centre of excellence. There may also be increasing returns in information about a technology as it diffuses across a wider group of users.

However, in periods during which there is a transformation in the types of technological activity which yield the greatest potential, there may be a change in the location of technological leadership as new centres become more dynamic than the previously established major centres (Cantwell, 1990a). What was once a source of success becomes a source of difficulty and failure. The established centres are 'locked in' to a path of technological development which has run its course. This is largely attributable to technological interrelatedness, by which it is costly to change one component of a production process or the methods prevailing in a local sector, or to start down quite new research avenues without complementary changes elsewhere. In this situation external diseconomies replace external economies. The pattern of research and production in a centre may become locked in to a course which eventually provides fewer technological opportunities than those which are available to other centres, but it is now costly and difficult for them to switch.

A second set of factors which regulate the geographical distribution of technological activity have to do with the internationalization of corporate research, as outlined in chapter 1. Due to the location-specificity of research in terms of the characteristics of technological activity as already described, leading multinationals have an incentive to carry out research programmes in the major centres of innovation in their industry. If so, the position of the centres themselves is likely to be strengthened, and technological activity tends to agglomerate in them in a cumulative fashion.

The creation of a virtuous circle of cumulative success can be viewed both in terms of the effects of the setting up of foreign owned research in a host centre, and in terms of the consequences of the foreign located research of firms that themselves originate from a home centre (Cantwell, 1987b). The benefits of inward investment mentioned in chapter 3 are likely to be further enhanced through the competitive stimulus which such an additional local presence provides for indigenous firms. Local firms may step up their own local research programmes in response, to ensure that they are able to exploit the opportunities open to them more rapidly and their technological development is not left behind.

With outward investment in research from a centre of excellence the home location may gain benefits. These follow from the improved competitiveness in international markets of the firm (higher sales promotes increased research), and from technological complementarities between research carried out at home and abroad. The firm is able to integrate complementary technologies initially developed in different environments. In so doing, it tends to widen the opportunities associated with the lines of research which have been pursued in the home country.

Although substitution effects between home and foreign research are possible, these tend to reinforce the agglomeration of technological activity. Foreign-owned research facilities are most likely to crowd out those of indigenous firms where local research has previously been ineffective, small scale by international standards, and poorly organized. Where local firms have an established technological tradition but the home environment deteriorates (due, say, to the decline of user firms in a related industry), then outward investment in research-related activity may also be an alternative to continued technological development at home. In each case, this is liable to strengthen the position of centres of excellence as against other locations.

The push towards the agglomeration of technological activity which internationalization provides depends not so much on an increase in the international dispersion of research as such, as on a rationalization or reorganization of existing networks. In an internationally integrated network the emphasis shifts towards the expansion of research facilities where the local environment is most conducive, given a steady change in the fields of greatest technological opportunity. This implies that the contribution of internationalization towards agglomeration may be constrained by impediments to the international integration of economic activity. It is well known that these barriers are greater in some industries than others (Cantwell, 1990b). Non-tariff barriers are now more important than tariff barriers in this respect; for example, national regulations, government purchasing policies, differences in quality control standards and procedures, and the need to differentiate products in national markets. Factors such as these may well attract research to countries with limited technological traditions, while making it more difficult to incorporate global research facilities located in centres of excellence into international networks.

The relative significance of these considerations, industry by industry, determines the degree to which the technological activity agglomerates in international centres. The next section provides a description of the data used to test the significance of the basic proposition that research tends to agglomerate geographically. In the following section (4.3) the statistical methodology is outlined, and the agglomeration proposition is shown to give rise to two more precise hypotheses. Sections 4.4 and 4.5 report the results of the statistical tests of the hypotheses, which can be formulated either in absolute or relative terms, and these are examined in turn. Having established the extent of agglomeration, section 4.6 assesses the role of foreign-owned research facilities as a contributory element towards it. As discussed above, the effects of internationalization are one of two sets of explanations behind the agglomeration proposition. Some conclusions are then drawn in a final section.

4.2 THE DATA

Technological activity is measured by a count of patents granted in the US over the period 1963 to 1986. In these data it is possible to separately identify the firm to which a patent has been granted, the location of the research facility originally responsible for the innovation, and an industrial classification of the technological activity with which each patent is associated. The tests of the agglomeration proposition rely on the second and third of these three dimensions, which can be used to indicate the relative importance of alternative locations for technological activity and how they change over time, sector by sector.

Since the US is the largest single national market it is common to patent there at around the same time or immediately after taking out a patent in the country of invention. The measure is improved by virtue of the fact that patents extended to the US by non-US firms are more likely to represent significant innovations than do purely domestic patents. Firms from different countries must also all meet the requirements of the US official patent assessment procedures, providing a standard for comparison. However, these same considerations imply that the US as a location for technological activity itself must be treated somewhat differently than other countries when using the data. Research facilities located in the US are more likely to give rise to US patents than similar facilities elsewhere.

It is well known that there are inter-industry differences in the propensity to patent. Scherer (1983), using US patent data, found that variations between firms in their propensity to patent relative to the value of the R&D expenditure were to be explained principally by such inter-industry differences. This major source of variations in the propensity to patent does not present a problem here, as the analysis is conducted at the level of individual sectors and not across them. However, for at least part of the study it has to be assumed that over relatively large numbers of patents, the propensity to patent from research facilities from a given non-US location (aggregating over the firms involved) does not have any systematic bias as compared to the average propensity to patent in that sector. This is critical when comparing the shares of foreign research centres in US patenting. To the extent, though, that there are variations between centres in the propensity to patent in the US which run across industries, this is allowed for when using a measure of the comparative advantage of centres as opposed to their absolute shares of patenting.

To test the agglomeration proposition the data were divided into 34 sectoral groups classified according to technological activity, and these are listed in table 4.1. In each of these sectors, patents were further classified to one of twelve countries, representing the location of the research from which the invention in question originated. The twelve countries of origin comprised

Table 4.1   The 34 sector classification

1	Food	20	Office equipment and
2	Drink		communications
3	Tobacco	21	Transmission equipment
4	Chemicals n.e.s.	22	Lighting and wiring
5	Synthetic resins	23	Radio and TV receivers
6	Cleaning agents	24	Motor vehicles
7	Dyestuffs and organic	25	Aircraft
	compounds	26	Other transport equipment
8	Agricultural chemicals	27	Textiles, clothing, leather and
9	Pharmaceuticals		footwear
10	Bioengineering	28	Paper products, printing and
11	Primary metals		publishing
12	Fabricated metal products	29	Rubber and plastic products
13	Mechanical engineering n.e.s.	30	Non-metallic mineral products
14	Agricultural machinery		(building materials)
15	Construction and mining	31	Coal and petroleum products
	equipment	32	Professional and scientific
16	Industrial engines		instruments
17	Nuclear reactors	33	Wood products
18	Electrical equipment n.e.s.	34	Other manufacturing
19	Semiconductors		

n.e.s. = Not elsewhere specified.

the US, Japan, West Germany, the UK, Italy, France, the Netherlands, Belgium, Denmark, Switzerland, Sweden, and all other countries as a group. In all these cases patenting in the US was significant during the 1963–86 period.

The data were prepared by the Office of Technology Assessment and Forecast in the US Patent and Trademark Office. It is important to emphasize again that in aggregating over firms and individuals, the basic data have been organized in accordance with the location of origin of inventions rather than the nationality of ownership of research facilities. This is possible as in completing the US patent application form the location of origin of invention must be recorded, even if the patent is granted to a firm (or an agent on their behalf) in another country.

This is sufficient to explore the agglomeration proposition itself. It is necessary, though, to organize the data in another way when examining the role of internationalization within any agglomeration process. In this case it is necessary to aggregate over the patenting of parent and affiliates in each major inter-national corporate group, to be able to distinguish between the home and foreign research of the group as a whole. In the present context it is a matter of indifference whether the patent is taken out by the parent, an affiliate, or an agent on their behalf; the policy on this may differ between companies for a variety of reasons. What is important is to gather information on all patents attributable to foreign research facilities owned by a multinational parent, irrespective of which part of the firm they are granted to. This is achieved through the aggregation of patents granted to parts of a common group, and then separating those due to research outside the home country of the parent company, according again to the country in which these facilities are located.

Through cooperation between researchers at the University of Reading and SPRU, University of Sussex, it has proved possible to establish the ultimate ownership of patents where they are granted to affiliates of multinationals. This consolidation of patenting by international corporate groups was carried out for the world's largest 792 industrial firms, measured by the value of their global sales in 1982. Of these, US patenting activity was rec-orded for 729 firms during the period 1969–86. The details of the composition of this group of firms, in terms of the nationality of parent companies and the industrial distribution of their output have been described by Dunning and Pearce (1985). Together, they account for nearly 43 per cent of all patents granted in the US between 1969 and 1986. Patel and Pavitt (1989) discuss further the significance of US patenting by this group of firms rela-tive to others. The role of foreign-owned research in the geo-graphical concentration or dispersion of technological activity was assessed using the evidence of this group.

4.3 THE STATISTICAL METHODOLOGY AND THE HYPOTHESES

The method followed was to begin by calculating the national shares of patenting in the US in 1978–86 (denoted period t) and

1963–72 (denoted t – 2). As described in the previous section, these national shares are defined by patents granted for inventions originating in the country in question, irrespective of the owner-ship of the patent or the location of the firm or agent which submitted the application. The relevant shares were obtained for each of the 34 industrial groups of technological activity listed in table 4.1.

Since these national shares were initially calculated for 12 countries (or 11 plus other countries), the mean value of share in any industry was 8.33 per cent. The degree of geographical con-centration of technological activity can then be measured by the variance of the cross-country distribution of patent shares (σ^2).

There are two reasons why the inclusion of the US may present problems which must be allowed for. Firstly, there may be a higher propensity to patent in the US from US-located research facilities than applies in the case of research outside the US, as alluded to above. Moreover, in recent years foreign patenting has been rising relative to domestic patenting in all countries. This implies that the observed decline in the US share of local patenting between 1963–72 and 1978–86 is not purely a result of a relative fall in the level of technological activity in the US. It is at least partly attributable to a rise in the propensity to patent in the US from research facilities located in other countries.

Secondly, in considering national shares including the US, in every industry US research clearly accounts for the largest propor-tion of patenting. It therefore dominates any analysis of the extent of the geographical concentration of technological activity measured by this means. The sectors which appear more concen-trated than others are simply those in which US research has a comparative advantage. Furthermore, the sectors in which tech-nological activity seems to become most dispersed over time are those in which the comparative advantage of the US has declined most. The interest to be found in this measure is therefore rather limited.

A greater reliance can be placed on trends in patenting in the US from inventions in foreign locations, which were again calcu-lated for the 1963–72 and 1978–86 periods. This was carried out across the 11 remaining countries (or 10 plus others), with a mean share of just over 9 per cent. However, even this construction is open to the objection that the focus of attention is the degree of concentration of technological activity in just a few major centres (principally Japan and Germany, and to a lesser extent the UK and France). Once again, this leading group of countries does not change very much across industries, although the distribution between different members of the leading group does.

While for some purposes this absolute measure of geographical concentration may be appropriate, a broader consideration of the performance of other potential centres can be brought in through estimating the comparative advantage of each location in innovative activity. This was achieved by drawing up an index of the revealed technological advantage (RTA) of locations, as discussed in chapter 1. Taking P_{ij} as the number of US patents granted in sector i attributable to research in country j, the RTA index is defined in the following way (Soete, 1987; Cantwell, 1989)

$$RTA_{ij} = (P_{ij}/\Sigma_j P_{ij})/(\Sigma_i P_{ij}/\Sigma_i\Sigma_j P_{ij})$$

The index varies around unity, so values greater than one suggest that a country is comparatively advantaged in research in the sector in question, while values less than one are indicative of a position of comparative disadvantage. The use of this measure also allows the US to be reintroduced into the study, as on average all countries are reduced to the same order of magnitude. However, the RTA index was calculated in a somewhat different way in the US case. For all other countries, the calculation was performed relative to inventions originating from all non-US locations, to allow for any differences in the domestic or against the foreign propensity to patent. For the US the index was obtained, as it had to be, by taking its position relative to all other countries.

The analysis then proceeded by running a cross-country regression of the national shares of patenting in the most recent period on the equivalent shares in the earliest period; or alternatively, a cross-country regression of the RTA index in the later years on the RTA index in the earlier years. Denoting the national share of patenting in the US due to research in country j by S_j, and using the term ε to represent a stochastic component, the

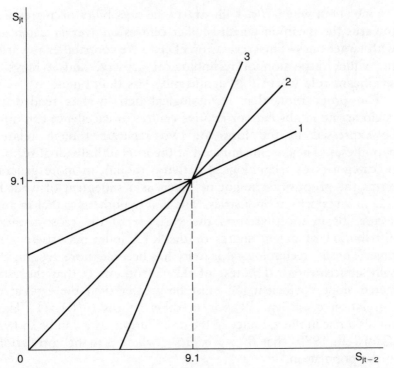

Figure 4.1 The regression of national shares of patenting in period t on the equivalent shares in period $t-2$

relevant equations can be written

$$S_{jt} = \alpha_1 + \beta_1 S_{jt-2} + \varepsilon_{1jt-2} \qquad (4.1)$$

$$RTA_{jt} = \alpha_2 + \beta_2 RTA_{jt-2} + \varepsilon_{2it-2} \qquad (4.2)$$

The first of these relationships is illustrated diagrammatically in figure 4.1. The regression line must pass through the point of means, which in this case are the same in both periods at just under 9.1 per cent. So if the slope coefficient β is equal to one the line passes through the origin as shown by line (2) in figure 4.1. Hence in the first regression $\beta = 1$ implies $\alpha = 0$. By comparison, for line (1) $\beta < 1$ and $\alpha > 0$, while for line (3) $\beta > 1$ and $\alpha < 0$. Industries can therefore be distinguished by the estimated value of β obtained.

Line (1) in which $\beta < 1$ illustrates the possibility of 'regression towards the mean' in which smaller centres on average catch up with larger ones. This 'regression effect' here contributes towards the wider dispersion of technological activity, and it plays a significant role where β is significantly less than one.

The proposition that technological activity has tended to agglomerate in absolute or relative centres of excellence can now be expressed in the form of two separate though related hypotheses. They are formulated at the level of individual sectors or categories of technological activity, though in more general terms the proposition might be taken as a statement of what is true in a majority of industries. The first hypothesis is that in any sector (or in most sectors) the variance of the cross-country distribution of patent shares or the RTA index has risen over time. That is, technological activity has become more geographically concentrated. The test of this hypothesis is that the estimated slope coefficient $(\hat{\beta})$ must be greater than the estimated correlation coefficient (R), or in other words $(\hat{\beta}/R) > 1$. This entails a rise in the variance of the distribution, as it can be shown (Cantwell, 1989) that $\beta^2/\rho^2 = \sigma^2/\sigma_{t-2}^2$, where ρ is the correlation in the population.

The second hypothesis is that locations which began as important centres for innovative activity in a sector remain at least as important in the later period, while locations with smaller shares of activity (or which are comparatively disadvantaged) on average remain smaller (or disadvantaged). This entails that the slope coefficient is greater than or equal to one, $\beta \geq 1$. There is a weak and a strong test of this hypothesis. The weak version is a t-test on whether β is significantly different from one. If according to this test $\hat{\beta}$ is not significantly less than one then the hypothesis that $\beta \geq 1$ cannot be rejected. However, this is a weak test as it does not necessarily imply that the hypothesis that $\beta \geq 1$ can be accepted either. If the standard error of the coefficient estimate is high, then the confidence interval surrounding the point estimate covers a wider band (including, perhaps, both zero and one). The strong test of the hypothesis is thus that the point estimate $\hat{\beta}$ is itself around one or greater, and the confidence interval surrounding it does not fall below some minimum level, say 0.5. The strength of this strong test can be varied according to the minimum value of the confidence interval around $\hat{\beta}$ deemed to be acceptable.

The strong version of the second hypothesis encompasses the first, since if $\beta \geqslant 1$ it follows that $(\beta/\rho) > 1$ as the maximum value of ρ is one. However, it is clearly possible to accept the first hypothesis while rejecting the second. This would imply that technological activity had become more geographically concentrated, but in the later period a different set of locations which had not previously been centres played a part in the higher degree of concentration. The first hypothesis concerns the degree of locational concentration of technological activity, while the second relates to the actual geographical composition of the international division of labour in any sector. If agglomeration is argued to be a cumulative process as suggested in the introduction, then it is necessary to examine both these aspects of the cross-country distribution of patenting from research facilities.

Having identified the sectors in which agglomeration is of the greatest significance, a similar set of cross-country regressions was run to establish the role of foreign-owned research in this. It is thus possible to examine the degree of similarity between the geographical distribution of foreign owned research and overall technological activity in a sector, and how they have changed over time.

4.4 THE GEOGRAPHICAL CONCENTRATION OF NATIONAL SHARES OF TECHNOLOGICAL ACTIVITY

The regression equation (4.1) was first run using the cross-country distributions of national shares of US patenting including the US, and the results are reported in table 4.2 for shares of total patenting. Estimated in this form, both the agglomeration hypotheses must be rejected. The locational concentration of technological activity has fallen ($\hat{\beta}/R < 1$), and the centres – in fact, centre – which was most important has declined ($\hat{\beta} < 1$).

As already mentioned, this reflects the major fall in the US

Table 4.2 The results of the regression of the national shares of patenting in the US in 1978–1986 on their shares in the 1963–1972 (for the total of all sectors)

$\hat{\alpha}_1$	$\hat{\beta}_1$	$t_{\beta 0}$	$t_{\beta 1}$	R	$\hat{\beta}/R$	$\hat{\sigma}_t^2$	$\hat{\sigma}_{t-2}^2$
2.133	0.744	14.84**	−5.11**	0.978	0.761	262.43	458.70

** Denotes $\hat{\beta}$ significantly different from zero or one at the 1 per cent level.
  Number of observations = 12.

share of patenting, which dominates this analysis. It is not possible to separate out that part of the US decline which is due to a fall in the technological competitiveness of the US, as opposed to that part which is due to an internationalization of patenting procedures. The share of US patenting originating from US research dropped from 76.1 per cent in 1963–72 to 58.3 per cent in 1978–86; and conversely, the non-US share rose from 23.9 per cent to 41.7 per cent.

The equivalent regression was then run excluding the US, for each of the 34 sectoral groups of technological activity set out in table 4.1, and for total patenting from non-US research. The results are recorded in table 4.3. Turning to the final row of the table first, which refers to total patenting, the first agglomeration hypothesis can be accepted, and the second finds at least some support. Concerning the first, the degree of geographical concentration of technological activity has risen. The standard deviation of the cross-country distribution rose by a third ($\hat{\beta}/R = 1.33$), and the variance $\hat{\sigma}^2$ nearly doubled. As to the second hypothesis, on a weak test $\hat{\beta}$ was not significantly less than one, suggesting that on average the most important centres retained their position. On a strong test, though, the evidence is rather more ambiguous. Despite a point estimate of β in the vicinity of unity ($\hat{\beta} = 0.934$), the standard error of this estimate is quite high. A value of β as low as 0.22 falls within the 95 per cent confidence interval.

What this result represents is that the geographical concentration of technological activity outside the US has risen, and on average the four major centres have just about retained their pos-

Table 4.3 The results of the regression of the national shares of foreign patenting in the US in 1978–1986 on their shares in 1963–1972, for each of 34 sectors and the total of all sectors

	$\hat{\alpha}_1$	$\hat{\beta}_1$	$t_{\beta 0}$	$t_{\beta 1}$	R	$\hat{\beta}/R$	$\hat{\sigma}_t^2$	$\hat{\sigma}_{t-2}^2$
1	0.623	0.932	8.21**	−0.60	0.939	0.992	62.16	63.20
2	−2.319	1.255	13.99**	2.84*	0.977	1.284	211.19	128.18
3	1.057	0.884	9.69**	−1.28	0.955	0.925	81.04	94.70
4	−0.419	1.046	3.25**	0.14	0.735	1.423	142.49	70.38
5	−0.818	1.090	4.50**	0.37	0.832	1.310	163.64	95.36
6	0.676	0.926	4.70**	−0.38	0.843	1.098	98.20	81.48
7	−0.278	1.031	6.20**	0.18	0.900	1.145	101.33	77.32
8	−1.681	1.185	6.08**	0.95	0.897	1.321	116.42	66.70
9	0.143	0.984	4.76**	−0.08	0.846	1.164	66.82	49.34
10	0.564	0.938	16.18**	−1.07	0.983	0.954	130.13	142.98
11	0.590	0.935	2.78*	−0.19	0.680	1.375	132.62	70.14
12	1.371	0.849	3.82**	−0.68	0.786	1.080	81.03	69.43
13	1.291	0.858	3.69**	−0.61	0.776	1.105	82.14	67.23
14	2.776	0.695	5.87**	−2.58*	0.891	0.780	63.31	104.06
15	1.405	0.845	12.67**	−2.32*	0.973	0.869	63.49	84.11
16	2.594	0.715	1.45	−0.58	0.435	1.642	275.37	102.12
17	6.015	0.338	1.06	−2.07	0.332	1.018	127.37	122.97
18	0.025	0.997	2.61*	−0.01	0.656	1.520	133.51	57.76
19	−4.375	1.481	3.73**	1.21	0.780	1.900	262.37	72.67
20	−3.996	1.440	2.90*	0.89	0.695	2.070	315.89	73.73
21	0.212	0.977	2.79*	−0.07	0.682	1.433	124.35	60.55
22	−0.646	1.071	3.59**	0.24	0.767	1.396	128.14	65.71
23	−2.436	1.268	2.46*	0.52	0.634	1.999	288.23	72.13
24	5.043	0.445	1.19	−1.48	0.369	1.206	164.12	112.80
25	2.601	0.714	4.03**	−1.61	0.802	0.890	113.45	143.18
26	1.858	0.796	3.58**	−0.92	0.767	1.038	85.41	79.34
27	2.292	0.748	5.12**	−1.72	0.863	0.867	69.16	92.00
28	0.680	0.925	4.29**	−0.35	0.819	1.129	146.50	114.88
29	−0.426	1.047	4.05**	0.18	0.803	1.303	107.30	63.23
30	0.569	0.937	4.15**	−0.28	0.810	1.157	66.24	49.49
31	0.440	0.952	3.95**	−0.20	0.796	1.195	93.03	65.11
32	0.480	0.947	2.53*	−0.14	0.645	1.469	179.91	83.36
33	2.317	0.745	2.67*	−0.91	0.665	1.121	96.73	76.98
34	−1.625	1.179	3.25**	0.49	0.734	1.605	165.48	64.25
Total	0.600	0.934	2.95*	−0.21	0.702	1.331	111.60	62.95

* Denotes $\hat{\beta}$ significantly different from zero or one at the 5 per cent level.
** Denotes $\hat{\beta}$ significantly different from zero or one at the 1 per cent level.
Number of observations = 11.

ition, but Japan has clearly outstripped the other three. Between 1963–72 and 1978–86 Japan's share of US patenting due to non-US research rose from 13.1 per cent to 34.6 per cent while Germany saw a fall from 26.0 per cent to 22.4 per cent, the UK from 17.8 per cent to 8.8 per cent, and France from 10.3 per cent to 8.0 per cent. So among the leading centres the tremendous rise in the Japanese share more than offsets a decline in the British position, promoting an increase in locational concentration.

A similar degree of support for the agglomeration proposition can be found from an inspection of the findings for each of the 34 sectors considered separately. The degree of geographical concentration rose in 27 of the 34 sectors ($\hat{\beta}/R > 1$), or around four-fifths of all industrial groups. The rise in concentration is hence fairly general. Moreover, the seven sectors in which concentration has fallen tend to be small. Between them, they account for just over 5 per cent of patenting activity.

The weak test of the second agglomeration hypothesis also yields an impressive result. For no less than 32 out of 34 sectors $\hat{\beta}$ was not significantly less than one, and at the 19 per cent level this was true of all 34 groups. So, in almost every case, the hypothesis cannot be rejected. However, on a stronger test the hypothesis can only be definitely accepted in a smaller number of cases. The point estimate of β was around one (0.97) or higher in 14 sectors, and over 0.9 in a further 8, which together comprise about two-thirds of all sectors. Imposing the still more restrictive test that β is around one and a value of 0.5 or lower can be rejected at the 5 per cent level of significance leaves just 6 sectors; widening this to those for which values of β of 0.3 or below can be rejected would include a further 5 sectors.

To summarize, a weak form of the agglomeration of technological activity was found in 27 out of 34 sectors. In these cases the geographical concentration of technological activity rose ($\hat{\beta}/R > 1$), and the hypothesis that the more important centres have on average retained their position cannot be rejected ($\hat{\beta}$ is not significantly different from one). Stronger positive evidence of agglomeration in the established centres was found in 22 of these 27 sectors, in which the estimated slope coefficient was over 0.9. The strongest evidence of all in favour of an agglomerative process of this kind appeared in 6 sectors, in which the point estimate of β was over 0.97 and the minimum value of the 95 per cent confidence interval for $\hat{\beta}$ (denoted by β_{min} in table 4.5) was greater than 0.5. These 6 sectors comprised drink, synthetic resins, dyestuffs, agricultural chemicals, pharmaceuticals and semi-conductors. Allowing for a 95 per cent confidence interval which spans down to 0.3 brings in a further 5 sectors; namely, other chemicals, office equipment, lighting and wiring, rubber and plastic products and other manufacturing. With the exception of drink, all 11 categories represent fields of substantial patenting activity.

In 10 of the 11 sectors in which technological agglomeration was of the strongest kind, the degree of geographical concentration was high by 1978–86. That is, the variance of the cross-country distribution of national shares of patenting activity ($\hat{\sigma}_i^2$) was over 100. The exception here was pharmaceuticals, in which despite a rise in locational concentration technological activity remained relatively dispersed by comparison with other sectors.

It is perhaps worth elaborating on the accuracy with which the slope coefficient of each industry regression can be estimated. A wider confidence interval around the point estimate (which makes it more difficult to accept the second agglomeration hypothesis) represents a high standard error on the coefficient estimate. This is indicative of a greater degree of mobility between centres in the cross-country distribution, which is why it plays a role in the stronger test of the second hypothesis. More precisely, in a bivariate regression a higher standard error relative to the estimate $\hat{\beta}$ entails a lower estimated correlation coefficient R. The extent of mobility between centres can thus be inversely measured by R.

Taking a value of R of less than 0.6 as representing a substantial mobility effect (which in this case is equivalent to a value of β which is not significantly different from zero), this involves three sectors in the analysis of national shares of patenting reported in table 4.3. These are industrial engines, nuclear reactors and motor vehicles. Not surprisingly, in view of trends in the overall shares of patenting from research in non-US locations, these are

Table 4.4 The results of the regression of the cross-country RTA index in 1978–1986 on the cross-country index in 1963–1972, for each of 34 sectors

	$\hat{\alpha}_2$	$\hat{\beta}_2$	$t_{\beta0}$	$t_{\beta1}$	R	$\hat{\beta}/R$	$\hat{\sigma}_t^2$	$\hat{\sigma}_{t-2}^2$
1	− 0.180	1.370	6.01[**]	1.62	0.885	1.548	0.89	0.37
2	0.060	0.927	3.16[**]	− 0.25	0.707	1.311	0.36	0.21
3	0.401	1.023	1.95	0.05	0.525	1.950	0.83	0.22
4	0.550	0.397	11.31[**]	− 17.18[**]	0.964	0.412	0.11	0.65
5	0.269	0.632	3.13[**]	− 1.82	0.704	0.898	0.19	0.24
6	0.391	0.753	1.61	− 0.53	0.453	1.664	0.26	0.09
7	0.037	0.984	11.03[**]	− 0.18	0.962	1.023	0.36	0.35
8	0.723	0.230	0.39	− 1.31	0.123	1.869	1.05	0.30
9	0.790	0.345	1.08	− 2.05	0.323	1.068	0.28	0.25
10	0.904	0.438	1.04	− 1.33	0.312	1.403	1.25	0.63
11	0.318	0.675	3.02[*]	− 1.46	0.691	0.976	0.05	0.05
12	0.083	1.041	7.43[**]	0.29	0.920	1.132	0.09	0.07
13	0.000	1.086	8.40[**]	0.66	0.936	1.160	0.08	0.06
14	0.893	0.863	1.12	− 0.18	0.335	2.577	4.71	0.71
15	0.468	0.841	5.69[**]	− 1.08	0.874	0.962	0.30	0.33
16	0.115	0.585	2.15	− 1.52	0.562	1.042	0.17	0.15
17	0.133	0.831	2.50[*]	− 0.51	0.619	1.341	0.89	0.49
18	0.028	0.919	6.71[**]	− 0.59	0.904	1.016	0.03	0.03
19	0.019	0.690	4.60[**]	− 2.07	0.824	0.837	0.18	0.26
20	− 0.368	1.123	7.55[**]	0.83	0.922	1.218	0.20	0.14
21	0.093	0.861	3.48[**]	− 0.56	0.740	1.163	0.14	0.10
22	− 0.351	1.483	10.55[**]	3.44[**]	0.958	1.548	1.62	0.67
23	− 0.072	0.891	7.29[**]	− 0.89	0.918	0.971	0.30	0.32
24	0.546	0.292	1.77	− 4.30[**]	0.489	0.597	0.08	0.23
25	− 0.004	1.352	5.16[**]	1.34	0.853	1.585	1.10	0.44
26	0.154	0.914	7.69[**]	− 0.72	0.925	0.988	0.17	0.18
27	0.011	1.290	3.14[**]	0.70	0.704	1.832	0.87	0.26
28	0.180	0.733	2.92[*]	− 1.06	0.678	1.081	0.13	0.12
29	0.745	0.330	1.06	− 2.15	0.318	1.038	0.10	0.09
30	0.819	0.351	3.23[**]	− 5.97[**]	0.715	0.491	0.17	0.69
31	0.320	0.783	4.32[**]	− 1.20	0.807	0.970	0.07	0.07
32	0.220	0.707	4.98[**]	− 2.77[*]	0.844	0.837	0.04	0.05
33	0.839	0.142	1.26	− 7.59[**]	0.371	0.384	0.14	0.96
34	0.296	0.611	4.13[**]	− 2.63[*]	0.794	0.769	0.08	0.13

[*] Denotes $\hat{\beta}$ significantly different from zero or one at the 5 per cent level.
[**] Denotes $\hat{\beta}$ significantly different from zero or one at the 1 per cent level.
Number of observations = 12.

all sectors in which the UK suffered substantial losses and (especially in engines and vehicles) Japan made major gains. In industrial engines and motor vehicles France lost as well as Britain, while in nuclear reactors France and Germany increased their shares of patenting alongside Japan. Despite this transformation the geographical concentration of technological activity increased in all three sectors. It was, though, a different group of centres which were responsible for the higher concentration in these cases.

4.5 THE GEOGRAPHICAL CONCENTRATION OF COMPARATIVE ADVANTAGE IN TECHNOLOGICAL ACTIVITY

In the analysis of national shares of patenting the prevailing trend towards technological agglomeration in most sectors reflects the growing importance of Japan as a research centre. Although this is not the only consideration which influences the results (the combined share of the top four centres rose from about two-thirds to nearly three-quarters of patenting), it is also of interest to examine the development of locational concentration in each sector relative to any general tendency towards agglomeration. Especially from the perspective of smaller countries, what matters is the pattern of their comparative advantage in innovative capability. Moreover, it might be argued that the substantial increase in the Japanese share of patenting is to some extent a consequence of an increasing propensity to patent in the US by the owners of Japanese research facilities. The measure of comparative advantage controls for any country-specific variations in the propensity to patent of this sort. Also, for the same reason, as remarked upon earlier, it then becomes possible to include the US as a research centre in the cross-country distribution.

The results of running the regression equation (4.2) with cross-country distributions of revealed technological advantage in each of the 34 sectors are shown in table 4.4. The first agglomeration hypothesis is accepted in 21 sectors ($\hat{\beta}/R > 1$), that is, in just

Table 4.5 The 95 per cent confidence intervals for the slope coefficients of the sector regressions of the national shares of foreign patenting and the cross-country RTA Index

	Foreign patenting shares (table 4.3)		Cross-country RTA (table 4.4)	
	β_{min}	β_{max}	β_{min}	β_{max}
1	0.675	1.188	0.862	1.878
2	1.052	1.458	0.274	1.580
3	0.677	1.090	−0.146	2.193
4	0.319	1.773	0.319	0.475
5	0.542	1.638	0.183	1.082
6	0.480	1.371	−0.292	1.798
7	0.655	1.406	0.785	1.183
8	0.744	1.626	−1.077	1.537
9	0.516	1.452	−0.368	1.057
10	0.807	1.069	−0.502	1.377
11	0.175	1.695	0.177	1.172
12	0.346	1.353	0.729	1.354
13	0.333	1.383	0.798	1.373
14	0.427	0.926	−0.847	2.574
15	0.694	0.996	0.511	1.170
16	−0.400	1.829	−0.022	1.192
17	−0.385	1.062	0.089	1.572
18	0.132	1.863	0.614	1.224
19	0.584	2.379	0.355	1.024
20	0.318	2.561	0.792	1.455
21	0.186	1.767	0.309	1.412
22	0.395	1.747	1.170	1.797
23	0.103	2.433	0.619	1.164
24	−0.400	1.291	−0.075	0.659
25	0.313	1.115	0.768	1.935
26	0.294	1.298	0.649	1.179
27	0.417	1.079	0.373	2.206
28	0.437	1.413	0.174	1.293
29	0.462	1.631	−0.363	1.023
30	0.426	1.449	0.109	0.593
31	0.406	1.497	0.379	1.186
32	0.100	1.794	0.391	1.023
33	0.114	1.377	−0.109	0.394
34	0.358	2.000	0.281	0.940
Total	0.219	1.649	n.a.	n.a.

n.a. = Not applicable.

under two-thirds of the total. The weak test of the second hypothesis provides support for the agglomeration viewpoint in 28 out of 34 sectors, in which $\hat{\beta}$ is not significantly less than one at the 5 per cent level. In all 21 sectors in which concentration has risen $\hat{\beta}$ is not significantly less than one, so for this group there is weak evidence in favour of an increasing degree of locational specialization as the consequence of a cumulative process. The hypothesis that greater specialization arises from a consolidation of centres already comparatively advantaged cannot be rejected.

Once again, a stronger test of this hypothesis narrows down the number of sectors for which it can be more certainly accepted. The point estimate of β is over 0.9 in 12 sectors, or just over a third. Of these, it was around one (0.97) or higher in 9 cases, in all of which, of course, concentration rose ($\hat{\beta}/R > 1$). From a check in table 4.5, in 8 of these sectors in turn the minimum value of the 95 per cent confidence interval for β was over 0.3. Indeed, in 7 sectors with a $\hat{\beta}$ of one or higher the value of β_{min} was over 0.7. In this group of 7 sectors the evidence in favour of the agglomeration of technological activity in comparatively advantaged locations is thus very strong. The 7 sectors consist of food products, dyestuffs, metal products, general industrial machinery, office equipment, lighting and wiring and aircraft. The eighth sector in which the 95 per cent confidence interval drops as low as 0.373 is textiles.

In most of the 8 sectors which experienced a strong form of technological agglomeration between 1963–72 and 1978–86, the degree of locational specialization (as measured by the variance of the cross-country distribution, $\hat{\sigma}_t^2$) was relatively high by the end of the period. It remained low, though, in metal products and other mechanical engineering or general industrial machinery. These are indeed fields in which one would expect a broader dispersion of activity rather than a heavy concentration in a few locations. In terms of absolute size, the general industrial equipment area accounts for the largest number of patents granted of any of the individual 34 sectors. However, there does seem to have been a trend towards an agglomerative consolidation of positions of comparative advantage and disadvantage in these cases.

Although there are around as many sectors subject to a strong form of agglomeration in the distribution of comparative advantage as in national shares of patenting, there are a greater number in which there is a significant mobility effect. A significant degree of mobility of locations up and down the comparative advantage distribution may again be measured by a value of R below 0.6, which here corresponds to a value of $\hat{\beta}$ which is not significantly different from zero on a t-test. The mobility effect was significant in 10 sectors; namely, tobacco, cleaning agents, agricultural chemicals, pharmaceuticals, bioengineering, agricultural machinery, industrial engines, motor vehicles, rubber products, and wood products.

For industrial engines and motor vehicles this was a reflection of changes in absolute patent shares as described in the previous section. Up to a point, the mobility observed in other sectors in comparative advantage terms was a consequence of mobility in these two. Japan's strong gains in comparative advantage in technological activity in engines and motor vehicles were balanced by a significant loss of comparative advantage in all the other 8 sectors mentioned except agricultural machinery and wood products (in which she remained comparatively disadvantaged throughout the period). In agricultural machinery a loss of comparative advantage was suffered by Switzerland, and in wood products by Denmark. Switzerland improved its comparative advantage in technological activity in agricultural chemicals and cleaning agents, building upon its traditional strengths; while Denmark made gains in bioengineering and tobacco (though its gain in bioengineering was matched by a loss in pharmaceuticals, perhaps reflecting a slight transition or even reclassification rather than a major shift).

Britain, which lost comparative advantage to Japan in industrial engines and motor vehicles, improved her position in cleaning agents, pharmaceuticals, rubber products and tobacco. In all these cases except pharmaceuticals she built upon an existing comparative advantage. In fact, in tobacco the evidence in favour of a significant mobility effect is rather ambiguous, since although the estimated correlation coefficient R was 0.525, the point estimate of $\hat{\beta}$ was greater than unity. Three of the four comparatively advantaged research centres at the beginning of the period (Britain, Germany and Italy) became still more advantaged, but the fourth (Sweden) lost out badly. A significant mobility effect contributed towards a rise in locational specialization ($\hat{\beta}/R > 1$) in 8 sectors, but in motor vehicles and wood products the geographical specialization of technological activity fell.

Dividing sectors into four groups according to the strength of the agglomeration effect as in table 4.6, it can be seen that the trend towards agglomeration has been stronger in absolute than in relative terms. This is not surprising as a consolidation of locational specialization in the form of a greater polarization of comparative advantage abstracts from any general cross-industry growth in technological activity in a rising centre such as Japan. At least a weak form of agglomeration can be established in 27 sectors in the distribution of national patent shares, and in 21 sectors for the RTA distribution. This requires $\hat{\beta}/R > 1$ and a value of $\hat{\beta}$ which is not significantly less than one. Within the category of weak agglomeration a distinction can be drawn between sectors which experienced a significant mobility effect ($\hat{\beta}$ is not significantly greater than zero, and $R < 0.6$), and those which did not ($\hat{\beta}$ is significantly greater than zero, and $R > 0.6$). At the top end a strong agglomeration effect can be represented by the presence of three conditions; that is, $\hat{\beta}/R > 1$, a value of $\hat{\beta}$ over 0.97, and a 95 per cent confidence interval for $\hat{\beta}$ whose minimum value is greater than 0.3.

It is apparent that with one exception (construction and mining equipment), the sectors in which the locational concentration of technological activity in absolute terms has fallen are different from those in which the RTA distribution becomes more broadly dispersed. In the case of sectors in which the geographical concentration of national shares of US patenting fell, one possibility is that smaller but comparatively advantaged countries have done well. This may have created a fall in concentration in terms of patent shares, but a rise in concentration in terms of RTA as comparative advantage is reinforced. This was a contributory factor in food products, in which the Netherlands, Switzerland and

Table 4.6 The division of sectors according to the strength of technological agglomeration in absolute and comparative terms over the 1963–1972 to 1978–1986 period

---

No agglomeration as locational concentration falls $(\hat{\beta}/R < 1)$

Foreign patenting shares (table 4.3)	*Cross-country RTA* (table 4.4)
1 Food	4 Chemicals n.e.s.
3 Tobacco	5 Synthetic resins
10 Bioengineering	11 Metals
14 Agricultural machinery	15 Construction and mining
15 Construction and mining equipment	equipment
25 Aircraft	19 Semiconductors
27 Textiles	23 Radio and TV receivers
	24 Motor vehicles
	26 Other transport equipment
	30 Non-metallic mineral products
	31 Coal and petroleum products
	32 Instruments
	33 Wood products
	34 Other manufacturing

Weak agglomeration but with a significant mobility effect $(\hat{\beta}/R > 1, \hat{\beta}$ not significantly less than one or greater than zero, $R < 0.6)$

Foreign patenting shares (table 4.3)	*Cross-country RTA* (table 4.4)
16 Industrial engines	3 Tobacco
17 Nuclear reactors	6 Cleaning agents
24 Motor vehicles	8 Agricultural chemicals
	9 Pharmaceuticals
	14 Agricultural machinery
	16 Industrial engines
	29 Rubber and plastic products

Table 4.6 (*continued*)

Weak agglomeration without a significant mobility effect ($\hat{\beta}/R > 1$, $\hat{\beta}$ not significantly less than one but significantly greater than zero, R > 0.6)

Foreign patenting shares (table 4.3)		*Cross-country RTA* (table 4.4)	
6	Cleaning agents	2	Drink
11	Metals	17	Nuclear reactors
12	Metal products	18	Electrical equipment n.e.s.
13	Mechanical engineering n.e.s.	21	Transmission equipment
18	Electrical equipment n.e.s.	28	Paper, printing and publishing
21	Transmission equipment		
23	Radio and TV receivers		
26	Other transport equipment		
28	Paper, printing and publishing		
30	Non-metallic mineral products		
31	Coal and petroleum products		
32	Instruments		
33	Wood products		

Strong agglomeration ($\hat{\beta}/R > 1$, $\hat{\beta} > 0.97$, $\beta_{min} > 0.3$)

Foreign patenting shares (table 4.3)		*Cross-country RTA* (table 4.4)	
2	Drink	1	Food
4	Chemicals n.e.s.	7	Dyestuffs
5	Synthetic resins	12	Metal products
7	Dyestuffs	13	Mechanical engineering n.e.s.
8	Agricultural chemicals	20	Office equipment
9	Pharmaceuticals	22	Lighting and wiring
19	Semiconductors	25	Aircraft
20	Office equipment	27	Textiles
22	Lighting and wiring		
29	Rubber and plastic products		
34	Other manufacturing		

Denmark made gains; bioengineering, in which the Danish share rose; and agricultural machinery, in which the Netherlands and Belgium built upon positions of initial comparative advantage.

In the aircraft and textiles sectors, though, smaller research centres have little role in explaining the combination of strong relative agglomeration but a fall in the absolute measure of geographical concentration. This has more to do with changes in the leading positions. In aircraft research the previous leader the UK lost ground to, and was overtaken by, France, resulting in a fall in concentration; but the UK's RTA remained static, and French technological advantage rose from a position of joint leadership, generating a rise in the RTA concentration. In textiles Germany and the UK as leaders were joined by Italy and France, as patent shares came closer; but in the RTA distribution, this meant that Italy strengthened its position of initial leadership.

The 13 sectors in which locational specialization as measured by the variance of the cross-country RTA distribution fell tended to represent cases in which Japan made strong absolute but not relative gains. In addition, the smaller country factor was sometimes important here as well. Belgium lost research from a comparatively advantaged position in chemicals and non-metallic mineral products, and Denmark did so in wood products. This weakening of comparative advantage reduced the cross-country variance of the RTA index, but had no such effect on the degree of concentration of patent shares as they began with below average shares.

There are three sectors in which strong evidence of agglomeration was found in both absolute and relative terms. In each case there were shifts between the leading research centres which were compatible with a reinforcement of the cross-country structure of comparative advantage. In dyestuffs and allied organic compounds Germany and Japan increased their share of patenting, while the UK, Switzerland and other smaller centres slipped back (though Switzerland remained in the leading group). However, in the RTA distribution, Switzerland consolidated its lead, and Germany and Italy improved upon positions of established advantage. In office equipment and lighting and wiring and allied electrical devices Germany and the UK lost to Japan and the Netherlands, which thereby also consolidated their leadership in comparative advantage terms.

4.6 THE ROLE OF FOREIGN-OWNED RESEARCH FACILITIES IN TECHNOLOGICAL AGGLOMERATION

Having identified the sectors in which technological agglomeration has been most pronounced, it is now possible to assess the contribution of foreign-owned research facilities towards this. The method used was to calculate the equivalent distributions of cross-country patent shares and RTA from the US patenting of the world's largest firms attributable to research outside their respective home countries. The data were again classified in accordance with the country of the research facilities responsible for the invention, rather than the country of the headquarters of the parent firm. The foreign or non-US patent shares thus included the patenting of US firms where it relied upon research carried out abroad.

However, the data on patenting by large firms from foreign research were only available from 1969 onwards, so the periods 1969–77 and 1978–86 were chosen for the comparison. In addition, it was not always possible to match the sectoral classification of the large firm data with that adopted in the earlier part of the study. Where it did prove feasible regressions were run for those sectors which demonstrated evidence of the strongest form of technological agglomeration as set out above. Taking FS_j to represent the national share of patenting in the US due to foreign owned research in country j, $FRTA_j$ to signify the value of the RTA index for country j calculated from patenting attributable to foreign owned research, and with t as 1978–86 and t − 1 as 1969–77, the estimated regression equations are as follows

$$FS_{jt-1} = \alpha_3 + \beta_3 S_{jt-1} + \varepsilon_{3jt-1} \qquad (4.3)$$

$$FS_{jt} = \alpha_4 + \beta_4 S_{jt} + \varepsilon_{4jt} \qquad (4.4)$$

$$FRTA_{jt-1} = \alpha_5 + \beta_5 RTA_{jt-1} + \varepsilon_{5jt-1} \qquad (4.5)$$

$$FRTA_{jt} = \alpha_6 + \beta_6 RTA_{jt} + \varepsilon_{6jt} \qquad (4.6)$$

The hypothesis tested is that the development of foreign-owned research contributes to technological agglomeration in the major centres. This implies that the cross-country distributions of patent shares or RTA become more similar over time, as foreign owned research tends to grow most rapidly in the leading research centres which are consolidating their position. It should be noted that this does not necessarily mean that foreign-owned research expands quickly in all such centres. If, for example, foreign-owned research began the period by being quite heavily concentrated in just one location, it is likely to become more dispersed across other important centres for technological activity. The test of the two distributions becoming more similar over time is whether the estimated correlation coefficient rises in moving from equation (4.3) to (4.4), and from (4.5) to (4.6).

The results are set out in table 4.7. They show that in terms of national shares of patenting from non-US research facilities, the value of R rose in 5 out of 7 sectors, and in terms of the cross-country RTA distribution, R rose in all 4 cases. However, although it seems that the trend of foreign-owned research has in general been in the same direction as overall technological activity, the extent of correlation was still only significant (β was significantly greater than zero) in 3 out of 7 sectors in terms of national shares, and in 3 out of 4 in the comparative advantage case. The relocation of foreign owned research has made a contribution towards technological agglomeration in most cases where it has occurred, but on this evidence it does not seem to have been a decisive one.

In the first set of regressions, the lack of a close degree of similarity is mainly a result of the limited level of international production and hence foreign-owned research so far established in Japan. Overall, the share of US patenting accounted for by foreign-owned research facilities in Japan increased from 7.0 per cent in 1969–77 to 9.2 per cent in 1978–86. This is well behind the rise from 21.6 per cent to 34.6 per cent over the same period in Japan's share of patenting from all non-US research. Moreover,

Table 4.7 The results of the regression of cross-country distributions of patenting from foreign owned research on the equivalent distributions from overall technological activity in selected sectors

FOREIGN PATENT SHARES (FS)

	1969–1977				1978–1986			
Sector	$\hat{\alpha}_3$	$\hat{\beta}_3$	$t_{\beta 0}$	R	$\hat{\alpha}_4$	$\hat{\beta}_4$	$t_{\beta 0}$	R
5	5.355	0.411	1.58	0.465	5.802	0.362	1.84	0.523
7	4.824	0.469	1.87	0.528	3.346	0.632	2.59*	0.653
8	4.505	0.505	1.99	0.552	2.921	0.679	2.43*	0.630
9	4.732	0.479	1.20	0.372	3.145	0.654	1.68	0.489
19	2.263	0.751	4.83**	0.849	6.140	0.325	1.47	0.440
29	3.302	0.637	2.89*	0.694	5.774	0.365	1.23	0.378
34	−0.945	1.104	3.36**	0.746	−3.564	1.392	3.94**	0.796

REVEALED TECHNOLOGICAL ADVANTAGE (FRTA)

	1969–1977				1978–1986			
Sector	$\hat{\alpha}_5$	$\hat{\beta}_5$	$t_{\beta 0}$	R	$\hat{\alpha}_6$	$\hat{\beta}_6$	$t_{\beta 0}$	R
7	0.754	0.312	1.18	0.348	0.470	0.403	2.55*	0.628
12	−0.970	2.060	2.56*	0.629	−0.408	1.261	2.80*	0.663
13	0.294	0.489	1.13	0.338	−00.65	0.901	2.64*	0.640
25	0.279	0.404	1.12	0.334	0.349	0.331	1.26	0.370

* Denotes $\hat{\beta}$ significantly different from zero at the 5 per cent level.
** Denotes $\hat{\beta}$ significantly different from zero at the 1 per cent level.
Number of observations = 11 (foreign patent shares) or 12 (RTA).

in semiconductors and rubber and plastic products Japan's share of foreign owned research measured in this way actually fell, and this is reflected in a fall in R in the regressions for these sectors.

Foreign-owned research may gradually be moving in the direction hypothesized, but until now the constraints on it doing so remain an important consideration. It has tended to become more similar to the geographical composition of other technological activity, and has contributed towards agglomeration in some sectors. A further discussion of the relationship between foreign-owned research and centres of excellence based on this evidence can be found in the next chapter.

4.7   CONCLUSION

The evidence suggests that there has been a tendency towards technological agglomeration, but with qualifications. Countervailing factors have also had a role to play. There has been some degree of international agglomeration of technological activity in around four-fifths of sectors in absolute terms, and about two-thirds in terms of the pattern of comparative advantage. In this latter group the locational concentration of research output as measured by patenting has risen, and the hypothesis that established centres have on average retained their position cannot be rejected. However, in a number of cases there is evidence of some mobility between centres in their shares of technological activity, and in some the mobility effect is a significant one. Just under a third of sectors, either in terms of shares of activity or comparative advantage, display a stronger form of technological agglomeration in which the hypothesis that existing centres have on average consolidated their position can be accepted.

To the extent that there has been a tendency towards the further development of established research centres, general economies of agglomeration would seem to have been the most important reason. The globalization of R&D within firms has contributed, but it is part of a broader phenomenon. It does seem, though, that the growth of foreign owned research facilities on average contributes towards the formation of research centres rather than inhibiting them. In this respect, they tend to be beneficial for locations with a tradition of scientific and technological strength.

5

Global R&D and UK Competitiveness

5.1 INTRODUCTION

It is widely held that one of the major benefits of multinationality – if not the principal benefit – is the capacity it provides to organize an international division of labour within the firm. Indeed, it seems that this facility has become steadily more important for MNEs over the last twenty years or so. MNEs have increasingly tended to rationalize their investments into globally integrated networks (Vernon, 1979; Dunning, 1988).

Clearly, this has implications for the competitiveness of both firms and countries. Among firms there may be pressure to become more multinational and to reorganize any existing network of international operations. The hypothesis that newer or less multinational firms attempt to 'catch up' with the more established MNEs has been investigated elsewhere (Cantwell and Sanna Randaccio, 1990).

At the level of countries those parts of local industry which are heavily influenced by MNE activity may find that the composition of local production moves in new directions. Foreign-owned affiliates may acquire a more specialized role, shifting away from the servicing of local markets and towards a greater involvement in intra-firm trade with other parts of their international networks. MNEs may concentrate research-related production in certain locations and assembly types of production in others, especially within an economically integrated region such as the

EC (Cantwell, 1987b). The production of indigenous firms which maintain contractual and other links with MNEs may be upgraded or downgraded accordingly. The growing interdependence between production locations and the potential to polarize research-related and other types of production helps to explain the attention which is currently paid to competitiveness by governments, policy makers and others.

The internationalization of research is obviously affected by (and affects) the organizational form of the MNE. Until recently it was common to view the MNE as comprising a parent company and a system of affiliates which were largely independent of one another. In this event the degree of geographical dispersion of R&D depends upon the relative strength of competing centripetal and centrifugal forces (for a review see Pearce, 1986, 1988).

The main centralizing force is the existence of scale economies in research. The main decentralizing force is the need for adaptation and a capacity to respond to local demand-side opportunities as reflected in local markets. Faced with these conditions a typical choice would be to concentrate the bulk of basic research in the parent company, while decentralizing adaptive research more widely. However, matters become rather more complicated once firms adopt strategies of technological specialization across affiliates, in the same way that they specialize in their productive operations.

There are two reasons why MNEs may take such an internationally integrated approach to technological development. Firstly, technological activity in any industry is locationally differentiated, as part of different national systems of innovation (Lundvall, 1988). The distinct characteristics of innovations in each country provide MNEs with an incentive to disperse research facilities to gain access to complementary paths of technological development, which they can then integrate at a corporate level. Secondly, it follows that the geographical dispersion of research to gain access to new lines of innovation may be related to technological diversification. It appears that in recent years there has been a growing interrelatedness between formerly separate technologies, and so to improve technological development even in its own immediate primary field of interest the firm may be obliged to broaden its technological activity through an international strategy.

In this case the emphasis shifts in discussions of the determinants of the internationalization of technological activity and its consequences. The chief concern is with the supply-side characteristics of locations (their potential for local technological development) rather than their demand-side characteristics (the degree of product adaptation required by local markets). This paper examines some new evidence on the internationalization of technological activity in this context. Data on the internationalization of technological activity by the world's largest firms are related to evidence on the wider geographical composition of innovation in each major manufacturing industry. Particular attention is paid to the internationalization of technological activity by British firms, and to the significance of the UK as a research centre.

5.2 THE INTERNATIONALIZATION OF TECHNOLOGICAL ACTIVITY AMONG THE WORLD'S LARGEST INDUSTRIAL FIRMS

The data on the technological activity of MNEs in general was reviewed in chapter 4. Patel and Pavitt (1989) elaborate upon the strengths and weaknesses of these data at the level of the individual firm. They offer the best (and in many cases the only) source of information on the sectoral and geographical composition of innovative activity across firms. Other recent studies have also supported the suitability of patent data in cross-firm empirical investigations. Griliches, Pakes and Hall (1987) argue that despite certain difficulties in using patents to describe time-series trends in innovation, patenting provides a good indicator of cross-firm variation in inventive activity, which is well correlated with R&D expenditure especially for large firms. Acs and Audretsch (1989) find that patenting varies across firms with R&D, skilled labour and size in the same manner as innovative activity when the latter is directly measured. Although there are differences in the relationship between patenting and measures of the appropriability of technology (such as concentration in the relevant industry) across firms, Acs and Audretsch conclude that overall patenting serves as a good proxy for innovative activity. In another survey, Pavitt (1987b) summarizes evidence in favour of using patenting in a third country when making international comparisons of technological activities, and particularly patenting in the US, which enforces common screening procedures and in which large firms generally patent first after their own home country.

There is, however, a drawback to the procedure used for consolidating the patents granted to corporate groups. This arises due to the regular changes in ownership of firms through mergers and acquisitions. To make the task manageable, it was necessary to identify corporate groups at a particular point in time, namely the year 1984. The patent data for the entire period 1969–86 were then consolidated on this basis. Consequently, changes in ownership links during the period were not allowed for.

This means that unfortunately it is difficult to assess the true extent of any trend over time towards the internationalization of technological activity. Any such trend is likely to be understated in the data on the patenting of the world's largest firms for two reasons. Firstly, where this internationalization is achieved through acquisition this is not recorded as a change in the geographical composition of the firm's technological development since the affiliate has been considered as part of the corporate group at both the beginning and the end of the period. A study of the foreign-located research of Swedish firms conducted by Hakanson suggested that around 60 per cent of the personnel they employed in foreign R&D facilities worked for affiliates which had been acquired by the parent firm. Secondly, where acquisitions have had motives other than the extension of research facilities (and there have been many of these), it may be expected that the new parent company would tend to wind down affiliate research. Any duplication with the existing research of the MNE may be eliminated, and other functions may be centralized in the technological headquarters. This would appear in the data as a move away from the internationalization of technological activity.

The evidence of table 5.1 must be viewed in this light. Note also that here patents are classified by the primary industry of output of the firms responsible, and not by the sector of technological activity as in chapter 4. Overall, it shows that the world's largest firms witnessed a mild trend towards the internationalization of technological activity over the 1969–86 period, even without allowing for the effects of acquisitions. The share of US patents granted to these firms attributable to research in foreign locations (outside the home country of the parent firm) rose from 9.8 per cent in 1969–72 to 10.6 per cent in 1983–6.

Table 5.1 The percentage share of US patents of the world's largest firms attributable to research in foreign locations (outside the home country of the parent company), organized by the industrial group of parent firms, 1969–1986

			Period		
Industry		1969–72	1973–7	1978–82	1983–6
1	Food products	16.63	20.04	22.66	23.96
2	Chemicals n.e.s.	12.18	12.90	12.60	12.73
3	Pharmaceuticals	17.69	20.24	18.42	17.79
4	Metals	10.64	8.70	10.61	9.18
5	Mechanical engineering	10.60	9.50	10.99	14.73
6	Electrical equipment n.e.s.	7.71	7.88	6.97	7.92
7	Office equipment	5.03	8.49	10.07	11.96
8	Motor vehicles	4.59	5.25	5.17	6.83
9	Aircraft	2.09	2.22	2.33	2.66
10	Other transport equipment	9.70	3.78	7.05	5.24
11	Textiles	5.88	5.72	5.17	3.90
12	Rubber and plastic products	6.53	7.18	6.06	5.13
13	Non-metallic mineral products	11.38	12.36	14.20	15.43
14	Coal and petroleum products	14.87	12.86	12.13	13.22
15	Professional and scientific instruments	6.68	4.61	3.70	3.31
16	Other manufacturing	5.03	7.46	10.39	12.69
Total		9.80	10.38	10.23	10.63

n.e.s. = Not elsewhere specified.

Source: The data on the geographical origins and industrial distribution of patents granted in the USA have been compiled at the University of Reading using data on patent counts obtained through the Science Policy Research Unit at the University of Sussex. The data on US patent counts were prepared by the Office of Technology Assessment and Forecast, US Patent and Trademark Office, with the support of the Science Indicators Unit, US National Science Foundation. The opinions expressed in this paper are those of the authors, and do not necessarily reflect the views of the Patent and Trademark Office or the National Science Foundation.

Table 5.2 The percentage share of US patents of the world's largest firms attributable to research in foreign locations (outside the home country of the parent company), classified by technological activity, 1969–1986

Industry	1969–72	1973–7	1978–82	1983–6
1 Food products	12.26	14.91	14.66	16.73
2 Chemicals n.e.s.	11.85	12.01	11.71	11.17
Inorganic chemicals	9.37	9.20	9.03	10.56
Organic chemicals	13.06	13.01	12.18	10.98
Agricultural chemicals	11.30	9.90	9.95	10.44
Chemical processes	9.59	10.08	11.33	11.49
Bleaching and dyeing	9.18	10.58	12.19	14.75
3 Pharmaceuticals	16.27	18.38	18.88	20.52
4 Metals	8.64	9.38	10.11	11.27
Metallurgical processes	7.69	8.07	8.28	7.72
Other metal products	9.30	10.47	11.60	14.46
5 Mechanical engineering	10.83	11.30	11.46	12.89
Chemical equipment	10.78	11.39	9.92	11.31
Metal working equipment	8.95	8.56	12.22	12.94
Construction equipment	11.35	12.15	12.46	11.64
Mining equipment	18.20	13.77	10.69	16.10
Specialized industrial equipment	13.56	14.69	16.00	15.89
General industrial equipment	7.45	9.03	9.32	11.96
6 Electrical equipment n.e.s.	7.08	7.55	7.32	8.39
Telecommunications	8.77	8.80	8.97	9.97
Semiconductors	6.35	8.63	6.20	7.03
Electrical systems	6.58	7.02	6.59	8.76
General electrical equipment	7.01	6.73	7.53	7.24
7 Office equipment	5.92	7.99	7.00	6.77
8 Motor vehicles	6.87	4.93	3.85	7.16
9 Aircraft	4.41	1.18	2.74	1.83
10 Other transport equipment	8.04	7.80	13.38	15.40
11 Textiles	10.94	14.00	18.46	11.25
12 Rubber and plastic products	9.01	10.42	9.81	9.92
13 Non-metallic mineral products	7.12	7.58	8.78	8.64
14 Coal and petroleum products	8.22	8.02	6.64	8.18
15 Professional and scientific instruments	9.44	9.72	8.35	9.02
Image and sound equipment	8.60	7.08	6.60	9.33
Photographic equipment	11.94	11.17	7.51	7.23
Other instruments	8.32	9.43	9.06	9.70
16 Other manufacturing	8.04	11.86	10.24	14.13
Total	9.80	10.38	10.23	10.63

Source: As for table 5.1.

Comparing industrial groups at each point in time is also revealing. Firms involved in the manufacture of food products, chemicals, pharmaceuticals, non-metallic mineral products (building materials) and coal and petroleum products were especially prone to international research strategies throughout the period. Of these, food and construction material companies experienced a clear trend towards the greater internationalization of technological activity during the period. By the mid-1980s about a quarter of the innovative activity of the major food firms was located outside their home countries. At the other extreme technological activity is most concentrated in the aircraft and aerospace sector, although it does seem to have become gradually more dispersed since around 1970.

It is also possible to look at the same data classified by the sectoral composition of the technological activity itself, and this is done for comparative purposes in table 5.2. What emerges most clearly is that the strong internationalization of research by food product, non-metallic mineral product and coal and petroleum product firms is not especially concentrated in those technological fields in which they are most immediately interested, but in other (presumably related) areas. Equally, although the major textile and instrument firms are not very highly internationalized in their overall technological development, textiles and instruments technologies themselves are rather more subject to the international dispersion of research.

It is worth briefly comparing the patent data with the most commonly used source of information on the internationalization of R&D, which refers to US MNEs. At first sight, table 5.3 suggests that a slightly higher share of patents are attributable to foreign locations than is R&D expenditure. However, this is a result of examining the distribution of R&D by US companies alone. Surprisingly, in view of their relatively high degree of multinationality, US firms tend to locate less technological activity abroad than firms of the other industrialized countries (table 5.4). In fact, the share of R&D expenditure abroad of US MNEs is greater than the share of patents of the largest US firms attributable to research in foreign locations. This is partly accounted for by the inclusion of a significant number of non-multinational firms among the world's largest industrial companies, whose research is obviously concentrated entirely at home. It may also be due to a greater propensity to patent in the USA from research carried out in the USA, which is for them their home location.

Table 5.3   The percentage share of the R&D expenditure of US multinational corporations located abroad, organized by industrial group of parent company, 1966–1982[1]

		Year		
Industry		1966	1977	1982
1	Food products	11.69	15.20	18.22
2	Chemicals n.e.s.	4.88	9.56	8.13
3	Pharmaceuticals	7.62	15.72	15.32
4	Metals	3.11	4.26	4.00
5	Mechanical engineering	13.51	7.56	6.25
6	Electrical equipment n.e.s.	5.37	3.38	3.30
7	Office equipment	6.98	4.09	4.68
8	Motor vehicles			
9	Aircraft	5.02	10.07[2]	13.04
10	Other transport equipment			
11	Textiles and wood products	53.04[3]	5.26	3.66
12	Rubber and plastic products	3.05	17.49	9.47
13	Non-metallic mineral products	3.74	7.69	8.81
14	Coal and petroleum products	n.a.	12.75	11.22
15	Professional and scientific instruments	5.34	9.80	10.97
16	Other manufacturing	6.15	11.03	4.43
Total		6.47	8.77	9.00

n.a. = Not available.

[1] In 1977 and 1982 expenditure on R&D for the company in question, including that locally subcontracted out by parents or affiliates.
[2] In 1977 the proportions were 13.71 per cent for motor vehicles, and 2.62 per cent for aircraft and other transport equipment.
[3] The Tariff Commission notes that the proportion of research attributed to foreign locations in wood products in 1966 appears to be overstated, probably due to a misallocation between industries.

Source: US Tariff Commission, 1973; US Department of Commerce, 1981, 1985.

Once this has been allowed for, the R&D evidence tells a remarkably similar story to that associated with the patent data. The internationalization of technological activity is again strongest in food products, pharmaceuticals and coal and petroleum products. Overall, there has been a trend towards internationalization which is clearest in the food and non-metallic mineral products sectors. However, for US companies at least, the building material producers do not have an above average international dispersion of R&D spending.

Table 5.4 shows that Japanese firms are even more inclined to concentrate their technological activity in their home country than are US firms. Indeed, whereas US firms have internationalized their research over the 1969–86 period, Japanese companies (in common with the Italian and Canadian groups) have moved towards a more centralized research strategy.

Table 5.4 The percentage share of US patents of the world's largest firms attributable to research in foreign locations (outside the home country of the parent company), organized by the nationality of parent firms, 1969–1986

	Period			
Country	1969–72	1973–7	1978–82	1983–6
US	4.28	5.47	6.03	7.40
Japan	2.85	1.90	1.25	1.24
West Germany	13.57	11.54	12.25	14.43
UK	43.27	40.45	38.67	44.91
Italy	20.11	18.32	13.68	11.72
France	10.23	9.43	8.84	10.92
Netherlands	63.93	68.77	64.08	70.04
Belgium	49.62	54.24	56.12	71.32
Switzerland	44.94	44.32	44.11	42.59
Sweden	20.94	17.77	25.87	31.30
Canada	42.06	39.98	39.76	35.52
Others[1]	32.76	26.39	27.39	23.10
Total	9.80	10.38	10.23	10.63

[1] Excluding companies registered in Panama.

Source: As for table 5.1.

UK firms are among the most multinational in their organization of technological activity. Around 40 per cent of the patents they are granted in the US are attributable to research facilities located outside the UK. This is a much greater share than for their German or French competitors, which acquire less than 15 per cent of their US patents through foreign research. It is higher even than the equivalent shares of Swedish or Canadian firms, though roughly on a par with the position of the largest Swiss firms. The greatest internationalization of technological activity of all has been undertaken by Dutch and Belgian firms. In 1983–6 nearly three-quarters of the patents they were granted in the US came from research outside their home countries. Patel and Pavitt (1988) have also noted the tendency for the firms of smaller industrialized countries to become substantially internationalized, and in a closer examination of the Swedish case they argue that foreign technological activities represent the cumulative extension of experience and skills first established in the home environment.

It is worth considering the other determinants of the internationalization of technological activity, apart from the nationality and industrial characteristics of the firm. In this respect as well, the patent data seem to mirror the pattern of innovation suggested by R&D data. Similar results can be obtained to those which have been observed in studies of the internationalization of R&D. This is seen from a cross-firm regression of the share of patenting attributable to foreign research (SPFR) on an index of technological competitiveness of the firm (TC), its foreign production ratio (FPR), and the overall size of its technological activity (STA). The index of technological competitiveness is defined as the firm's share of patenting in its industry in 1969–72 relative to its share of industry sales in 1972 among the world's largest firms. An adjustment was made to allow for the higher propensity of US firms to patent in the US. The foreign production ratio is represented by the sales from international production (foreign affiliate sales less intra-firm exports from the parent company) relative to the global sales of the corporate group. The overall size of technological activity is measured by the total number of US patents granted to the firm in the period in question, divided by a constant factor to make its coefficient easier to handle. The results of the regression run for patenting over the 1969–86 period were as follows, with absolute values of t-statistics in brackets:

$$SPFR = -0.014 + 0.001 \text{ TC} + 0.760^* \text{ FRP} - 0.159\dagger \text{ STA}$$
$$ (0.46) \quad (0.01) \quad (12.60) \quad (2.65)$$

No. of observations = 140 $\qquad$ $R^2 = 0.53$

F = 51.73 $\qquad\qquad\qquad$ $\overline{R}^2 = 0.52$

* Denotes coefficient significantly different from zero at the 1 per cent level.
† Denotes coefficient significantly different from zero at the 2 per cent level.

Predictably enough, the degree of multinationality of the firm is very strongly related to the extent of internationalization of its technological activity. A positive association might also have been expected with the technological competitiveness of the firm, but it was not significant. The negative sign of the coefficient on the overall size of technological activity is in line with the study of Pearce (1986) using R&D data. He reported that the size of the firm as measured by its sales was negatively related to the extent of decentralization of R&D, though at a declining rate as size increased. However, although this is consistent with what others have found using evidence on the location of R&D expenditure, it remains somewhat surprising. It seems reasonable to hypothesize the reverse, whether due to the existence of scale economies in R&D or the greater capacity to engage in an international research strategy as the size of technological activity rises. It may be that this is the consequence of the composition of firms in the sample. US and Japanese firms have the highest levels of patenting (between them they account for nearly three-quarters of all patents granted in the USA to the largest firms), but their technological activities are the most highly centralized.

5.3 THE GEOGRAPHICAL COMPOSITION OF INNOVATIVE ACTIVITY

Largely because of the size of technological activity of US and Japanese firms, and the significance of their home based operations, the bulk of the research of the world's largest firms is concentrated in the US or Japan. In 1978–86, of US patents granted to the largest firms 55.5 per cent were attributable to research facilities in the US. Of those attributable to innovations in non-US locations, 44.8 per cent were from Japan, 25.2 per cent from Germany, and 9.1 per cent from the UK. European locations collectively accounted for 52.1 per cent of innovations outside the US.

This also illustrates the high of degree of concentration of the technological activity of the largest firms in the industrial centres. Taking all patents granted in the US in 1978–84 (not just to this group of firms), of those due to research outside the US 32.5 per cent were attributable to Japan, 23.0 per cent to Germany, 9.2 per cent to the UK, and 55.3 per cent to the European countries as a group. This left 12.2 per cent due to research outside Europe or Japan, as opposed to 3.1 per cent of patents granted to the biggest firms.

Perhaps more interesting is the comparative advantage of different locations as hosts to innovative activity, in terms of which industrial types of activity they are most likely to attract. To examine this in more detail an index of comparative advantage, or what is termed revealed technological advantage, has been constructed for the major industrialized countries as locations for innovative activity (see chapters 1 and 4). This is defined as the share of patents attributable to research in the country in question in a given industry, relative to the share of all patents which can be traced to that country. The index thus varies around unity, with those industries in which the country is especially attractive as a location for research assuming values of the index greater than one. Owing to the differences involved in patenting US as opposed to non-US inventions in the US, the index is compiled relative to all patents granted for the US, but relative to all patents attributable to foreign locations for all other countries.

The results of this exercise for the patenting of the world's largest firms are reported in tables 5.5 and 5.6. The data are classified by the nature of the underlying technological activity with which each patent is associated, rather than by the industrial characteristics of the firms responsible. This allows for a more direct comparison with the sectoral composition of overall innovative activity, country by country. The same procedure was repeated for patenting attributable to research in foreign locations for the same group of firms, as set out in tables 5.7 and 5.8. In this case the position of each country depends entirely upon the distribution of the innovative activity of foreign-owned firms carried out locally. The index here therefore serves as an indicator of the attractiveness of a particular country for a given technological activity as a location for the research of foreign multinationals.

The location of innovative activity by the world's largest firms needs to be examined in the context of the wider role of locations as centres for technological development. It was argued above that the major MNEs have an incentive to locate research facilities in all the most important international centres of innovation in their industries. The revealed technological advantage of locations in overall innovative activity, as measured by all patents granted in the US attributed to the country in which the research originally responsible for the invention was located, is set out in tables 5.9 and 5.10.

It is noticeable that technological activity is much more locationally concentrated among the world's largest firms than overall. This is hardly surprising, given that national technological strengths are quite well related to the pattern of innovative activities of home based large firms, who contribute a sizeable share of national innovation (Patel and Pavitt, 1989), and an even higher share in the areas of local comparative advantage in which they themselves tend to be concentrated. The technological activity of the world's largest firms has been based especially in the UK in seven fields; food products, pharmaceuticals, aircraft, textiles, rubber and plastic products, coal and petroleum products and other manufacturing. With two exceptions (aircraft and to a lesser extent coal and petroleum products) these are all sectors in which the research programmes of the largest firms have become quite significantly internationalized as shown in table 5.2.

Data on the location of US-owned foreign affiliate R&D suggest that US MNEs have been relatively drawn to research in the UK in certain of these same fields of local capability. Table 5.11 shows that US foreign affiliate R&D is especially attracted to the UK in food products, chemicals (including pharmaceuticals), metals and other manufacturing. However, this is compiled on the basis of a classification by industrial group of firm rather

Table 5.5 The revealed technological advantage of locations in the innovation of the world's largest firms, classified by technological activity, 1969–1977

Sector	Countries								
	US	Japan	Germany	UK	Italy	France	Switzerland	Others (Europe)	Others
1 Food Products	1.17	0.84	0.37	2.07	0.57	0.24	0.42	2.17	2.90
2 Chemicals n.e.s.	0.96	0.73	1.22	0.89	0.84	0.87	1.97	0.76	0.91
Inorganic	1.05	0.86	1.16	0.82	0.74	1.40	0.36	1.32	1.51
Organic	0.92	0.67	1.25	0.84	0.94	0.86	2.32	0.69	0.85
Agricultural	1.03	0.45	1.36	0.86	0.11	0.83	3.00	0.64	1.01
Processes	1.06	1.00	1.06	1.08	0.63	0.85	0.80	0.99	1.11
Bleaching	0.69	0.37	1.64	0.90	0.49	0.63	3.05	0.24	0.26
3 Pharmaceuticals	0.90	0.80	0.97	1.09	0.94	1.23	2.25	0.38	0.98
4 Metals	1.07	1.01	0.80	1.22	0.84	1.21	0.55	1.20	1.53
Metallurgical	1.00	1.20	0.82	1.08	0.71	0.83	0.46	1.12	1.62
Other products	1.13	0.81	0.78	1.38	0.99	1.63	0.65	1.28	1.44
5 Mechanical engineering	1.04	0.85	0.96	1.19	1.29	0.95	0.65	1.41	1.38
Chemical equipment	1.08	0.94	0.91	0.96	1.26	0.81	0.60	1.79	1.71
Metals equipment	0.95	0.90	0.83	0.95	1.24	1.17	0.83	1.93	1.37
Construction equipment	1.05	1.17	0.90	0.78	2.04	0.82	0.38	1.22	1.60
Mining equipment	1.28	0.37	0.43	1.32	0.77	2.00	0.31	3.19	3.98
Specialized equipment	1.05	0.82	0.94	1.23	1.50	0.91	0.73	1.28	1.65
General equipment	0.99	0.72	1.14	1.58	0.98	0.93	0.66	0.90	0.66

6	Electrical equipment n.e.s.	1.01	1.25	0.85	0.95	0.93	1.29	0.47	0.97	0.94
	Telecommunications	0.99	1.15	0.77	0.98	0.68	1.89	0.30	1.04	1.38
	Semiconductors	1.00	1.85	0.85	0.56	0.46	0.53	0.43	0.54	0.45
	Systems	1.01	1.14	0.87	1.08	1.03	1.26	0.53	0.99	0.95
	General equipment	1.02	1.19	0.89	0.91	1.22	1.25	0.52	1.11	0.80
7	Office equipment	1.04	1.54	0.63	0.80	3.09	1.51	0.33	0.62	0.25
8	Motor vehicles	0.71	1.37	1.30	0.62	0.95	1.16	0.06	0.22	0.28
9	Aircraft	1.10	0.11	0.95	3.19	0.47	1.92	0.08	0.54	0.37
10	Other transport equipment	0.97	0.97	1.28	0.79	0.75	1.44	0.27	0.87	0.80
11	Textiles	1.08	0.92	1.03	1.36	2.23	1.83	0.08	0.44	0.35
12	Rubber products	0.94	1.01	0.78	1.60	2.01	1.00	0.18	0.87	1.15
13	Non-metallic minerals	1.09	1.17	0.82	1.36	0.52	0.72	0.32	1.18	1.18
14	Coal and petroleum	1.23	0.84	0.67	1.48	1.82	0.50	0.12	1.77	3.03
15	Professional instruments	0.95	1.49	0.87	0.73	0.62	0.82	0.48	1.21	0.56
	Image equipment	0.87	2.29	0.41	0.64	0.26	0.90	0.12	0.45	0.30
	Photographic	0.83	1.83	0.89	0.34	0.42	0.19	0.32	1.64	0.17
	Other instruments	1.01	1.11	0.94	1.00	0.83	1.23	0.65	1.05	0.87
16	Other manufacturing	1.15	0.51	1.20	1.28	0.41	0.59	0.50	1.90	2.19

Source: As for table 5.1.

Table 5.6 The revealed technological advantage of locations in the foreign research of the world's largest firms (outside the home country of the parent company), 1969–1977

Sector	Country								
	US	Japan	Germany	UK	Italy	France	Switzerland	Others (Europe)	Others
1 Food Products	1.13	1.09	0.74	0.71	0.86	0.27	0.68	1.84	1.36
2 Chemicals n.e.s.	1.18	1.06	0.83	1.08	1.04	1.00	0.89	0.98	1.11
Inorganic	0.93	0.23	1.18	0.78	0.53	0.41	1.02	1.43	1.40
Organic	1.21	1.00	0.83	1.07	1.26	1.08	0.86	0.89	1.15
Agricultural	1.14	1.81	0.82	0.78	0.00	1.97	0.00	0.88	1.21
Processes	1.11	1.27	0.77	1.16	0.53	0.82	0.97	1.22	0.98
Bleaching	0.99	1.79	0.82	1.58	1.10	0.85	1.52	0.50	0.58
3 Pharmaceuticals	1.30	1.13	0.30	1.46	1.62	2.22	0.18	0.51	1.04
4 Metals	0.95	0.65	1.05	1.24	0.74	0.80	0.98	0.84	1.10
Metallurgical	0.98	1.06	0.73	1.30	1.06	0.47	0.63	0.87	1.39
Other products	0.94	0.41	1.24	1.21	0.54	1.00	1.19	0.83	0.93
5 Mechanical engineering	0.94	0.69	1.37	0.87	0.99	0.84	1.24	0.82	1.04
Chemical equipment	0.97	1.07	0.91	0.87	1.31	0.66	1.33	1.19	1.09
Metals equipment	0.71	0.25	1.11	0.90	1.58	0.92	3.76	0.72	0.86
Construction equipment	0.98	1.06	1.49	0.67	1.33	0.77	0.83	0.61	1.24
Mining equipment	1.57	0.00	0.36	0.56	0.14	0.80	1.07	1.97	2.10
Specialized equipment	0.95	0.50	1.63	0.92	0.90	0.93	0.86	0.60	1.02
General equipment	0.70	0.68	1.80	0.98	0.51	0.92	0.65	0.62	0.78

6 Electrical equipment n.e.s.	0.92	1.58	1.08	0.96	1.33	1.02	1.34	0.57	0.95
Telecommunications	1.17	0.54	0.71	1.05	0.20	2.44	1.66	0.56	1.16
Semiconductors	0.99	3.79	1.45	0.84	1.18	0.38	1.42	0.50	0.20
Systems	0.70	1.47	1.13	1.00	1.66	0.79	1.39	0.56	0.93
General equipment	1.01	1.50	1.12	0.88	1.77	0.55	0.91	0.64	1.21
7 Office equipment	0.70	0.69	0.88	1.15	1.69	2.44	2.39	0.63	0.19
8 Motor vehicles	0.74	0.48	1.21	1.35	0.98	1.81	0.18	0.42	0.81
9 Aircraft	0.45	0.00	2.84	0.27	0.00	1.26	1.57	0.00	1.01
10 Other transport equipment	0.85	0.80	1.65	0.60	0.75	0.87	0.50	1.01	1.03
11 Textiles	1.06	0.26	0.89	2.57	0.90	0.20	0.50	0.69	0.32
12 Rubber products	0.75	1.69	0.75	0.70	0.88	1.56	0.12	1.02	1.30
13 Non-metallic minerals	0.89	1.15	0.88	0.78	0.37	1.60	0.40	1.90	1.02
14 Coal and petroleum	0.95	0.24	0.56	0.36	0.40	0.58	0.33	1.91	2.29
15 Professional instruments	0.70	1.16	0.84	1.01	0.67	0.85	0.94	1.80	0.55
Image equipment	1.37	3.04	0.72	1.33	0.00	0.67	2.67	0.62	0.50
Photographic	0.27	1.57	0.60	0.86	0.74	0.45	0.21	2.93	0.17
Other instruments	0.89	0.64	1.06	1.12	0.65	1.21	1.44	0.90	0.88
16 Other manufacturing	1.19	1.34	0.38	1.09	0.38	0.84	0.63	0.73	2.05

Source: As for table 5.1.

Table 5.7 The revealed technological advantage of locations in the innovation of the world's largest firms, classified by technological activity, 1978–1986

Sector	Country							Others (Europe)	Others
	US	Japan	Germany	UK	Italy	France	Switzerland		
1 Food Products	1.33	0.61	0.61	2.48	0.59	0.61	1.04	2.43	4.00
2 Chemicals n.e.s.	1.08	0.63	1.45	1.05	1.23	0.94	2.10	0.96	1.05
Inorganic	1.09	0.58	1.42	0.88	0.94	1.77	0.41	1.47	2.51
Organic	1.08	0.61	1.55	0.95	1.38	0.89	2.32	0.87	0.80
Agricultural	1.05	0.42	1.60	1.08	0.81	0.38	5.39	0.24	1.24
Processes	1.11	0.77	1.19	1.33	1.11	0.99	1.02	1.25	1.37
Bleaching	0.54	0.22	1.96	0.69	0.62	0.81	6.51	0.19	0.18
3 Pharmaceuticals	0.95	0.44	1.12	2.56	2.16	1.29	2.53	0.71	0.70
4 Metals	1.07	0.98	0.87	1.06	0.71	1.15	0.89	1.56	1.30
Metallurgical	0.96	1.10	0.74	0.87	0.58	1.00	1.00	1.61	1.29
Other products	1.16	0.84	1.02	1.27	0.87	1.32	0.77	1.50	1.30
5 Mechanical engineering	1.04	0.82	1.08	1.09	1.34	0.98	0.76	1.83	1.33
Chemical equipment	1.12	0.84	1.06	0.89	1.50	0.82	0.73	2.17	1.55
Metals equipment	0.86	0.86	0.98	0.72	0.99	1.14	1.12	2.49	0.86
Construction equipment	1.05	1.03	0.89	0.67	0.93	0.88	0.42	2.12	1.47
Mining equipment	1.42	0.27	0.71	2.55	2.30	1.61	0.40	3.52	3.61
Specialized equipment	1.04	0.72	1.16	1.17	2.39	0.81	1.00	1.60	1.77
General equipment	0.95	0.85	1.20	1.33	0.78	1.09	0.62	1.12	0.81

6	Electrical equipment n.e.s.	1.01	1.17	0.80	0.83	0.60	1.43	0.58	0.72	1.16
	Telecommunications	1.00	1.03	0.72	0.97	0.36	2.14	0.53	0.80	1.98
	Semiconductors	1.00	1.53	0.71	0.37	0.05	0.95	0.39	0.11	0.60
	Systems	1.06	1.07	0.88	0.97	0.80	1.56	0.56	0.75	1.07
	General equipment	0.95	1.24	0.79	0.74	0.78	0.92	0.73	0.89	0.87
7	Office equipment	0.96	1.55	0.50	0.47	1.16	1.26	0.18	0.26	0.43
8	Motor vehicles	0.43	1.46	0.92	0.49	0.85	0.50	0.11	0.23	0.18
9	Aircraft	1.39	0.11	1.33	2.99	0.35	4.61	0.00	0.39	0.91
10	Other transport equipment	0.82	1.00	0.99	0.68	0.95	0.58	0.56	2.41	0.95
11	Textiles	1.01	1.13	0.63	1.46	0.73	0.83	0.63	1.83	0.35
12	Rubber products	0.97	0.89	0.99	1.29	2.41	0.89	0.34	1.51	1.08
13	Non-metallic minerals	1.07	1.20	0.82	0.97	0.45	0.97	0.48	0.83	1.07
14	Coal and petroleum	1.52	0.64	0.89	1.50	0.84	0.78	0.10	2.76	4.24
15	Professional instruments	0.82	1.41	0.73	0.67	0.46	0.71	0.48	0.60	0.59
	Image equipment	0.67	1.72	0.42	0.40	0.23	0.87	0.16	0.12	0.49
	Photographic	0.66	1.68	0.56	0.39	0.30	0.15	0.43	0.45	0.41
	Other instruments	0.92	1.17	0.91	0.90	0.62	1.00	0.59	0.80	0.72
16	Other manufacturing	1.24	0.52	1.10	1.71	0.81	0.79	0.40	1.84	4.94

Source: As for table 5.1.

Table 5.8 The revealed technological advantage of locations in the foreign research of the world's largest firms (outside the home country of the company), classified by technological activity, 1978–1986

Sector		Country								
		US	Japan	Germany	UK	Italy	France	Switzerland	Others (Europe)	Others
1	Food Products	1.24	0.52	0.54	0.78	0.00	0.75	2.39	1.65	1.87
2	Chemicals n.e.s.	1.33	0.99	0.75	1.13	0.98	1.04	0.63	1.19	1.12
	Inorganic	0.98	0.44	0.79	0.69	0.39	0.61	0.17	1.06	2.72
	Organic	1.42	1.22	0.74	1.11	1.04	1.13	0.36	1.17	1.03
	Agricultural	1.37	3.10	0.72	0.75	0.00	0.68	0.00	0.37	1.89
	Processes	1.20	0.57	0.72	1.27	1.08	0.88	1.14	1.42	1.01
	Bleaching	1.21	0.12	1.24	1.43	0.85	2.41	1.89	0.14	0.39
3	Pharmaceuticals	1.11	0.82	0.53	2.13	1.23	1.56	0.25	0.66	0.60
4	Metals	0.84	0.52	1.43	0.86	0.88	0.91	0.81	0.94	0.91
	Metallurgical	0.96	1.11	1.07	0.77	1.44	0.79	0.79	1.00	1.17
	Other products	0.78	0.24	1.60	0.90	0.61	0.96	0.82	0.92	0.78
5	Mechanical engineering	0.76	0.66	1.39	0.77	1.25	0.65	1.06	0.95	1.04
	Chemical equipment	1.02	0.47	1.11	0.61	1.50	0.63	1.51	1.31	1.32
	Metals equipment	0.49	0.57	1.66	0.71	1.15	0.61	2.10	0.88	0.61
	Construction equipment	0.77	0.89	1.02	0.76	0.88	0.87	1.26	1.26	1.13
	Mining equipment	1.36	0.00	0.52	1.50	0.00	0.58	0.99	1.16	2.28
	Specialized equipment	0.74	0.44	1.30	0.94	2.20	0.71	0.81	0.87	0.97
	General equipment	0.50	1.10	1.82	0.64	0.63	0.57	0.40	0.65	0.84

6 Electrical equipment n.e.s.	0.99	1.33	1.09	0.73	1.20	1.26	1.81	0.55	1.07
Telecommunications	1.00	1.08	0.62	0.76	0.30	2.51	3.19	0.51	1.17
Semiconductors	1.14	1.85	1.68	0.74	0.14	0.87	2.06	0.17	0.59
Systems	1.07	1.31	1.16	0.87	1.79	0.84	0.94	0.63	1.00
General equipment	0.79	1.41	1.24	0.52	1.65	0.78	1.56	0.61	1.22
7 Office equipment	0.78	0.98	0.92	0.92	1.13	2.78	1.51	0.32	0.63
8 Motor vehicles	0.69	3.11	0.86	0.83	0.82	1.52	0.22	0.40	0.63
9 Aircraft	0.58	0.00	1.41	0.00	2.35	1.81	0.00	0.00	2.60
10 Other transport equipment	0.69	0.27	0.78	0.39	1.01	0.21	0.73	3.18	0.84
11 Textiles	0.92	0.00	0.39	1.99	0.86	0.33	3.43	2.10	0.24
12 Rubber products	0.83	0.63	0.95	0.66	1.15	0.71	0.46	1.77	1.18
13 Non-metallic minerals	0.98	0.96	1.17	0.79	0.31	0.88	0.75	1.12	1.17
14 Coal and petroleum	0.98	0.10	0.37	0.36	0.24	0.61	0.00	2.60	2.47
15 Professional instruments	0.86	1.52	0.84	1.08	0.64	0.78	1.52	1.11	0.67
Image equipment	0.97	4.25	0.88	0.99	0.25	0.53	1.65	0.15	0.48
Photographic	0.50	1.73	0.38	1.58	1.25	0.30	1.66	1.61	0.52
Other instruments	0.97	1.43	1.05	0.88	0.45	1.04	1.44	1.05	0.77
16 Other manufacturing	0.68	0.48	0.34	0.95	0.32	0.37	0.64	0.79	3.57

Source: As for table 5.1.

Table 5.9 The revealed technological advantage of locations in overall innovation, classified by technological activity, 1969–1977

Sector		US	Japan	Germany	UK	Italy	France	Switzerland	Others (Europe)	Others
1	Food Products	1.07	1.00	0.66	1.24	0.70	0.70	1.23	1.43	1.31
2	Chemicals n.e.s.	0.92	1.00	1.18	0.91	1.16	0.91	1.59	0.74	0.70
	Inorganic	0.93	0.97	1.13	0.79	1.30	1.14	0.27	0.77	1.32
	Organic	0.87	0.99	1.23	0.84	1.39	0.88	1.99	0.63	0.57
	Agricultural	1.00	0.90	1.22	0.83	0.63	0.68	2.39	0.64	0.88
	Processes	1.02	1.10	1.03	1.09	0.70	0.89	0.72	1.06	0.92
	Bleaching	0.78	0.54	1.53	0.94	0.58	1.41	2.54	0.31	0.39
3	Pharmaceuticals	0.83	1.11	0.88	0.96	1.14	1.32	1.63	0.74	0.70
4	Metals	1.08	0.76	0.93	1.06	1.00	1.03	0.71	1.19	1.42
	Metallurgical	0.98	1.08	0.87	1.05	0.80	0.88	0.58	1.23	1.23
	Other products	1.12	0.60	0.97	1.07	1.11	1.11	0.79	1.16	1.53
5	Mechanical engineering	0.99	0.68	1.08	1.04	1.15	0.96	0.98	1.15	1.23
	Chemical equipment	1.00	0.72	1.08	0.88	1.22	0.86	0.89	1.33	1.30
	Metals equipment	0.93	0.66	1.13	0.95	0.96	0.97	0.94	1.02	1.41
	Construction equipment	1.02	0.77	1.06	0.94	1.21	0.94	1.07	1.23	1.14
	Mining equipment	1.13	0.44	0.91	1.13	0.61	1.36	0.30	1.37	1.85
	Specialized equipment	0.98	0.63	1.05	0.96	1.54	0.86	1.29	1.05	1.35
	General equipment	0.99	0.70	1.13	1.38	0.80	1.11	0.79	1.08	0.87

Country

6	Electrical equipment n.e.s.	1.03	1.24	0.84	1.06	0.86	1.13	0.71	1.10	0.85
	Telecommunications	1.07	1.23	0.70	1.10	1.05	1.57	0.50	1.00	0.87
	Semiconductors	1.01	1.90	0.86	0.87	0.43	0.74	0.49	1.04	0.46
	Systems	1.05	1.19	0.86	1.09	0.85	1.05	0.75	1.24	0.80
	General equipment	0.98	1.08	0.90	1.05	0.87	1.04	0.91	1.00	1.04
7	Office equipment	1.04	1.75	0.72	0.92	1.36	1.02	0.53	0.97	0.49
8	Motor vehicles	0.89	1.30	1.21	0.95	0.78	1.23	0.17	0.36	0.84
9	Aircraft	1.10	0.17	1.15	1.93	0.44	2.10	0.32	0.64	0.99
10	Other transport equipment	1.02	0.64	1.01	0.89	0.79	1.50	0.72	0.83	1.59
11	Textiles	1.12	0.60	0.83	0.99	2.05	1.06	0.68	0.93	1.86
12	Rubber products	0.89	1.11	0.85	1.35	1.35	1.20	0.46	0.80	0.87
13	Non-metallic minerals	1.04	1.07	0.87	1.20	0.69	0.91	0.64	1.18	1.10
14	Coal and petroleum	1.18	1.27	0.62	1.21	1.38	1.17	0.15	0.99	1.21
15	Professional instruments	0.98	1.51	0.90	0.85	0.58	0.83	0.93	0.95	0.80
	Image equipment	0.99	2.09	0.53	0.91	0.43	0.71	0.30	1.06	0.80
	Photographic	0.82	2.44	0.99	0.39	0.36	0.22	0.35	1.13	0.22
	Other instruments	1.02	1.09	0.93	0.99	0.68	1.06	1.24	0.88	1.00
16	Other manufacturing	1.20	0.58	0.91	0.88	0.92	0.95	1.03	1.31	1.83

Source: As for table 5.1.

Table 5.10 The revealed technological advantage of locations in overall innovation, classified by technological activity, 1978–1986

Sector		US	Japan	Germany	UK	Italy	France	Switzerland	Others (Europe)	Others
1	Food Products	1.07	0.69	0.75	1.43	1.36	1.09	1.77	1.59	1.27
2	Chemicals n.e.s.	0.99	0.87	1.27	1.03	1.05	0.95	1.50	0.82	0.76
	Inorganic	0.97	0.74	1.26	0.89	0.62	1.37	0.28	0.96	1.47
	Organic	0.97	0.91	1.35	0.90	1.31	0.89	1.69	0.64	0.61
	Agricultural	0.97	0.69	1.40	1.19	0.53	0.49	3.92	0.33	0.75
	Processes	1.04	0.90	1.10	1.25	0.80	1.00	0.94	1.15	0.93
	Bleaching	0.68	0.38	1.85	0.79	0.58	1.24	4.64	0.29	0.35
3	Pharmaceuticals	0.83	0.74	0.96	1.72	1.84	1.36	1.48	0.83	0.77
4	Metals	1.11	0.74	1.00	1.06	1.02	1.09	0.95	1.25	1.53
	Metallurgical	0.97	1.07	0.85	0.95	0.78	0.98	0.91	1.10	1.17
	Other products	1.16	0.57	1.08	1.12	1.14	1.15	0.96	1.32	1.70
5	Mechanical engineering	1.00	0.69	1.18	1.01	1.31	0.98	1.09	1.24	1.30
	Chemical equipment	1.00	0.69	1.18	0.94	1.49	0.89	1.03	1.36	1.35
	Metals equipment	0.91	0.73	1.23	0.77	1.12	0.97	1.11	1.10	1.41
	Construction equipment	1.03	0.77	1.15	0.91	1.32	0.82	1.14	1.39	1.20
	Mining equipment	1.21	0.30	1.10	1.74	0.71	1.54	0.30	1.48	1.98
	Specialized equipment	0.97	0.63	1.19	0.95	1.78	0.85	1.55	1.22	1.32
	General equipment	1.01	0.77	1.18	1.20	0.84	1.21	0.75	1.13	1.10

6	Electrical equipment n.e.s.	1.03	1.21	0.79	0.95	0.74	1.24	0.76	1.02	0.81
	Telecommunications	1.07	1.12	0.65	1.17	0.98	1.68	0.64	0.98	0.91
	Semiconductors	0.99	1.72	0.70	0.68	0.34	0.96	0.39	0.67	0.31
	Systems	1.06	1.15	0.87	0.97	0.77	1.21	0.74	1.23	0.73
	General equipment	0.94	1.19	0.83	0.85	0.66	1.04	0.99	0.92	1.00
7	Office equipment	0.95	1.80	0.53	0.64	0.78	0.74	0.40	0.83	0.37
8	Motor vehicles	0.69	1.54	1.06	0.68	0.71	0.60	0.31	0.32	0.54
9	Aircraft	1.24	0.18	1.06	2.10	0.35	3.64	0.05	0.82	1.32
10	Other transport equipment	1.01	0.69	0.94	0.90	0.89	1.34	0.91	0.99	1.91
11	Textiles	1.18	0.61	0.93	0.94	2.65	1.12	0.88	1.06	1.81
12	Rubber products	0.91	0.98	1.01	1.22	1.51	1.05	0.48	1.13	0.84
13	Non-metallic minerals	1.01	1.11	0.88	1.00	0.73	0.92	0.68	1.08	1.11
14	Coal and petroleum	1.35	0.81	0.71	1.13	0.81	1.75	0.16	1.51	1.55
15	Professional instruments	0.92	1.44	0.80	0.83	0.56	0.73	0.85	0.77	0.70
	Image equipment	0.89	1.77	0.50	0.79	0.37	0.71	0.51	0.92	0.46
	Photographic	0.63	2.14	0.56	0.38	0.24	0.15	0.44	0.47	0.25
	Other instruments	0.99	1.11	0.96	1.00	0.71	0.95	1.08	0.85	0.91
16	Other manufacturing	1.29	0.51	0.84	1.09	0.89	0.93	1.03	1.59	2.39

Source: As for table 5.1.

Table 5.11   The revealed comparative advantage of the UK in US majority-owned foreign affiliate R&D expenditure, classified by industry of affiliates, 1982

Industry	RCA index
Food products	1.59
Chemicals	1.11
Metals	1.43
Mechanical engineering and office equipment	0.92
Electrical equipment n.e.s.	0.33
Transport equipment	0.73
Other manufacturing	1.90

Source: US Department of Commerce, (1985).

than technological activity. When the equivalent of tables 5.5 and 5.6 were rearranged on the same basis (allocating all of a firm's patents to its primary sector of output), results similar to the existing tables 5.5 and 5.6 were obtained. In comparing tables, anomalies appeared in the case of metals, in which US MNEs appear to favour a UK research location more than large firms in general (although technological activity in metals itself has been relatively attracted to the UK, at least until recently); and non-metallic mineral products, in which industry it seems that large firms favour a UK research location, but not especially to carry out technological activity in this specific field.

The UK as a location seems to have experienced a high degree of mobility in the pattern of its technological advantage between 1963–70 and 1978–84 as have UK firms (Cantwell, 1989). This reflects changes in the UK research activities of the world's largest firms. Between 1969–77 and 1978–86 the index of revealed technological advantage for the UK for the technological activity of this group as a whole rose from 1.09 to 2.56 in pharmaceuticals, from 1.32 to 2.55 in mining equipment, while in non-metallic mineral products it fell from 1.36 to 0.97.

In general, the geographical composition of the research of the world's largest firms follows a broadly similar pattern to the locational distribution of all technological activity. To examine this more closely, cross-sectoral regressions were carried out for each country of the distribution of innovative activity of large firms, as described in tables 5.5–5.8 on the distribution of overall technological advantage in that country over the same period, as captured in tables 5.9 and 5.10. These regressions were run across 33 technological activities, consisting of the 31 fields shown in the tables in question (using subsectors where possible rather than broader aggregate groupings), together with nuclear reactors and power plants. In all cases the distribution of large firm innovation in the country, as reported in tables 5.5 and 5.6, was positively and significantly correlated with the pattern of overall innovation in the same country, as recorded in tables 5.9 and 5.10. This applied for both the 1969–77 and 1978–86 periods. The results are summarized in table 5.12.

Matters are not so simple in the more interesting case of the sectoral composition of foreign owned research. Here too, as a rule, the distribution of foreign-owned research activity was positively related to the overall pattern of innovation in the major industrialized countries, though it was not always significantly so. The outstanding exception was the UK in the earlier 1969–77 period. For the UK at this time there was a significant negative association between the distribution of foreign-owned technological activity and the composition of overall innovation of all UK located firms and individuals. In other words, in the late 1960s and early 1970s foreign firms were especially prone to carry out research in the UK in areas of technological activity in which the country was comparatively disadvantaged, or at least much less advantaged. The most striking sector is aircraft, in which the revealed technological advantage of the UK was 1.93 overall as against 0.27 in foreign-owned research activity; foreign firms were also less likely to undertake technological projects in the UK than were indigenous concerns in food products, construction and mining equipment, general industrial equipment, rubber and plastic products, nonmetallic mineral products, and coal and petroleum products. Their research efforts were relatively stronger, though, especially in textiles, but also in pharmaceuticals, metals, office equipment and motor vehicles.

However, the negative relationship between foreign-owned and

Table 5.12   The estimated slope coefficients from bivariate regressions of the cross-sectoral RTA indexes from all large firm research, and from foreign-owned research, on the equivalent overall national RTA index

	Dependent variable			
Host country	Largest firms research in country, 1969–77	Largest firms research in country 1978–86	Foreign firms research in country 1969–77	Foreign firms research in country, 1978–86
US	0.997***	1.265***	0.953**	0.177
	(8.06)	(9.40)	(2.05)	(0.58)
West Germany	1.218***	1.035***	1.069**	0.591*
	(6.62)	(10.34)	(2.27)	(1.89)
UK	1.423***	1.794***	−0.633**	0.333
	(5.90)	(13.93)	(2.46)	(1.34)
Italy	1.260***	0.648***	0.122	0.212
	(6.30)	(3.66)	(0.50)	(1.01)
France	0.595***	0.657***	0.346	0.319
	(2.81)	(4.16)	(1.18)	(1.60)
Japan	0.814***	0.793***	0.890***	1.374***
	(10.52)	(9.73)	(3.40)	(4.17)

Number of observations: 33.
Figures in brackets are absolute values of t-statistics, showing:
*** coefficient significantly different from zero at the 1 per cent level;
** coefficient significantly different from zero at the 5 per cent level;
* coefficient significantly different from zero at the 10 per cent level.

overall technological activity in the UK from 1969–77 disappeared once two other considerations were taken into account. Firstly, in sectors in which international production is relatively low only small numbers of patents are granted to foreign-owned research facilities. The problems of calculating the RTA index where only small numbers of patents are involved are familiar (Cantwell, 1989). Essentially, the cross-sectional RTA distribution becomes skewed and its variance rises, while stochastic factors play a greater role in influencing the composition of the distribution. In this instance, particular problems arise in the case of aircraft and nuclear reactors, in which little research (or production) is carried on outside the home country.

Secondly, the extent of the international integration of economic activity discussed above in the opening section varies across industries. Where national markets remain substantially differentiated, or where government regulations and other non-tariff barriers are significant, progress towards integration may be prevented. In such cases, the international rationalization of technological activity concentrated in the major centres of excellence may not be feasible. Instead, research facilities may be dispersed in large part in accordance with the requirements of local markets (food products) or national procurement policies (pharmaceuticals), or concentrated especially at home where political and business contacts enable contracts to be won (aircraft).

The first factor was allowed for by dropping the two sectors with small numbers of patents from the regression of the sectoral distribution of foreign-owned RTA (tables 5.7 and 5.8) on the equivalent overall RTA distribution (tables 5.9 and 5.10). The second issue was dealt with by the introduction of an additional independent variable which measured the degree of integration of activity achieved by multinationals across industries. This was proxied by the ratio of exports to sales of the foreign affiliates of US multinationals in the relevant sector in 1982, reflecting their international as against their local role. The effect of the first change was to eliminate the significantly negative relationship in the UK in 1969–77. The second change worked in the same direction, but the integration variable did not itself exercise a significant effect on the distribution of foreign-owned research.

In any case, the comparison between foreign-owned and overall technological activity in Britain had turned around by 1978–86. In this later period, as for other countries, there was a positive relationship between the sectoral distribution of foreign-owned firm and overall research in the UK, though it was still not a statistically significant one. It seems that this transformation can be largely explained by changes in two fields of technological activity, namely pharmaceuticals and motor vehicles. In pharmaceuticals foreign firms became still more attracted to locate research in the UK, while local firms also steadily improved their innovative performance; while in motor vehicles foreign firms reduced their UK research in line with indigenous producers. The respective virtuous and vicious circles which characterized the organization of these two sectors in the UK have been described elsewhere (Cantwell, 1987a). It remained the case, though, that foreign firms were virtually absent from work on aircraft technology in the UK; they did not carry out any research in the UK in this field which led to US patenting in the years 1978–86. This is despite the strength of UK-owned firms in this area, but as noted in tables 5.1 and 5.2 it is a field in which research is heavily oriented towards the domestic locations of the companies responsible. In this sector there does not seem to be any particular incentive to locate research in other international centres of innovation; this may be because of its linkage with defence related R&D in which the pull of home country government contracts is important.

Briefly reviewing the position of other countries, the research of foreign firms is more heavily concentrated in the US than the distribution of all technological activity would suggest in chemicals and pharmaceuticals, but (like the UK) less so in aircraft. The association between the pattern of foreign- and domestically-owned research was closest or most significant in Japan, and became stronger still between 1969–77 and 1978–86. Foreign firms are especially keen to invest in research in the major fields of local technological strength in Japan, namely electrical equipment, motor vehicles and professional and scientific instruments. The switching of foreign-located research towards Japan has been most dramatic in the motor vehicles area. In this sector the revealed technological advantage of Japan as a location for foreign-owned research rose from 0.48 (table 5.6) in 1969–77 to 3.11 (table 5.8) in 1978–86.

In Germany and Switzerland the puzzle is why foreign firms have not been relatively drawn to undertake research in the chemicals and pharmaceuticals fields (though see chapter 8). Aside from the significance of government regulations in pharmaceuticals which have drawn foreign firms to other countries such as France, the very strength of German firms may have inhibited entry for some time. However, recent trends suggest that this may be changing. Technological activity has been attracted in the bleaching and dyeing fields especially in the 1980s, which are the areas of the greatest traditional strength of German and Swiss firms. Foreign-owned research has also been pulled towards Germany in the field of general industrial equipment, and to Switzerland in chemical equipment, and more recently in food products, which are all areas of indigenous capability. In Italy foreign firms have shown an increasing propensity to locate technological activity in specialized industrial equipment, in which the country is comparatively advantaged. In France the overlap between foreign and indigenous research is most obvious in the telecommunications field, but foreign firms are also drawn to local technological activity in office and computing equipment in which the overall French record is unimpressive.

It should be noted that the RTA index is a relative measure, averaged over a range of companies, and foreign firms in chemicals and pharmaceuticals are carrying out important research in Germany. For some, their German R&D facilities contribute a good deal, so it may be that it is only the technologically strongest or those which most require access to the particular German research strengths who have so far become firmly established there. For example, of the 47 large US chemicals and pharmaceuticals firms granted US patents between 1969 and 1986, 36 had patents attributable to German research. Of these, the share of patents due to German based inventions were important (over 1 per cent of the total) for 11 firms, and highly significant for three firms (over 8 per cent of their total US patenting, and in one case 16 per cent).

On the whole, therefore, it does seem that the technological activity of the world's largest firms is quite frequently drawn to the main centres of innovation for their industries. In line with the general tendency towards international integration this seems to have become stronger, though in some sectors more than others. Of course, this is an iterative rather than a one-way process, in that the establishment of research by this crucial group of companies itself contributes to the overall technological activity of a location, both directly and indirectly through the spur that they provide to the local research of other firms, whether competitors or contractual partners.

The question which then arises is whether the companies which have adopted international research strategies to take advantage of the innovative potential of different locations have achieved better overall performance as a result. A first approximation to whether this is so can be achieved through a cross-firm regression of the proportional growth in sales between 1972 and 1982 (PGS) as a measure of performance on the share of patenting attributable to foreign research at the start of the period 1969–72 (SPFR) and the index of technological competitiveness at the beginning of the period as previously described (TC). The results of this regression were as follows, with absolute values of the t-statistics in brackets as before:

$$PGS = -0.995^* + 0.143\dagger \ SPFR + 0.097^* \ TC$$
$$\quad\ (24.87) \quad (1.59) \qquad\qquad (4.85)$$

No. of observations $= 320 \quad R^2 = 0.07$
$F = 11.45 \qquad\qquad\qquad \bar{R}^2 = 0.06$

* Denotes coefficient significantly different from zero at the
  1 per cent level.
† Denotes coefficient significantly different from zero at the
  15 per cent level.

The share of patenting attributable to foreign research is positively associated with the growth of the firm in the ensuing period, as hypothesized. So firms with a greater international dispersion of research have tended to have a better record of performance. However, the coefficient on SPFR is not significantly different from zero at the statistical levels which are customarily employed. Although the measure of technological competitiveness is positively and significantly related to growth as expected, the overall explanatory power of the equation is quite weak.

One reason for the weakness of this association may be that SPFR is a rather crude measure of the capacity of the firm to capture the benefits of an international research strategy. It takes no account of the actual geographical composition of the technological activity of the firm (the extent to which it is in centres of innovation), nor does it allow for differences in the appropriability of innovations across firms. These matters need to be investigated more closely in future research.

5.4 THE CONSEQUENCES FOR BRITISH FIRMS AND INDUSTRIES

From the perspective of the UK, the internationalization of technological activity can be viewed in two ways. Firstly, there is the role of research carried out abroad by British MNEs. This may improve their competitiveness but not necessarily the performance of their UK operations. Secondly, the UK is host to the research facilities of foreign-owned firms. It has been suggested above that where foreign MNEs locate more extensive fundamental research in Britain this is generally associated with a beneficial impact upon local industry (Cantwell, 1987b). The share of research-related production tends to rise and export performance to improve, setting in motion a positive interaction with the local research and production of indigenous firms. An alternative argument has recently been advanced by Stoneman (1989). As noted in chapter 1, he contends that the research of foreign-owned firms in Britain represents a potential internal brain drain in which the UK's scientific and technological resources are used by foreign MNEs to support production elsewhere in the world, with few spin-off benefits for local British industry.

A full examination of these issues awaits further research, but it is possible to extend the discussion here to survey in rather more detail how the internationalization of technological activity has impinged upon British firms and industries. Considering British firms first, table 5.4 has already indicated their relatively heavy dependence upon foreign research facilities. A more comprehensive treatment of these data is provided in table 5.13. It is clear that the UK producers of food products, machinery and mechanical equipment and coal and petroleum products are particularly obliged to rely on research outside the UK. Of the US patents granted to them in 1983–6, 62.9 per cent, 65.8 per cent and 82.2 per cent respectively were attributable to research conducted abroad. This is reflected in a heavy internationalization of these same three fields at the level of technological activity, as shown in table 5.13. In these terms UK firms carrying out research in textiles and in certain areas of chemicals have also displayed a strong propensity towards foreign locations.

Table 5.13   The percentage share of US patents of the largest UK firms attributable to research outside the UK, organized by the industrial group of parent firms, 1969–1986

Industry	Period			
	1969–72	*1973–7*	*1978–82*	*1983–6*
1 Food products	68.06	68.68	62.96	62.94
2 Chemicals n.e.s.	28.77	29.52	26.66	31.77
3 Pharmaceuticals	21.25	15.71	15.78	18.28
4 Metals	48.37	39.34	36.48	39.94
5 Mechanical engineering	62.50	50.69	49.66	65.83
6 Electrical equipment n.e.s.	28.98	35.31	24.94	20.12
7 Office equipment	3.33	14.12	33.33	10.00
8 Motor vehicles	10.99	14.39	23.51	33.33
9 Aircraft	2.03	0.00	2.12	6.32
10 Other transport equipment	0.00	0.00	0.00	0.00
11 Textiles	18.45	19.12	25.76	34.48
12 Rubber and plastic products	12.62	8.74	4.00	2.33
13 Non-metallic mineral products	12.12	28.07	39.88	42.11
14 Coal and petroleum products	85.92	80.85	83.29	82.16
15 Professional and scientific instruments	n.a.	n.a.	n.a.	n.a.
16 Other manufacturing	0.00	0.00	2.56	13.75
Total	43.27	40.45	38.67	44.91

n.a. = Not applicable.

Source: As for table 5.1.

In addition, it seems that a clear trend towards the internationalization of technological activity has been under way in the motor vehicles, textiles and non-metallic mineral products sectors. It should be noted that for UK textile firms this is true in the textile field, even though other UK firms outside the sector have reduced their share of foreign technological activity from a very high level, as can be seen from table 5.14. However, the rising share of foreign research for UK textile firms is also partly associated with technological diversification, and is partly a function of a strong internationalization of technological activity in the field of professional and scientific instruments (the other

Table 5.14 The percentage share of US patents of the largest UK firms attributable to research outside the UK, classified by technological activity, 1969–1986

		Period			
Sector		1969–72	1973–7	1978–82	1983–6
1	Food products	67.86	54.87	61.64	69.43
2	Chemicals n.e.s.	48.16	42.77	46.47	53.73
	Inorganic chemicals	59.05	65.25	62.04	69.09
	Organic chemicals	46.22	38.43	47.78	54.60
	Agricultural chemicals	59.38	30.77	51.25	53.85
	Chemical processes	51.84	50.44	41.58	50.00
	Bleaching and dyeing	27.59	29.31	18.18	31.58
3	Pharmaceuticals	54.29	35.52	24.62	24.38
4	Metals	40.47	49.91	52.22	51.09
	Metallurgical processes	32.65	46.29	35.86	34.15
	Other metal products	47.16	52.61	63.26	59.67
5	Mechanical engineering	49.05	46.99	43.46	55.10
	Chemical equipment	60.87	57.51	59.79	59.79
	Metal working equipment	37.85	28.43	39.47	53.49
	Construction equipment	65.00	61.63	44.93	57.69
	Mining equipment	90.40	81.86	53.47	84.15
	Specialized industrial equipment	47.49	51.79	45.78	55.49
	General industrial equipment	23.41	29.51	25.06	40.13
6	Electrical equipment n.e.s.	35.46	31.46	23.08	27.20
	Telecommunications	45.73	50.52	32.04	38.81
	Semiconductors	28.57	22.22	10.34	8.70
	Electrical systems	25.05	21.56	18.24	18.42
	General electrical equipment	42.73	28.10	23.11	27.78
7	Office equipment	31.94	15.65	26.13	28.57
8	Motor vehicles	8.89	13.39	16.15	21.31
9	Aircraft	6.12	2.08	15.79	8.33
10	Other transport equipment	32.81	27.96	29.69	48.94
11	Textiles	80.95	61.90	63.64	53.85
12	Rubber and plastic products	31.11	23.26	30.41	36.49
13	Non-metallic mineral products	30.92	34.70	40.39	40.00
14	Coal and petroleum products	56.35	57.30	65.65	70.16
15	Professional and scientific instruments	35.77	34.98	29.01	31.75
	Image and sound equipment	23.73	27.66	22.22	35.71
	Photographic equipment	63.04	56.81	35.71	25.00
	Other instruments	34.50	33.74	29.06	31.82
16	Other manufacturing	54.22	56.84	55.74	63.86
Total		43.27	40.45	38.67	44.91

Source: As for table 5.1.

instruments and controls category). Textiles is indeed the most interesting case, since in motor vehicles and to a lesser extent in non-metallic mineral products that there has been a relative decline of innovation in the UK. Tables 5.5 and 5.6 reveal that for the world's largest firms there has actually been an increase in the comparative importance of Britain as a location for technological activity in the textiles field. In other words, it would seem that whereas in motor vehicles British firms have simply followed the trend and moved their research facilities elsewhere (or closed down local research anyway), in textiles the internationalization of their research has been part of a much more positive process. Either research abroad has been supportive of an extension of their UK research, or non-UK firms have increased their British research operations. To the extent that this has happened it may be partly in response to the expansion of the technological activity of British companies abroad.

Table 5.15 shows that the role of foreign research stands out relatively more for US companies (and is increasing) in pharmaceuticals and other transport equipment, but relatively less in food products and coal and petroleum products. The relative internationalization of research by British firms compared to the largest firms of all other nationalities can be seen in tables 5.16 and 5.17. Table 5.16 shows that by the standards of others UK firms are especially reliant upon technological activity located abroad in chemicals, metals, electrical equipment, motor vehicles, textiles and non-metallic mineral products, apart from the cases of food products, mechanical engineering and coal and petroleum products already mentioned. As previously suggested they have become more so in motor vehicles, textiles and non-metallic mineral products. However, non-UK firms have been catching up their high degree of international dispersion of technological activity in food products, while UK companies themselves have been reducing the significance of research done abroad in electrical equipment and rubber and plastic products. Due to the sectoral complexity of research by all these groups of firms, it is difficult to discern such distinct differences in international strategies as between technological fields as described in table 5.17. UK firms are more dependent upon foreign research in every field, but only in coal and petroleum products do they stand out as being particularly so even relative to the average.

Turning now to the implications of foreign research by non-UK firms for British industry, table 5.18 presents some evidence on the share of such research which has been directed to the UK. Overall, the share of US patents of the largest non-UK firms attributable to research in the UK has fallen as a proportion of non-UK firm patenting due to research in all foreign locations between 1969–72 and 1978–86. However, for these firms the significance of the UK as a research centre has slipped back rather less than has the British share of all technological activity. For the largest non-UK firms the share of US patents due to foreign research which emanated from British inventions fell from 17.4 per cent in 1969–72 to 14.3 per cent in 1978–86. By contrast, the UK's share as a host country for technological activity in the US patenting of the world's largest firms fell from 19.3 per cent to 9.1 per cent of foreign patents, and from 5.0 per cent to 4.0 per cent of all patents over the same period.

The continued interest of non-UK firms in technological activity in Britain has been particularly true of the pharmaceuticals sector. In this industry the US patents of non-British MNEs due to UK research facilities as a proportion of patents due to all foreign research facilities rose from 10.7 per cent to 23.6 per cent between 1969–72 and 1978–86. Table 5.19 shows that this is reflected in a similar rise in foreign owned research located in the UK in pharmaceuticals itself, in which the share of US patenting increased from 9.1 per cent in 1969–72 to 22.7 per cent in 1983–6. This was associated with an improvement in the relative importance of pharmaceuticals research in Britain, as illustrated in tables 5.5–5.10. However, the significance of the UK as a technological centre for foreign firms declined quite sharply in electrical equipment, motor vehicles, aircraft, textiles, rubber and plastic products, coal and petroleum products and other manufacturing. This is also true in the equivalent fields of technological activity, although research in aircraft and other manufacturing behaved more erratically. In this group of sectors the lessening interest of foreign companies reflected the general fall in innovative activity in the UK.

Table 5.15 The percentage share of US patents of the largest UK firms attributable to research outside the US, classified by technological activity, 1969–1986

			Period		
Sector		1969–72	1973–7	1978–82	1983–6
1	Food products	3.28	4.53	5.74	6.47
2	Chemicals n.e.s.	4.49	5.24	4.60	4.59
	Inorganic chemicals	3.48	3.04	3.17	3.86
	Organic chemicals	5.05	5.86	4.51	4.34
	Agricultural chemicals	4.46	2.93	2.07	1.34
	Chemical processes	3.47	4.38	5.37	5.50
	Bleaching and dyeing	5.08	4.88	1.96	2.94
3	Pharmaceuticals	4.42	8.86	13.43	12.46
4	Metals	4.17	4.62	5.24	7.51
	Metallurgical processes	3.65	3.44	4.02	5.26
	Other metal products	4.50	5.46	6.03	9.19
5	Mechanical engineering	4.47	6.46	7.10	9.04
	Chemical equipment	4.30	5.38	3.72	5.80
	Metal working equipment	3.38	4.05	5.43	9.37
	Construction equipment	3.90	7.15	7.19	9.87
	Mining equipment	3.71	3.96	5.13	6.92
	Specialized industrial equipment	6.01	9.03	11.51	13.15
	General industrial equipment	4.62	6.78	8.43	9.80
6	Electrical equipment n.e.s.	3.64	4.69	5.28	6.85
	Telecommunications	3.87	4.62	6.27	8.10
	Semiconductors	3.30	5.25	5.08	5.16
	Electrical systems	4.11	5.27	5.08	6.72
	General electrical equipment	2.87	3.39	4.91	6.79
7	Office equipment	3.65	6.90	7.41	7.57
8	Motor vehicles	5.11	4.28	3.59	10.85
9	Aircraft	2.88	0.92	1.73	1.19
10	Other transport equipment	4.85	5.87	14.07	20.67
11	Textiles	4.80	10.06	15.74	8.54
12	Rubber and plastic products	5.22	8.14	6.65	7.31
13	Non-metallic mineral products	2.65	2.81	3.65	5.62
14	Coal and petroleum products	3.39	3.73	2.34	3.55
15	Professional and scientific instruments	5.35	5.81	6.64	9.91
	Image and sound equipment	3.00	3.64	6.49	15.76
	Photographic equipment	6.29	7.53	6.65	10.05
	Other instruments	5.24	5.36	6.66	9.01
16	Other manufacturing	2.30	3.73	5.09	6.94
Total		4.28	5.47	6.03	7.40

Source: As for table 5.1.

Table 5.16 The percentage share of US patents of the largest UK firms attributable to research abroad relative to the equivalent share of the world's largest firms considered together, for each industrial group of parent firms, 1969–1986

		Period			
Industry		1969–72	1973–7	1978–82	1983–6
1	Food products	4.09	3.43	2.78	2.62
2	Chemicals n.e.s.	2.36	2.29	2.12	2.50
3	Pharmaceuticals	1.20	0.78	0.86	1.03
4	Metals	4.55	4.52	3.44	4.35
5	Mechanical engineering	5.90	5.34	4.52	4.47
6	Electrical equipment n.e.s.	3.76	4.48	3.58	2.54
7	Office equipment	0.66	1.66	3.31	0.84
8	Motor vehicles	2.39	2.74	4.55	4.88
9	Aircraft	0.97	0.00	0.91	2.38
10	Other transport equipment	0.00	0.00	0.00	0.00
11	Textiles	3.14	3.34	4.98	8.84
12	Rubber and plastic products	1.93	1.22	0.66	0.45
13	Non-metallic mineral products	1.07	2.27	2.81	2.73
14	Coal and petroleum products	5.78	6.29	6.87	6.21
15	Professional and scientific instruments	n.a.	n.a.	n.a.	n.a.
16	Other manufacturing	0.00	0.00	0.25	1.08
Total		4.41	3.90	3.78	4.23

n.a. = Not applicable.

Source: As for table 5.1 and table 5.13.

Given that overall foreign firms have held the UK share of their technological activity more consistently than the UK has held its share of all such activity, it follows that the proportion of British research due to foreign companies will have risen. This suggestion is supported by tables 5.20–5.22. The share of US patents of the largest non-UK firms attributable to British research facilities, as a proportion of patenting by all the world's largest firms due to UK research, rose from 24.0 per cent to 31.7 per cent from 1969–72 to 1983–6. In all technological activity located in the UK the share of the largest foreign firms measured in the same way increased from 10.9 per cent in 1969–72 to 15.2 per cent in

Table 5.17 The percentage share of US patents of the largest UK firms attributable to research abroad relative to the equivalent share of the world's largest firms considered together, classified by technological activity, 1969–1986

Sector	Period 1969–72	1973–7	1978–82	1983–6
1 Food products	5.54	3.68	4.20	4.15
2 Chemicals n.e.s.	4.06	3.56	3.97	4.81
Inorganic chemicals	6.30	7.09	6.87	6.55
Organic chemicals	3.54	2.95	3.92	4.97
Agricultural chemicals	5.25	3.11	5.15	5.16
Chemical processes	5.41	5.01	3.67	4.35
Bleaching and dyeing	3.01	2.77	1.49	2.14
3 Pharmaceuticals	3.34	1.93	1.30	1.19
4 Metals	4.69	5.32	5.17	4.53
Metallurgical processes	4.24	5.74	4.33	4.42
Other metal products	5.07	5.02	5.45	4.13
5 Mechanical engineering	4.53	4.16	3.79	4.28
Chemical equipment	5.65	5.05	6.03	5.29
Metal working equipment	4.23	3.02	3.23	4.13
Construction equipment	5.73	5.07	3.61	4.96
Mining equipment	4.97	5.94	5.00	5.23
Specialized industrial equipment	3.50	3.53	2.86	3.49
General industrial equipment	3.14	3.27	2.69	3.35
6 Electrical equipment n.e.s.	5.01	4.17	3.15	3.24
Telecommunications	5.21	5.74	3.57	3.89
Semiconductors	4.50	2.57	1.67	1.24
Electrical systems	3.81	3.07	2.77	2.10
General electrical equipment	6.09	4.17	3.07	3.84
7 Office equipment	5.40	1.96	3.73	4.22
8 Motor vehicles	1.29	2.71	4.20	2.98
9 Aircraft	1.39	1.76	5.76	4.54
10 Other transport equipment	4.08	3.58	2.22	3.18
11 Textiles	7.40	4.42	3.45	4.79
12 Rubber and plastic products	3.45	2.23	3.10	3.68
13 Non-metallic mineral products	4.34	4.58	4.60	4.63
14 Coal and petroleum products	6.85	7.14	9.89	8.58
15 Professional and scientific instruments	3.79	3.60	3.47	3.52
Image and sound equipment	2.76	3.91	3.37	3.83
Photographic equipment	5.28	5.09	4.75	3.46
Other instruments	4.15	3.58	3.21	3.28
16 Other manufacturing	6.74	4.79	5.44	4.52
Total	4.41	3.90	3.78	4.23

Source: table 5.2 and table 5.14.

Table 5.18 The percentage share of US patents of the largest non-UK firms attributable to research in the UK, as a proportion of non-UK firm patenting due to research in all foreign locations, organized by the industrial group of parent firms, 1969–1986

	Industry	Period	
		1969–72	1978–87
1	Food products	26.45	18.31
2	Chemicals n.e.s.	12.71	12.38
3	Pharmaceuticals	10.69	23.55
4	Metals	13.56	12.73
5	Mechanical engineering	20.91	16.35
6	Electrical equipment n.e.s.	18.47	9.90
7	Office equipment	19.41	14.88
8	Motor vehicles	29.94	12.89
9	Aircraft	52.99	19.23
10	Other transport equipment	0.00	0.00
11	Textiles	10.53	3.70
12	Rubber and plastic products	30.89	15.59
13	Non-metallic mineral products	11.05	5.64
14	Coal and petroleum products	18.05	9.32
15	Professional and scientific instruments	29.25	24.62
16	Other manufacturing	41.71	12.39
	Total	17.38	14.33

Source: As for table 5.1.

1983–6. This essentially reflects a wider decline in the technological activities of British companies. They have lost out in both UK and non-UK research, consistent with their roughly constant degree of internationalization of technological activity over the period in question. The overall share of UK firms in the US patenting of the world's largest companies fell from 6.7 per cent in 1969–72 to 4.8 per cent in 1978–86.

The greatest increases in foreign participation in British research were recorded in chemicals, mechanical engineering and office equipment industries (table 5.20), and in the mechanical engineering, office equipment and non-metallic mineral product

Table 5.19 The percentage share of US patents of the largest non-UK firms attributable to research in the UK, as a proportion of non-UK firm patenting due to research in all foreign locations, classified by technological activity, 1969–1986

Sector	Period 1969–72	1973–7	1978–82	1983–6
1 Food products	14.52	20.79	14.10	23.53
2 Chemicals n.e.s.	13.60	15.97	14.38	12.68
Inorganic chemicals	13.51	22.83	14.77	15.38
Organic chemicals	11.99	14.65	12.54	11.53
Agricultural chemicals	9.09	12.16	10.34	10.81
Chemical processes	19.38	20.49	18.73	14.48
Bleaching and dyeing	26.00	24.29	16.85	13.64
3 Pharmaceuticals	9.09	19.21	28.26	22.74
4 Metals	24.20	23.30	16.29	13.74
Metallurgical processes	24.64	24.38	8.59	14.53
Other metal products	23.95	22.61	21.50	13.29
5 Mechanical engineering	17.90	16.11	12.35	14.18
Chemical equipment	19.95	14.67	10.30	10.57
Metal working equipment	19.59	15.54	10.99	13.61
Construction equipment	9.64	14.43	10.71	11.93
Mining equipment	14.75	16.00	17.98	41.41
Specialized industrial equipment	15.46	15.85	14.20	15.54
General industrial equipment	23.12	19.30	12.33	11.94
6 Electrical equipment n.e.s.	21.96	13.22	10.96	8.42
Telecommunications	22.75	16.55	12.90	8.81
Semiconductors	19.20	7.36	8.40	7.73
Electrical systems	23.45	14.89	13.06	8.58
General electrical equipment	20.18	11.39	7.49	8.08
7 Office equipment	31.14	14.13	12.75	12.84
8 Motor vehicles	24.68	20.34	13.39	12.45
9 Aircraft	0.00	25.00	0.00	0.00
10 Other transport equipment	12.00	9.16	6.11	5.73
11 Textiles	47.37	42.00	31.71	31.03
12 Rubber and plastic products	17.78	11.97	13.04	7.96
13 Non-metallic mineral products	13.00	16.27	12.85	10.94
14 Coal and petroleum products	11.96	7.14	11.94	6.59
15 Professional and scientific instruments	21.41	15.12	17.05	13.61
Image and sound equipment	16.67	11.58	13.08	12.12
Photographic equipment	22.25	13.16	24.31	24.60
Other instruments	21.36	16.82	14.44	10.09
16 Other manufacturing	24.56	15.24	28.13	15.87
Total	17.38	16.03	15.29	13.33

Source: As for table 5.1.

technological fields (tables 5.21 and 5.22). Some industries, against the trend, witnessed a rise in the share of British firms in British research over the 1969–86 period. This was achieved in food products, pharmaceuticals, aircraft, textiles, rubber products, coal and petroleum products and other manufacturing; but in none of these cases was there a clear increase in the corresponding technological areas. Pharmaceuticals represents a case in which both British firms and British industry have been successful. UK companies have retained their share of around 50 per cent of the US patents of pharmaceutical firms due to UK research facilities, despite the increasing attractiveness of the UK as a location for the research of foreign firms shown in table 5.18. They hold

Table 5.20 The percentage share of US patents of the largest non-UK firms attributable to research in the UK, as a proportion of the number due to research in the UK by UK or non-UK large firms, organized by the industrial group of parent companies, 1969–1986

		Period	
Industry		*1969–72*	*1978–86*
1	Food products	16.00	12.33
2	Chemicals n.e.s.	21.96	30.88
3	Pharmaceuticals	52.27	49.29
4	Metals	22.48	22.78
5	Mechanical engineering	37.72	54.47
6	Electrical equipment n.e.s.	20.96	22.33
7	Office equipment	57.66	79.19
8	Motor vehicles	11.10	12.83
9	Aircraft	15.54	9.38
10	Other transport equipment	0.00	0.00
11	Textiles	2.33	2.25
12	Rubber and plastic products	17.43	15.18
13	Non-metallic mineral products	12.65	13.02
14	Coal and petroleum products	22.93	20.28
15	Professional and scientific instruments	100.00	100.00
16	Other manufacturing	82.02	27.95
Total		23.96	29.89

Source: As for table 5.1.

Table 5.21 The percentage share of US patents of the largest non-UK firms attributable to research in the UK, as a proportion of the number due to research in the UK by UK or non-UK large firms, classified by technological activity, 1969–1986

Sector	Period			
	1969–72	1973–7	1978–82	1983–6
1 Food products	16.67	17.07	16.42	25.00
2 Chemicals n.e.s.	26.83	31.61	31.51	32.10
Inorganic chemicals	18.87	33.87	24.07	26.09
Organic chemicals	27.68	32.47	31.72	34.25
Agricultural chemicals	18.75	25.00	13.33	21.05
Chemical processes	26.67	29.62	32.67	30.88
Bleaching and dyeing	23.64	29.31	45.45	40.91
3 Pharmaceuticals	29.67	40.40	42.13	39.75
4 Metals	26.45	30.93	31.75	27.53
Metallurgical processes	20.48	28.49	15.45	24.30
Other metal products	32.02	32.87	44.37	30.00
5 Mechanical engineering	21.61	26.34	25.38	34.71
Chemical equipment	31.65	32.71	22.00	26.88
Metal working equipment	25.68	21.08	30.30	50.00
Construction equipment	17.20	40.00	41.54	54.17
Mining equipment	27.27	24.49	19.28	58.57
Specialized industrial equipment	26.91	36.91	40.00	50.32
General industrial equipment	13.80	17.45	15.98	19.88
6 Electrical equipment n.e.s.	20.28	20.48	18.89	21.72
Telecommunications	17.59	24.21	22.22	20.13
Semiconductors	26.97	32.69	29.73	40.00
Electrical systems	20.76	19.72	18.77	21.85
General electrical equipment	19.25	15.53	13.76	18.75
7 Office equipment	34.67	34.46	34.92	48.28
8 Motor vehicles	31.67	17.91	12.10	25.58
9 Aircraft	0.00	2.08	0.00	0.00
10 Other transport equipment	17.31	15.19	19.64	27.27
11 Textiles	69.23	72.41	61.90	60.00
12 Rubber and plastic products	14.68	9.34	14.88	16.07
13 Non-metallic mineral products	12.56	16.53	19.58	26.67
14 Coal and petroleum products	12.22	9.52	15.09	13.95
15 Professional and scientific instruments	38.97	35.53	32.47	39.87
Image and sound equipment	21.05	24.44	28.57	57.14
Photographic equipment	85.09	77.91	74.53	83.70
Other instruments	28.13	28.70	23.21	26.09
16 Other manufacturing	26.92	28.07	40.00	25.00
Total	23.96	27.41	28.56	31.66

Source: As for table 5.1.

a still higher share of pharmaceutical patents themselves, though one which has slipped back since the 1969–72 period.

Tables 5.22–24 offer a comparison between the role of foreign-owned research in the UK and in two other large EC countries, Germany and France. Just as UK firms are more heavily internationalized in their technological activity then German or French firms (table 5.4), so too are local UK industries relative to German or French. Of US patents attributable to research in each of these three countries in 1983–6, 15.2 per cent were granted to foreign-owned firms in the UK, 8.8 per cent in Germany and 8.9 per cent in France. However, the increasing role of foreign-owned research was evident in all three countries, as can be seen from the equivalent shares of patenting in the earlier 1969–72 period, which were 10.9 per cent in the UK, 5.6 per cent in Germany and 6.3 per cent in France. The sectoral composition of this internationalization by the type of technological activity involved is also similar across this group of countries, but especially between Britain and France. The share of foreign firms in local innovation is especially high in both the UK and France in chemicals (particularly organic chemicals), pharmaceuticals and office equipment; and it is relatively low in aircraft, other transport equipment and other manufacturing.

Differences arose in the case of textiles, in which foreign-owned technological activity is comparatively low in France but not in the UK, and in rubber and plastic products which is the other way round. Foreign firms have also been relatively weakly represented in patenting originating from research in Germany in the textiles field, so here it seems that Britain is the exception rather than the rule. As in the UK or France, foreign-owned research facilities in Germany account for a high share of US patenting in office equipment, and low shares in aircraft and other manufacturing. By contrast, though, foreign firms are especially prominent in technological activity in the coal and petroleum products field in Germany.

It may also be recalled from tables 5.13 and 5.16 that UK firms had increased the internationalization of their technological activity in the textiles and non-metallic mineral products industries, despite an improvement in the relative share of large firm

Table 5.22 The percentage share of US patents of the largest non-UK firms attributable to research in the UK, as a proportion of the total number due to research in the UK by all firms or individuals, classified by technological activity, 1969–1986

Sector	Period 1969–72	1973–7	1978–82	1983–6
1 Food products	10.71	11.05	8.94	14.81
2 Chemicals n.e.s.	18.02	22.55	21.86	20.33
Inorganic chemicals	9.43	17.95	12.26	18.18
Organic chemicals	21.19	26.37	25.27	25.04
Agricultural chemicals	12.50	20.93	8.82	16.00
Chemical processes	14.22	16.11	19.53	16.37
Bleaching and dyeing	16.46	19.54	28.30	25.71
3 Pharmaceuticals	18.75	30.30	35.16	31.48
4 Metals	9.91	10.75	10.36	9.96
Metallurgical processes	10.15	13.46	7.56	12.75
Other metal products	9.78	9.44	11.52	8.77
5 Mechanical engineering	7.61	9.97	9.21	13.70
Chemical equipment	10.58	11.66	6.98	9.89
Metal working equipment	7.41	7.29	10.03	18.35
Construction equipment	3.68	10.63	8.65	13.47
Mining equipment	8.33	7.23	8.29	26.80
Specialized industrial equipment	8.39	11.85	12.73	15.51
General industrial equipment	6.64	8.78	7.95	10.28
6 Electrical equipment n.e.s.	9.64	9.12	8.98	10.02
Telecommunications	8.14	10.11	9.59	8.88
Semiconductors	13.48	11.49	10.89	15.91
Electrical systems	11.14	9.78	10.12	11.06
General electrical equipment	7.53	6.39	6.31	8.16
7 Office equipment	18.31	16.35	16.42	24.45
8 Motor vehicles	10.05	9.27	6.52	14.80
9 Aircraft	0.00	1.16	0.00	0.00
10 Other transport equipment	3.95	4.33	6.29	6.00
11 Textiles	11.11	19.44	17.80	13.85
12 Rubber and plastic products	9.76	5.88	8.82	7.89
13 Non-metallic mineral products	6.79	7.55	9.41	11.25
14 Coal and petroleum products	10.38	8.60	12.31	10.53
15 Professional and scientific instruments	15.79	13.24	13.94	15.34
Image and sound equipment	9.60	5.24	6.93	16.90
Photographic equipment	55.75	46.21	50.32	62.10
Other instruments	10.11	10.72	9.94	9.19
16 Other manufacturing	6.11	6.25	8.04	4.85
Total	10.94	13.11	14.22	15.15

Source: As for table 5.1.

Table 5.23 The percentage share of US patents of the largest non-German firms attributable to research in W. Germany, as a proportion of the total number due to research in W. Germany by all firms or individuals, classified by technological activity, 1969–1986

Sector		1969–72	1973–7	1978–82	1983–6
		Period			
1	Food products	6.19	15.23	6.17	10.81
2	Chemicals n.e.s.	5.13	7.35	6.26	6.18
	Inorganic chemicals	7.55	7.99	6.34	6.59
	Organic chemicals	4.91	8.08	6.59	5.61
	Agricultural chemicals	14.71	4.86	5.00	5.64
	Chemical processes	5.19	6.10	6.47	6.47
	Bleaching and dyeing	3.83	2.51	1.86	11.62
3	Pharmaceuticals	5.33	2.75	7.30	9.36
4	Metals	5.05	5.45	7.56	12.09
	Metallurgical processes	4.44	4.19	5.83	11.09
	Other metal products	5.31	6.10	8.23	12.49
5	Mechanical engineering	6.04	7.68	8.94	9.87
	Chemical equipment	4.36	5.41	6.36	6.65
	Metal working equipment	3.39	4.50	9.72	12.32
	Construction equipment	6.54	8.09	6.50	5.78
	Mining equipment	1.22	4.64	4.28	5.95
	Specialized industrial equipment	7.61	9.45	9.03	7.92
	General industrial equipment	7.87	10.18	13.24	15.43
6	Electrical equipment n.e.s.	6.73	7.33	8.64	10.09
	Telecommunications	3.81	6.14	7.32	7.68
	Semiconductors	10.51	12.54	15.94	15.84
	Electrical systems	7.87	8.01	8.40	9.01
	General electrical equipment	5.82	5.21	7.63	11.50
7	Office equipment	7.60	9.71	12.45	14.07
8	Motor vehicles	1.75	4.51	2.29	5.63
9	Aircraft	8.25	2.41	3.85	3.28
10	Other transport equipment	4.20	5.94	5.81	7.59
11	Textiles	2.80	3.87	1.73	1.71
12	Rubber and plastic products	2.35	9.67	9.60	6.60
13	Non-metallic mineral products	4.43	6.85	8.17	10.64
14	Coal and petroleum products	10.87	19.35	7.45	12.87
15	Professional and scientific instruments	6.09	5.88	5.83	7.17
	Image and sound equipment	3.95	2.94	5.43	11.59
	Photographic equipment	7.20	8.02	4.43	5.65
	Other instruments	5.74	5.54	6.22	6.92
16	Other manufacturing	0.53	1.51	0.97	2.32
Total		5.64	6.94	7.38	8.77

Source: As for table 5.1.

Table 5.24 The percentage share of US patents of the largest non-French firms attributable to research in France, as a proportion of the total number due to research in France by all firms or individuals, classified by technological activity, 1969–1986

Sector		1969–72	1973–7	1978–82	1983–6
		\multicolumn{4}{c}{*Period*}			
1	Food products	0.00	6.85	8.33	9.52
2	Chemicals n.e.s.	12.04	11.16	11.71	13.99
	Inorganic chemicals	4.85	1.59	5.69	4.35
	Organic chemicals	14.69	13.67	14.21	18.00
	Agricultural chemicals	10.00	41.38	17.86	12.50
	Chemical processes	9.16	7.27	7.63	12.01
	Bleaching and dyeing	5.80	2.78	22.08	10.64
3	Pharmaceuticals	15.19	19.76	19.38	17.76
4	Metals	3.04	4.95	6.81	5.80
	Metallurgical processes	3.28	2.97	8.76	3.37
	Other metal products	2.92	5.72	6.00	6.85
5	Mechanical engineering	˙5.09	5.88	4.91	6.76
	Chemical equipment	5.10	5.24	3.93	7.03
	Metal working equipment	2.94	5.48	4.28	6.99
	Construction equipment	5.16	4.86	9.48	6.11
	Mining equipment	6.74	4.79	3.11	6.03
	Specialized industrial equipment	7.21	6.71	5.30	9.26
	General industrial equipment	3.95	6.50	4.40	5.20
6	Electrical equipment n.e.s.	4.15	6.76	7.68	7.39
	Telecommunications	7.12	10.24	12.95	12.53
	Semiconductors	2.67	4.84	8.66	4.39
	Electrical systems	3.97	6.17	5.20	4.70
	General electrical equipment	1.60	3.66	4.93	5.59
7	Office equipment	5.81	27.07	41.92	21.46
8	Motor vehicles	4.88	6.77	8.81	18.79
9	Aircraft	1.45	1.67	0.00	2.41
10	Other transport equipment	1.83	2.33	0.80	2.14
11	Textiles	0.00	1.08	0.00	2.78
12	Rubber and plastic products	12.07	10.59	5.70	7.78
13	Non-metallic mineral products	4.41	4.36	7.52	7.30
14	Coal and petroleum products	13.46	7.06	6.33	8.79
15	Professional and scientific instruments	6.89	7.87	7.20	7.15
	Image and sound equipment	1.45	3.42	2.83	5.00
	Photographic equipment	37.31	19.05	22.58	5.71
	Other instruments	4.79	7.68	6.82	7.55
16	Other manufacturing	1.37	3.46	1.16	2.52
Total		6.32	8.02	8.76	8.86

Source: As for table 5.1.

technological activity in textiles located in the UK over the same period (tables 5.5 and 5.6). In textiles the foreign firm share of British research has not altered very much. In terms of the activity of the largest firms as recorded in table 5.21 the foreign share in the textiles field has fallen, suggesting that more foreign research (in a variety of areas) has been associated with an extension in the domestic research facilities of British textiles companies in the textiles field. In non-metallic mineral products the foreign share has risen slightly at the industry level as shown in table 5.20, and has risen significantly in the building materials technological field as can be seen in tables 5.21 and 5.22. This may indicate some withdrawal from the UK by indigenous companies in non-metallic mineral products (like in motor vehicles), but it may also show some response on the part of foreign firms to the internationalization of technological activity by the largest UK firms.

5.5   CONCLUSION

A wide range of new evidence on the internationalization of tech-nological activity has been reviewed here. It can be concluded that this is an important phenomenon which deserves closer attention that it has typically been paid in the existing literature. One impression that clearly emerges from the data is that previous writers may well have understated the role of the internationaliz-ation of research due to the reliance of most work in this field on evidence from US companies alone.

In general, it seems that US and Japanese MNEs have made comparatively little use of international research strategies by the standards of European firms. However, it also appears that US firms have begun to appreciate the benefits of a wider dispersion of technological activity, and they have increasingly made use of foreign research facilities. Where the world's largest industrial firms have dispersed their research they have as a rule been especially attracted to the main centres of innovation for their primary sector of activity, although there are exceptions as in the aircraft industry.

UK firms and UK industry have both been heavily involved in the internationalization of technological activity. It is fairly clear that in pharmaceuticals this has been associated with an improvement in competitive performance, while in motor vehicles there has been a competitive deterioration. However, it remains to consider the relationship between the internationalization of technological activity and other indicators of competitiveness in greater detail.

6

The Overseas Laboratory

6.1 INTRODUCTION

It has long been a central tenet of much thinking on MNEs that their competitiveness stems from their expertise in the internal diffusion of centrally generated technology. The more recent thinking which underlies the present research suggests that this essentially sequential strategy – centralized creation of technology followed by diffusion and adaptation – may be collapsing into a more internationally integrated parallel programme of research which recognizes the need both to respond continually (rather than through a technological 'trickle down' effect) to the needs of a range of important markets and to involve geographically dispersed scientific capabilities.

An MNE's growing knowledge of international environments, through overseas marketing and production, may lead to recognition of distinctive scientific capabilities which could serve specialized needs in its research programme. Furthermore, experience of particular local environments may indicate a degree of incompatibility between the MNE's existing products and processes and local needs. R&D work may then be carried out locally to adapt MNE products and processes in ways that enhance their suitability to indigenous consumer requirements and productive potentials. In some cases the distinctive scientific capabilities accessible to MNEs in a country may exceed those needed for adaptive or evolutionary work, and may be better harnessed to the more ambitious creative programmes of the group. By contrast the locally focused adaption or evolution work can often be performed by routinely capable members of the local scientific labour force in conjunction with expatriate MNE personnel.

The type of R&D performed by an overseas laboratory can be divided into three types.

1   *R&D undertaken to adapt an existing product, or production process, to the needs of a particular host country*   R&D units predominantly committed to this type of work are called Support Laboratories (SL), since it is their function to support the efficient local assimilation of current technology.

2   *R&D to derive new products or processes which go beyond mere assimilation of products derived elsewhere in the group*   Because effective performance of this type of work is predicated upon feedback from local marketing personnel and engineers, the unit involved is characterized as a Locally Integrated Laboratory (LIL). An important variant of the work of an LIL occurs when it functions within a subsidiary that has been given a world product mandate (WPM). In this case the subsidiary has been endowed with the responsibility for deriving, producing and marketing a distinctive product in the MNE's range for the global (or at least a large regional) market. The LIL, though probably still operating within the broad confines of the MNE group's existing technology, works with subsidiary marketing and production/engineering personnel to derive the product to fulfil this mandate.

3   *Long-term R&D*   When an MNE feels it has located a source of scientific capability whose competence exceeds the demands of SL or LIL work it may incorporate it into a wider programme of more basic research focused on the derivation of future generations of products. Units performing this type of work are described as Internationally Interdependent Laboratories (IIL). The IIL participates in an R&D initiative which is likely to involve several similar units in other locations. The IIL may not be significantly involved with producing and marketing units in the same host country, and, therefore, there is no reason to expect the results of its work to directly benefit them.

6.2   THE SAMPLE

The sample derives from 560 major enterprises, these being divided into three sub-samples, termed A, B and C. Within each enterprise (except in subsample C) it was intended, where relevant, to survey the parent and all the overseas laboratories.

Parent laboratories are either corporate level R&D units (either physically located at corporate headquarters, or distinguished as the corporate unit) or the main R&D facilities of major divisions in diversified enterprises. The expectation, investigated in the questionnaires, is that such units may (a) perform the more basic R&D work from which spin-offs may be picked up for development by subsidiary laboratories, including those overseas, and (b) conceive, initiate and coordinate integrated research programmes involving, among others, overseas laboratories.

Overseas laboratories are non-parent laboratories which are likely to support local engineering or marketing needs, or make a specialized contribution to a globally integrated research programme.

Sample A. The 500 companies in sample A are the 500 largest industrial enterprises in the world in 1986 as derived from the Fortune listings. A number of the leading directories of R&D facilities were scrutinized to find the parent and overseas subsidiaries of sample A companies (Bowker, 1987; Longman, 1987, 1988a,b). Since, as noted above, large divisionalized companies were often considered to have more than one parent R&D facility, more than 500 parent laboratories were found for sample A companies. On the other hand, not all had overseas facilities and the total of these came to less than 500. To cover cases with no overseas R&D a section of the parent questionnaire is directed at such enterprises, seeking elucidation of the lack of such decentralization. In a small number of cases the R&D directories did not even produce addresses for parent facilities. For these companies parent questionnaires were sent to corporate headquarters, using addresses from *Dun and Bradstreet Principal International Businesses*.

Table 6.1 Characteristics of the sample of laboratories surveyed, and of the sample of respondents

	Location			Ownership		
	Foreign-dependence of research: percentage of foreign-owned laboratories in sample surveyed	Response rate		Internationalization of research: percentage of overseas laboratories in sample surveyed	Response rate	
Country		Indigenous laboratories	Foreign laboratories		Home laboratories	Overseas laboratories
US	39	26	30	30	26	40
Europe	48	33	44	60	33	—
UK	50	42	57	60	42	27
West Germany	43	21	41	66	21	35
France	39	8	6	37	8	33
Italy	62	40	38	50	40	40
Netherlands	55	80	50	81	80	24
Sweden	15	36	50	15	36	50
Switzerland	44	40	25	78	40	47
Other Europe	70	43	50	22	43	0
Japan	3	23	67	8	23	38
Canada	62	45	11	15	45	50
Australia	76	25	46	0	25	—
Rest of the World	31	27	0	0	27	—

Sample B. In reviewing the directories to locate facilities for the 500 enterprises of sample A a number of companies outside this sample were discovered which seemed to constitute relevant cases of international decentralization of R&D. A sample of 30 of these companies was distinguished (as sample B) and parent and subsidiary units surveyed as for sample A.

Sample C. Since sample B is a self-selecting sample of companies with some commitment to international R&D, sample C was assembled from 30 companies with no apparent overseas R&D operations. The firms in sample C were selected to match those in sample B by industry and home country as closely as possible. Unless otherwise stated, the results reported in this book refer to the consolidated sample of A, B and C.

Each parent firm and each laboratory was associated with a particular industry and a particular country (bi-national firms were arbitrarily allocated to one country – Unilever to the Netherlands and Shell to the UK). For the purposes of statistical analysis 20 industry groups were used, and these were further aggregated into eight groups for the regression analysis in chapter 7. A total of 1028 questionnaires was sent out, and 296 usable replies were received – an overall response rate of 28.8 per cent. Parents supplied 163 of the responses, and subsidiaries 133. The response rate was slightly higher for subsidiaries than for parents – 32.8 per cent compared to 26.2 per cent. The response rate was particularly good for foreign laboratories in the UK, and notably poor for laboratories in France (see table 6.1). Results pertaining to Japan need to be treated with caution because although the coverage of Japanese-owned laboratories is quite satisfactory (at least in respect of home laboratories), there were only a small number of responses from foreign laboratories in Japan.

For the most part, results pertaining to home and overseas laboratories are reported separately. There are significant differences not only in the motives for establishing these different types of laboratory but also in the general scale of the establishments. Table 6.2 presents a frequency distribution of size of laboratory, showing that in both the US and the UK the headquarters laboratories of local firms are on average much larger than the laboratories of foreign firms. The difference is particularly marked in the

Table 6.2 Percentage size distribution of laboratories located in the US and UK by employment

	US		UK	
Size range	Parent	Subsidiary	Parent	Subsidiary
1–24	0	32	4	18
25–49	1	18	7	35
50–99	17	16	21	18
100–249	24	20	21	18
250–499	25	2	18	6
500–999	11	11	18	4
1000–4999	20	0	11	0
5000–	1	0	0	0
Column total	100	100	100	100
Average size	1061	137	498	196
Number sampled	66	44	28	28

US because the headquarters laboratories are much larger, while the foreign laboratories are somewhat smaller, than in the UK.

The analysis in this chapter relies on simple cross-tabulations. For many purposes these are sufficient to demonstrate the main points that arise from a more sophisticated analysis such as that used in chapter 7. They are particularly useful in handling questions for which a relatively small number of responses is available. More complex issues on which a large amount of data is available are deferred until chapter 7.

6.3 A PROFILE OF THE SAMPLE

A simple cross-tabulation by ownership and location of the laboratories associated with the parent firms in sample A affords a useful overview of global R&D. Table 6.3 shows the number of laboratories owned by parents of a given nationality in a given country. There are only twelve countries that are involved in overseas research by the leading 500 firms, and these are listed in the table. The 'Rest of the World' simply refers to countries where some of these leading firms are domiciled but which do not source overseas research. The most obvious point is the dominance of the US in terms of large-firm R&D. This is hardly surprising, of course, since the US is not only the world's major economy, with a major technological orientation, but it is also the home of many of the world's largest MNEs. It is still notable, though, that 51 per cent of all laboratories in the sample are located in the US, while 46 per cent are owned by US firms.

The discrepancy between these two percentages arises because the US actually hosts more foreign laboratories than it owns overseas. The difference is captured, more generally, by the distinction between the foreign dependence ratio, which measures the percentage of all domestic laboratories that are foreign owned, and the internationalization ratio, which measures the proportion of all domestically-owned laboratories that are located overseas. The relation between foreign dependence and internationalization is illustrated in figure 6.1. Three main groups of countries can be identified by dividing up the square with two parallel lines. The countries in the central division are those which are equally 'open' in the two respects. Countries such as Japan and Sweden, which lie close to the origin, are relatively closed, while a country such as Italy, which is remote from the origin, is relatively open in both respects. The US, together with France, occupies a middle position, having a modest and balanced openness compared with other countries.

Four countries – Switzerland, Netherlands, West Germany and the UK – are significantly more open in terms of internationalization than they are in terms of foreign dependence. Four other units – Australia, Canada, Other Europe and the Rest of the World – exhibit the reverse situation where foreign dependence is high relative to internationalization. Firms based in these countries have made only limited attempts to exploit the potential of overseas R&D, even though their home countries host R&D themselves.

A simple count of laboratories, however, pays no heed to

Table 6.3 International distribution of the laboratories owned by 500 major firms

Ownership	US	CN	UK	FR	GR	IT	NL	SW	SZ	OE	JP	AL	RW	O/S	All	International ratio
US	282	17	41	12	14	7	3	1	6	11	1	6	5	124	416	30
Canada		11	1									1		2	13	15
UK	68	1	55	1	3		2		1	1	1	4		81	136	60
France	12		1	25		1			1					15	40	38
West Germany	50		4		29					2		1		57	86	66
Italy	3		1			5		1						5	10	50
Netherlands	12		4	2	2		5	1						21	26	81
Sweden	1						1	11						2	13	15
Switzerland	26		2	1	3		1		10	1	1	1		36	46	78
Other Europe	2									7				2	9	22
Japan	7		1								96			8	104	8
Australia												4		0	4	0
Rest of World													11	0	11	0
Total foreign	181	18	55	16	22	8	6	3	8	15	3	13	5	353		
Grand total	463	29	110	41	51	13	11	14	18	22	99	17	16		914	
Foreign dependence ratio	39	62	50	39	43	62	55	21	44	68	3	76	31			

Note: The key to the locations at the head of the table is given by the listing in the ownership column.

Source: Authors' investigations.

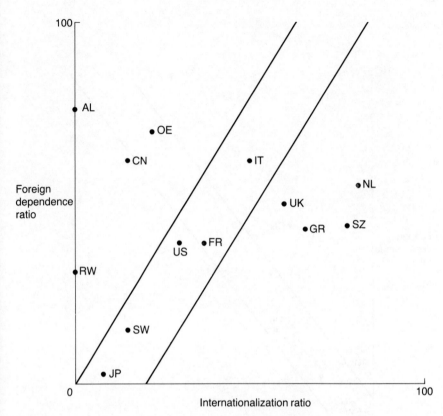

Figure 6.1   Foreign dependence and internationalization, based on the
frequency distribution of laboratories

Key: See table 6.1.

Source: Table 6.1.

differences in size of establishment. Size differences can be quite
significant, as table 6.2 shows. The smaller size of subsidiary
facilities means that conversion to an employment basis considerably reduces the estimated openness of most economies as figure
6.2 shows. This is particularly true of the US and Japan, where
the discrepancy in size is particularly great. It is less true of, say,
Canada, where laboratories of both kinds are relatively small.
The internationalization of the UK is considerably reduced relative to its foreign dependence because UK laboratories overseas

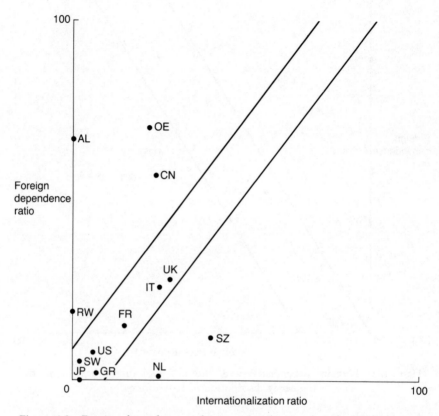

Figure 6.2 Foreign dependence and internationalization based on estimates of employment in parent and subsidiary laboratories

Key: See table 6.1.

Note: It was not possible to estimate from sample data the average employment of parents based in Australia, or in the Rest of the World. Nor was it possible to estimate subsidiary employment in the Rest of the World. On the basis of information for other countries, it was assumed that the missing averages were respectively 200, 100 and 50.

Source: Table 6.1 and sample data on employment.

are on average smaller than overseas laboratories in the UK. This is because overseas laboratories in the UK are among the largest overseas laboratories in the world. The openness of West Germany is more generally reduced because both German overseas laboratories and overseas laboratories in Germany are relatively small compared to German parent laboratories. This is mainly accounted for by the relatively large size of the parent laboratories by world standards. Only Switzerland and the Netherlands clearly retain their position as countries whose internationalization considerably exceeds their foreign dependence. This outcome cannot be attributed solely to their 'small country' status, since the 'Other European' category includes several small countries – notably Belgium – in which foreign dependence considerably exceeds internationalization.

6.4   ORIGINS OF OVERSEAS LABORATORIES

The most prevalent origin was as a 'fresh installation for specific purposes' which accounted for 69 per cent of the 132 responding units. This origin was clearly most associated with the more research-oriented activities. Thus 80 per cent of the IILs covered were 'fresh installations', compared with 62 per cent of both SLs and LILs. Similarly 86 per cent of facilities 'regularly' doing basic research had this origin compared with 64 per cent of those performing such work either 'never' or 'occasionally'.

Overseas laboratories which had been acquired as part of a company involved in a merger or takeover accounted for 20 per cent of respondents. This type of origin was most important among units in the US (29 per cent) and Europe (excluding the UK) (23 per cent) and relatively scarce in the UK (6 per cent). By contrast only 7 per cent of the overseas laboratories of US MNEs had been acquired as part of a merger or takeover, compared with 33 per cent of those of European parent companies and 29 per cent of UK owned facilities. One responding unit was an 'acquired independent existing R&D facility', while another involved collaboration in a joint venture with another company. The remaining respondents (10 per cent) attributed their origin to some other unspecified cause.

6.5   SPECIALIZATION BETWEEN PARENTS AND SUBSIDIARIES

Parent laboratories were asked to assess a number of categories of R&D according to whether they were perceived as being relatively more or less important in overseas laboratories compared to the parent laboratory.

Basic Research

Of the 79 respondents to the question about basic research 16 (20 per cent) did not carry out basic research in either the parent unit or any overseas units. Where such work was done it tended to be mostly strongly focused on the parent units, with 45 (57 per cent) believing this type of work to be relatively less important in overseas units than the parent, 16 (20 per cent) equally important in both types of unit, and only 2 per cent believing it to be relatively more important in subsidiary units.

Applied Research to Derive New Products in the Present Industry

All but two of the 83 respondents to this question felt that this type of research was performed somewhere in the group. By comparison with basic research, overseas laboratories played a more prominent role. Thus 52 (62 per cent) of respondents felt this type of work was equally important in overseas and parent units, 19 (23 per cent) relatively more important in the parent and 10 (12 per cent) relatively more important overseas. Parent units seemed to retain an above average commitment to such work in US companies, while subsidiaries were relatively more prominent in European companies.

Applied Research to Derive New Production Technology in the Present Industry

Five (6 per cent) of 83 responding units (all five being of US origin) felt that no work on the derivation of new production technology was performed in the group. The location of such work was quite similar to that for product development work, with 47 (57 per cent) of the 83 units believing it to be of equal importance in parent and subsidiary units, 21 (25 per cent) of greater importance in the parent and 10 of greater importance overseas. A particular overseas focus on this type of work seemed most prevalent in European and Japanese companies, and least noticeable in US and UK enterprises.

Applied Research to Improve Existing Products and/or Techniques

All 83 respondents felt that work to improve existing products and/or techniques was performed in their group. The pervasiveness of this type of work means that it was regarded as of equal importance in parent and subsidiary units by 57 (69 per cent) of the respondents. Where some degree of specialization was reported this adaptive work emerged as the only type of research with an overseas orientation. Thus 16 (19 per cent) of respondents felt this work was relatively more important in overseas units, and 10 (12 per cent) relatively more important in parent units. The overseas orientation was most pronounced in European firms and relatively weak for US companies.

Research to Derive Additional Products in New Areas of Specialization

Overall 75 of the 80 respondents undertook research aimed at extending the product range into new areas of specialization. Of the various types of research this ranked just below basic in terms of a centralized (parent laboratory) orientation. Thus 33 (42 per cent) of respondents considered this type of research to be relatively more important in parent laboratories than overseas ones, and only 8 (10 per cent) rated it as relatively more important in subsidiary laboratories.

6.6   PARENT LABORATORY PERSPECTIVES ON FACTORS INFLUENCING THE TYPE OF WORK DONE IN OVERSEAS LABORATORIES

Parent laboratories were questioned about their views on the factors influencing the type of work done overseas. Respondents were requested to grade each factor as 'never relevant' (score of unity), 'sometimes relevant' (score of two) or 'nearly always relevant' (score of three).

A Distinctive Local Scientific, Educational or Technological Tradition Conducive to Certain Types of Research Project

Overall only 12 (15 per cent) of 82 respondents rated this as 'nearly always' a relevant influence, while 26 (32 per cent) felt it was 'never relevant' (mean 1.83). Industries in which such distinctive characteristics had above average relevance were photographic equipment and scientific instruments (mean 2.50), electronics and electrical appliances (2.15) and pharmaceuticals (2.11), with such factors least relevant in food, drink and tobacco (1.29) and metal manufacture (1.50). Japanese MNEs seemed most attracted by such characteristics (2.25) and US MNEs (1.65) least so.

Cost Factors

Cost factors were perceived by parent laboratories as having relatively little influence on the work done in overseas subsidiary units. Thus only 12 (15 per cent) of 81 respondents rated this as 'nearly always relevant' to decisions, and 24 (29 per cent) saw it as 'never relevant' (mean 1.85). The industries most responsive to cost conditions were metal manufacture (mean 2.25), industrial and agricultural chemicals (2.13) and food, drink and tobacco (2.10), with petroleum (1.33) and photographic equipment and scientific instruments (1.50) least so. The parent country of

MNEs seemed to have little influence on their degree of response to cost conditions.

Only Room for a Small Number of Basic R&D Laboratories

It has often been alleged that decentralized R&D would, in many industries, be limited to low profile adaptive work, since more advanced work required such large units that the adequate realization of economics of scale would restrict the number of units that could effectively be used. In fact 36 (48 per cent) of 75 respondents felt this to 'never' be relevant as an influence on overseas R&D, and only 22 (29 per cent) rated it as 'nearly always relevant' (mean 1.81). Industries where this influence did seem to be a constraint on decentralization were petroleum (2.33), industrial and agricultural chemicals (2.79), and food, drink and tobacco (2.14), with its relevance lowest in metal manufacture (1.00), photographic equipment and scientific instruments (1.50) and other manufacturing (1.50). Once again the parent country of the MNE had little influence on the relevance of this influence.

Need to Adapt the Product to the Local Market

With supply-side influences and technical characteristics of R&D rated as of limited influence on geographically decentralized R&D, it is perhaps not surprising that more weight seems to be placed on demand-side factors. Thus of 84 respondents 56 (67 per cent) believed 'the need to adapt the product to the local market' was 'nearly always relevant' to decisions on overseas R&D, with only 9 (11 per cent) rating this influence as 'never relevant' (mean 2.56). Product adaptation was rated as particularly crucial in industrial and agricultural chemicals (2.82), motor vehicles (2.83) and electronics and electrical appliances (2.77), and was less pervasively influential in pharmaceuticals (2.22), photographic equipment and scientific instruments (2.00) and other manufacturing (2.00).

Need to Adapt Production Techniques to Local Conditions

Process adaptation was also seen as a key influence on decisions with regard to overseas R&D. Thus 43 (53 per cent) of 81 respondents felt it was 'nearly always' relevant, and only 13 (16 per cent) 'never' (mean 2.37). Process adaptation was recognized as most widely relevant in food, drink and tobacco (2.75), metal manufacture (2.75), and industrial and agricultural chemicals (2.67) and least so in pharmaceuticals (1.89), industrial and farm machinery (2.00) and other manufacturing (2.00). UK MNEs had the most notable recognition of the relevance of 'process adaptation' in overseas R&D (2.50) and US (2.25) least.

Need to Develop Distinctive New Products for the Local Market

Though seen by parent R&D units as somewhat less influential than the adaptation of current products, the development of new products in recognition of distinctive needs of local markets was also rated high. Thus 32 (41 per cent) of 78 respondents believed this to be 'nearly always' relevant and only 11 (14 per cent) thought it 'never relevant' (mean 2.27). Such local needs seemed most relevant to subsidiary R&D work in food, drink and tobacco (2.67) and metal manufacture (2.50), and least so in photographic equipment and scientific instruments (1.75), pharmaceuticals (2.00) and industrial and farm equipment (2.00). MNEs from European countries seemed most responsive to such overseas product development opportunities (mean 2.53) and those from the US (2.11) least so.

6.7 COORDINATION AND INTERDEPENDENCE IN GLOBALIZED R&D

A number of questions probed parents' perceptions of the nature of coordination between themselves and overseas laboratories. One question asked if the parent unit felt that interaction took the form of (1) systematic coordination, (2) *ad hoc* consultations, or (3) infrequent interaction. 'Systematic coordination' clearly predominated with 68 per cent of 85 respondents opting for this. It was strongest in pharmaceuticals (91 per cent), petroleum (89 per cent) and motor vehicles (86 per cent) and relatively infrequent in photographic equipment and scientific instruments (25 per cent) and industrial and agricultural chemicals (45 per cent). There was little difference in the use of this approach according to the nationality of the parent company. *Ad hoc* consultation was used by 25 per cent of respondents, being notably prevalent in photographic equipment and scientific instruments (75 per cent), but absent in metal manufacture and pharmaceuticals and relatively little used in petroleum (11 per cent) and motor vehicles (14 per cent). Only 7 per cent of respondents accepted 'infrequent interaction' as describing their coordination approach, with metal manufacture (40 per cent) making most use of it.

In another question respondents were asked what proportion of their foreign R&D units they considered to be 'closely coordinated' with the parent units. Of 67 respondents 25 (37 per cent) believed that all their subsidiary units were 'closely coordinated' and 15 (22 per cent) considered that none were. In response to a complementary question 28 (52 per cent) of 54 parents said that none of their overseas units were 'autonomous', and only 2 (4 per cent) believed all such subsidiaries were so.

Further questions investigated particular aspects of intra-group specialization and coordination of R&D in the form of project mobility. With various perspectives and skills accessible in a wide range of locations, projects initiated in one location may benefit from being moved to other laboratories to facilitate completion. The parents were asked 'are promising projects shifted from an affiliate to the parent at crucial stages of their development?' Of 82 respondents 15 (18 per cent) said this 'never' happened and 39 (48 per cent) said it happened 'rarely', with 7 (8 per cent) saying it occurred 'sometimes', 17 (21 per cent) 'frequently' and only 4 (5 per cent) 'automatically'. Sixty of the respondents who admitted to some project diversion to the parent answered a question relating to the motive behind such mobility. Of these 33 (55 per cent) considered that the parent 'could better complete the research', 17 (28 per cent) felt that the move was in response to the belief that 'the parent country is the most likely market for innovation of a new product', and the remaining 10 (17 per cent) believed the move to be motivated by 'other reasons'.

Similarly parent laboratories were asked if 'promising projects were shifted from parent R&D units to a foreign R&D unit?' This in fact seemed to happen to a slightly greater degree than the pull of projects towards the centre. Thus of 81 respondents 7 (9 per cent) 'never' allowed such project movement, 33 (41 per cent) said it happened 'rarely', 6 (7 per cent) 'sometimes', 32 (40 per cent) 'frequently' and 3 (4 per cent) 'automatically'. The motives for this outward movement of projects differed quite notably from that described for the opposite direction. Thus only 8 (11 per cent) of 74 respondents believed that shifting projects to subsidiary units was intended to 'better complete research work' while 59 (80 per cent) saw it as aiming 'to ensure that the outcome is best directed to a particular market', with 7 (10 per cent) noting 'other reasons'.

Parent laboratories were also asked if they foresaw any changes in the international location of R&D within their company. Of 119 respondents 79 (66 per cent) felt that an 'increased emphasis on a globally integrated R&D network' was likely. Industries where such a shift was particularly favoured were office machinery (both of 2 respondents), pharmaceuticals (92 per cent), motor vehicles (86 per cent), aerospace (80 per cent) and industrial and agricultural chemicals (76 per cent). Relatively little enthusiasm for such a change was discerned in industrial and farm machinery (30 per cent), metal manufacture (40 per cent) and food, drink and tobacco (46 per cent). Japanese MNEs seemed most disposed towards the further evolution of a globally integrated R&D network (81 per cent) (confirming the remarks in chapter 1) and UK MNEs least (48 per cent).

By contrast only 11 (9 per cent) of the respondents saw 'more emphasis on autonomous overseas laboratories' as a likely future development, with this most favoured by industrial and farm machinery (20 per cent) and UK (20 per cent) respondents. Increased centralization in the form of 'more use of the centralized facility' was favoured by 24 (20 per cent) of respondents, this being most prevalent in industrial and farm machinery (50 per cent), metal manufacture (40 per cent), and food, drink and tobacco (39 per cent) among industries and by UK MNEs (28 per cent). Finally 5 (4 per cent) of respondents perceived no notable changes as being likely.

6.8 SOURCES OF PROJECT IDEAS INITIATED IN OVERSEAS LABORATORIES

To further investigate the roles of overseas laboratories, overseas laboratories themselves were questioned about the sources of the ideas incorporated into their projects. They were asked to grade nine sources of ideas as never, occasionally or regularly used (with scores of one, two and three respectively).

Of 128 respondents 21 (16 per cent) 'never' initiated project ideas suggested by the parent, 90 (70 per cent) did so 'occasionally' and 17 (13 per cent) 'regularly' (mean 1.97). As expected, ideas from the parent are most influential in IIL units. Even so only 24 per cent of ILLs (compared with 12 per cent for SLs and 3 per cent for LILs) found the parent a regular source of ideas. It seems that parents are more interested in coordinating projects suggested by creative IILs abroad, rather than taking sole responsibility for initiation.

The position of laboratories regularly doing basic work is particularly distinctive. Thus 19 per cent of such laboratories found parent suggestions 'a regular source of ideas', which was more than for any other type. However, these same laboratories provided the highest incidence (29 per cent) of never using parent suggestions as a source of ideas. Thus basic research has a tendency to provide an extreme position of either strong parental influence or strong autonomy. Other forms of research are associated with more *ad hoc* suggestions from the parent.

Suggestions by Other Laboratories

Ideas suggested by other overseas laboratories were less relevant than those from the parent, with only 4 (3 per cent) of 129 respondents rating them a 'regular' source of ideas and 79 (6 per cent) an 'occasional' source (mean 1.67). This source of ideas varied relatively little between types of unit, with LILs producing the highest mean (1.72) followed by IILs (1.67) and SLs (1.58). Units regularly doing basic work were the least dependent on suggestions from sister R&D units, with a mean response of 1.52 compared with a range of from 1.73 to 1.84 for other types of research. Thus laboratories whose predominant motivation is to adapt or develop existing technology are the most amenable to suggestions from similar units elsewhere in the MNE network, probably reflecting the applicability of the advice of units which have dealt with similar problems. This emphasizes that where an MNE has committed itself to a geographical dispersion of R&D good communications are not only essential among units involved in an integrated programme of basic research, but of considerable value among those with apparently more autonomous objectives.

Own Proposals Approved by Parent

Of 129 respondents 99 (77 per cent) said that their 'own pro- posals approved by the parent' were a 'regular' source of ideas, while 22 (17 per cent) rated them an 'occasional' source; only 8 (6 per cent) 'never' provided their own ideas for their work (mean 2.71). Units operating in the UK (mean 2.91) were particularly likely to implement their own ideas, while those in the US (2.58) had a below average tendency to do so. By contrast units of US parents were most likely to implement their own ideas (mean 2.83) and those of UK parents least likely to do so (2.55).

IILs were most likely to implement their 'own proposals approved by parent', with 83 per cent rating this a 'regular' source of ideas (mean 2.79), compared with 75 per cent (2.69) for LILs and 65 per cent (2.50) for SLs. An explanation for this rather sur- prising prevalence of their own ideas in the work of IILs has already been noted, namely that parents are seeking to obtain dis- persed sources of creative ideas as well as research skills, and seek to *approve* a balanced programme of work rather than themselves *initiate and impose* such a programme. Laboratories regularly doing basic research had a mean response of 2.81, compared with

2.75 for those 'occasionally' doing such work and 2.60 for those 'never' doing it.

Feedback from Local or Foreign Production Units

Of 127 respondents 34 (27 per cent) 'never' found feedback from local production units to be a source of ideas, 68 (53 per cent) found it to be an 'occasional' source and 25 (20 per cent) a 'regular' source (mean 1.93). Local production units were notably important as sources of ideas in motor vehicles (2.40), other manufacturing (2.33), metal manufacture (2.30), and food, drink and tobacco (2.27) and least so in office equipment (1.25) and pharmaceuticals (1.47). By contrast there was relatively little variation between host countries or between parent countries.

Predictably feedback from local production units is of least relevance in units 'regularly' doing basic work, where the mean response is 1.45 compared to 2.03 for those 'occasionally' doing such work and 2.00 for those 'never' doing it. The highest mean responses are found among units regularly doing applied research. IILs are least dependent of local production unit feedback with a mean response of 1.66 compared with 2.20 for LILs and 2.15 for SLs. Generally 'feedback from foreign production units' is of limited relevance to the work done in overseas laboratories, with only 7 (5 per cent) of 129 respondents believing it to be a 'regular' source of ideas, while 81 (63 per cent) rated it as 'never' a source (mean 1.43).

Feedback from Local or Foreign Marketing Units

Local marketing units were found to play a very significant role. Thus 62 (48 per cent) of 130 respondents rated 'feedback from local marketing units' as a 'regular' source of project ideas, with a further 49 (38 per cent) believing such feedback to 'occasionally' be an influence (mean 2.33). Marketing units were notably important in food, drink and tobacco (2.73) and electronics and electrical appliances (2.67), and least so in pharmaceuticals (1.93) and office equipment (1.87). Marketing units were particularly likely to influence projects in the US (2.52) and marketing feed-back was also influential on subsidiaries of UK (2.62) and Japanese (2.75) parents.

This influence was rated highly by both SLs (2.65) and LILs (2.67) and, as would be expected, much less so for IILs (1.98). Similarly the mean response for units regularly doing basic research was only 1.62 for local marketing feedback, compared with a range of 2.41 to 2.55 for those regularly performing adaptive or developmental work.

The possibility of foreign marketing units influencing the work done by a laboratory may be strong where it holds a WPM. Though only 19 (15 per cent) of 130 respondents found foreign marketing units' feedback to be a 'regular' source of ideas, 71 (55 per cent) found them an 'occasional' source (mean 1.84). Thus in petroleum the mean response for foreign marketing inputs was 2.50 and in office equipment it was 2.33 (compared with a well-below-average 1.87 for local marketing feedback), while sub-sidiary units in the UK (2.14) and Europe (1.96) and from US parents (2.08) also seemed to be responding to wider market needs. IILs were most likely to be 'regularly' influenced by foreign market needs (20 per cent compared with 12 per cent for SLs and 6 per cent for LILs) but also recorded the highest proportion 'never' influenced by this source (35 per cent compared with 31 per cent for LILs and 37 per cent for SLs). As would be expected basic research was least influenced by this source of ideas, with a mean response of 1.50 compared with a range of from 1.75 to 1.94 for other types of work.

Feedback from Local or Foreign Sales Channels

Local sales channels also provided a significant source of ideas, though less so than marketing. Thus of 128 respondents 43 (34 per cent) found feedback from sales channels a 'regular' source of ideas and another 44 per cent an 'occasional' source (mean 2.02). Sales channels were notably influential in petroleum (2.60), indus-trial and farm machinery (2.50), food, drink and tobacco (2.36) and industrial and agricultural chemicals (2.25) and least so in pharmaceuticals (1.43) and office equipment (1.62). Units in the

UK (2.18) were particularly influenced by local sales channels, as were those with UK (2.24) or Japanese (2.25) parents.

Foreign sales channels were of relatively little importance. Thus while only 14 of 129 respondents (11 per cent) rated them a 'regular' influence, 65 (50 per cent) said they 'never' were (mean 1.61). As in the case of marketing feedback, foreign sales channels emerged as of notable influence in petroleum (2.40) and office equipment (2.00). There was little difference between laboratory types with regard to the influence of foreign sales channels (which notably boosts the *relative* position of IILs, as might be expected), while units doing basic work had a mean response of 1.35 compared to a range from 1.61 to 1.73 for other types of work.

Feedback from Local or Foreign Customers

Of the various forms of local feedback influencing the work done in overseas laboratories, customer feedback is most important. Thus of 130 respondents 68 (52 per cent) rated feedback from local customers a 'regular' source of project ideas, with another 46 (35 per cent) finding it an 'occasional' source (mean 2.40). Industries with a notable dependence on this source of influence (and on most other types of local market feedback) were industrial and farm machinery (2.75) and petroleum (2.67). Also of note is the just-above-average rating (2.44) for local customer feedback in the office equipment industry, in which all other types of local feedback rank well below average. The most notably below-average rating of local customer feedback is in the pharmaceutical industry (1.90). Though this is in line with the usually low rating of local feedback in the industry, it is surprising that local health service regulations and standards are not more influential.

Customer feedback was the most influential of the foreign sources of ideas as well. Thus 37 (29 per cent) of 128 respondents assessed foreign customer feedback to be a 'regular' source of project ideas, and 52 (41 per cent) rated it an 'occasional' source (mean 1.98). This source of ideas was most influential in petroleum (2.80) and office equipment (2.67), in the latter case making this the most influential of all ideas sources (alongside 'own ideas approved by parent') and also reflecting the greater foreign rather than local relevance of the market side influences in that industry.

Collaborative Research with Another Enterprise

The possibility that ideas for work done in the overseas laboratory will derive from that unit's role in collaborative research with another enterprise found little support. Thus only 9 (7 per cent) of 122 respondents rated this a 'regular' source of ideas, while 47 (39 per cent) said it 'never' was (mean 1.69). Such collaboratively derived ideas were relatively most prevalent in electronics and electrical appliances (1.91) and least so in office equipment (1.50). Units with Canadian or Australian parents were most likely to derive ideas from collaboration (2.33), with UK parents somewhat above average (1.81), and US parents below (1.53).

Ideas derived in collaborative work were predictably most influential in IILs (mean 1.80), and were also relatively significant in LILs (1.73), compared to SLs (1.46). Such ideas were of most influence in laboratories regularly doing basic work (mean 1.90) and 'research to derive additional products in new areas of specialization' (1.89).

Independent Local Researchers

Ideas originating from independent local researchers played a very limited role. Only 12 (9 per cent) of 129 respondents rated such researchers a 'regular' source of ideas, while 79 (61 per cent) felt they 'never' were (mean 1.48). Their influence was relatively most pervasive in food, drink and tobacco (1.73) and pharmaceuticals (1.63) and least so in metal manufacture (1.18) and industrial and farm machinery (1.25). Units operating in Europe were most likely to tap this source (1.65).

The ideas of independent local researchers were most likely to influence the work of IILs (mean 1.67), followed by LILs (1.47) and SLs (1.27). Also local researchers were most likely to present ideas incorporated in basic R&D (1.86).

6.9 SOURCES OF FINANCE FOR RESEARCH PROJECTS IN OVERSEAS LABORATORIES

Respondents were asked to grade four likely sources of finance for their project as 'of no importance', 'of some importance', 'of major importance', or 'the only source of financing' (with scoring from one to four).

Parent

The parent company proved to be the most important source of funding. Thus 23 per cent of respondents reported this as the only source of financing, while 32 per cent considered it of 'major' importance and another 32 per cent of 'some importance' (mean 2.63).

As expected, IILs are most likely to be funded by the parent (mean 2.93), though SLs (2.72) and LILs (2.34) were also more dependent on this source than on any other. Similarly units regularly performing basic work, which is least likely to have direct applicability locally, are the most reliant on parent funding (3.05). Laboratories in office equipment (3.22), pharmaceuticals (2.97) and electronics and electrical appliances (2.83) were most dependent on parent funding, and those in industrial and farm machinery (2.25), metal manufacture (2.33), industrial and agricultural chemicals (2.36) and food, drink and tobacco (2.36) least so. Units in the UK (2.97) were the most dependent on parental finance and those in the US (2.46) least so; while those with Japanese (1.75) parents were least likely to receive parental funding, and those with US parents most likely to (2.78).

Associated Local Manufacturing Units

Though notably less relevant than parent support, funding from associated local manufacturing units is the second main source of finance. While only 7 per cent of respondents were solely dependent on this source 28 per cent considered it a 'major' source and 24 per cent of 'some importance' (mean 2.00).

The two types of laboratory which predominately focus on locally oriented work are also most reliant on local manufacturing funding – SLs (2.23) and LILs (2.12) – while the IILs are least so (1.77). In line with this, laboratories regularly performing 'applied research to adapt existing production technology to the local environment' are most often supported financially by local manufacturing units (2.13) and those regularly performing basic work least so (1.82).

Sister Affiliates Overseas

Funding support from other affiliates in the group (excluding the parent) played a small role, with no respondents reporting it as the only source of financing and only 6 per cent as a 'major' source; 71 per cent rated it as of 'no importance' (mean 1.35). Of the 6 units which reported sister affiliates as a 'major' source of financing and also specified their laboratory type, 5 were IILs.

Host Government

Host governments play a very small role in funding overseas R&D. Thus 77 per cent of respondents considered it of 'no importance', 22 per cent of 'some importance' and only 1 per cent of 'major importance' (mean 1.23). Where it did occur, government funding was most likely to support work aimed at developing new locally oriented products or processes. Thus, although LILs accounted for 33 per cent of respondents answering this question and specifying their laboratory type, they provided the only instance in which the host government was considered a 'major' source of funding.

6.10 LOCAL PERSONNEL IN TOTAL EMPLOYMENT

Out of 125 respondents 94 (75 per cent) reported that over 80 per cent of their employment comprised local personnel, and a further 13 (10 per cent) reported between 60 per cent and 80 per cent. Use of local personnel was most pervasive (over 80 per cent) in food, drink and tobacco, motor vehicles, and industrial and farm machinery (100 per cent of respondents) and metal manufacture too (89 per cent). Local personnel were least prevalent in industrial and agricultural chemicals, where 28 per cent of respondents (compared with a sample average of 14 per cent) had less than 60 per cent local personnel.

A notable influence on employment patterns seems to be the prevalence of basic research. Thus of units 'regularly' performing basic research only 65 per cent had over 80 per cent local personnel while 20 per cent had less than 40 per cent local personnel. For units 'occasionally' performing basic work the comparable figures were 76 per cent and 5 per cent, and for those 'never' performing such work 80 per cent and 4 per cent. Thus even though it might be anticipated that the quality of local personnel might be a key influence attracting such work to a particular location, a relatively strong commitment of external personnel is also involved. These may be necessary to facilitate the effective integration of the local capabilities with those elsewhere in the group, matching skills and ensuring the full realization of the complementarities sought in a global R&D programme. LILs make the most use of local personnel with 89 per cent of them employing over 80 per cent and only 6 per cent less than 60 per cent, while IILs report comparable figures at 76 per cent and 15 per cent. Somewhat surprisingly, only 60 per cent of SLs reported over 80 per cent local personnel, and 24 per cent of them less than 60 per cent. One explanation is that the foreign personnel are technicians on short-term secondment to the unit, for the purpose of introducing local personnel to the technology.

6.11   SUMMARY

A preliminary analysis of questionnaire responses indicates that despite a significant diffusion of applied research to overseas laboratories, basic research is still relatively concentrated in the parent laboratory.

On average, respondents indicated that parent and subsidiary laboratories were equally prominent where applied research was concerned. So far as overseas laboratories are concerned, applied research to derive new production technology is marginally more important than applied research to derive new products, which in turn is marginally more important than applied research to derive additional products in new areas of specialization.

Applied research to develop new products depends on close links with marketing, while the adaptation of products to local markets involves some interaction with local sales channels too. Applied research to develop new technologies depends on links with production – but less significantly so. Links with production appear to be more selective, being prominent in mass production continuous flow industries such as motor vehicles but of limited significance in batch production industries such as pharmaceuticals.

The conduct of basic research in overseas laboratories is more characteristic of high-technology industries such as photographic equipment, electronics and pharmaceuticals than it is of low technology industries such as food and metals. The propensity to engage in basic research is a significant influence on the motivation for locating research overseas. Thus the existence of a distinctive research tradition is much more important in attracting basic research in high technology industries than in other cases. The cost of scientific labour is sometimes a factor too, but mainly in relatively low-technology industries.

In the majority of overseas laboratories, where applied research is dominant, it is the pull of the market which is the key factor in location. In some cases this pull is related to the overall size of the market, whereas in others – such as office equipment – the need to maintain contact with key customers is an important consideration too. There is some evidence that in service-oriented activities such as bespoke software development, the research laboratory 'follows the customer' overseas. In almost all cases of applied research being pulled abroad by the market, it is the adaptation of the product or process to local conditions that is the key consideration.

Very few parents seemed to regard overseas laboratories as

either purely autonomous, on the one hand, or purely subordinate on the other – with the possible exception of overseas laboratories oriented to pure research, where instances of both attitudes were found. In most cases the role of the parent laboratory was to orchestrate the programmes of all the laboratories within the group – though sometimes this would be done by a research director with no responsibility for any particular parent laboratory. Most respondents reported that systematic interaction between laboratories was very strong, and was expected to become even stronger in future. There was little concern that the proliferation of research laboratories would result in loss of economies of scale at the individual laboratory level.

The central coordination role did not necessarily involve the initiation of every project – in many cases the coordinator would merely decide whether to approve proposals formulated in individual laboratories. The coordinator assesses how far different research proposals are likely to synergize to further the overall goals of the firm. Projects begun at one laboratory can sometimes be moved to another. Typically a promising project may be moved to the parent because of the wider range of special expertise available at the parent laboratory, while the parent may delegate relatively self-contained components of R&D (such as writing software or testing reliability through trial use) to an overseas laboratory.

The coordination of group R&D also involves planning the movement of personnel between laboratories. About three-quarters of research personnel at an overseas laboratory are usually recruited locally, although the figure may be somewhat lower if significant basic research is being done. The parent laboratory is likely to take a close interest in some (but not all) types of basic research and may seek to monitor and support overseas activities by seconding its own personnel. This tends to result in a relatively high proportion of foreign personnel (say 40 per cent) working in an overseas laboratory devoted to basic research.

Overall, these results are consistent with the view that overseas laboratories are capable of sustaining much more than just a subordinate satellite role. Laboratories with local access to high quality scientific labour and led by an energetic intrapreneur can win for themselves a significant role, not only in adaptive work, but in general applied research, the investigation of new areas of specialization, and even in basic research too. The fact that corporate research networks increasingly allow for intensive systematic interaction between laboratories affords overseas laboratories with considerable potential for claiming a key role in the research activity of the firms as a whole.

7

Business Strategy and Overseas R&D

7.1 INTRODUCTION

This chapter uses regression analysis to make international comparisons of the factors influencing the behaviour of overseas laboratories. The focus is on the responses to the subsidiary questionnaires. Focusing on the subsidiaries makes it easier to identify the separate effects of the ownership of the subsidiary and its location. It is difficult to identify separate effects for a parent laboratory because its ownership and location coincide.

Differences in behaviour that seem to be due to location could in fact be caused by particular industries agglomerating in different places. Similarly, differences attributed to ownership could also be due to industry effects instead. For example, if US overseas research is dominated by chemical firms, and chemical firms concentrate their overseas laboratories in West Germany, the peculiarities of the chemical industry may be wrongly imputed to US ownership or German location. It is therefore important to control for industry as well.

Industry is also important in its own right: high-technology industries such as pharmaceuticals have long-term projects and carry out more fundamental research than do low-technology industries such as food and drink (as noted in chapter 1). The location of laboratories in high-technology industries may therefore be more sensitive to the availability of scientists and engineers and less sensitive to market proximity than in low-technology industries. Industry therefore interacts with location in a non-trivial way.

7.2 THE NATURE OF OVERSEAS RESEARCH

Table 7.1 analyses the type of R&D done in overseas laboratories. The technique used is ordinary least squares regression analysis. The dependent variables are categorical variables, ranging in value from one (no research of a given type) to three (regular participation in research of that type). The categorical nature of the dependent variable does not bias the regression results, but it means that significance tests must be interpreted with caution, as the usual assumption of normality is violated. While the t-tests of significance are fairly robust to such deviations, the F-tests are not. It is possible to decompose a categorical regression into a set of regressions with zero-one dependent variables and apply a logit transformation to each, but the results obtained from this more sophisticated approach only lead to similar inferences to the ones indicated here.

Location, ownership and industry effects are captured using dummy variables. To avoid losing too many degrees of freedom, and having too many categories with only a small number of members, countries were consolidated into eight groups: US, Canada, Japan, UK, European Community (excluding UK), Scandinavia (Sweden, Norway, Finland), Other Europe (Switzerland and Austria) and the Rest of the World (mainly Australia, India and Brazil). The Rest of the World is used as a control group. Because there are no responses from foreign-owned laboratories in Scandinavia, Scandinavia appears only in the ownership and not the location category.

Eight industrial groups are also used. Five high-technology industries are separately identified: pharmaceuticals, office equipment, motor vehicles, aircraft, and professional and scientific instruments. Chemicals, coal and petroleum products and pulp and paper are consolidated into a 'process industry' category in which technology-intensity is medium-high. Chemical firms dominate this category. Mechanical and electrical engineering firms are similarly combined into a single 'engineering' category. The remaining industries – represented in the sample mainly by food and metals firm – form a 'low-technology' control group.

The figures in brackets in each table represent, as before, the absolute values of the t-statistics. Significance is reported at three levels: 10 per cent (one asterisk), 5 per cent (2 asterisks) and 1 per cent (3 asterisks). The overall significance of location, ownership and industry effects is indicated by the three F-statistics near the bottom of each column. The F-statistic for the regression as a whole is also shown. Because some questions achieved a better response rate than others, the number of observations, together with the overall goodness of fit, R^2, is shown at the foot of each column.

Five categories of research are identified in the table, out of the seven identified in the questionnaire. Results relating to local adaptation of the product, and local adaptation of the process have been suppressed because in almost all cases they are simply an average of those pertaining to product development or process development on the one hand, and technical support on the other.

The results confirm that the conduct of basic research is a minority interest so far as the respondents are concerned. The sample mean of 1.80 is below the mid-point of the measurement scale – indeed, this figure is the lowest of the five mean responses shown in the table. None of the three major R&D centres – US, Japan and the EC – is significantly oriented to basic R&D carried out by foreign firms, compared to the Rest of the World control group. This is because the control group is responsible for quite a lot of overseas basic research – much of it in Australia. Only Canada has a significant bias towards foreign-owned basic research. Canadian firms themselves, on the other hand, are less inclined than the control group to carry out their basic research overseas. The importance of basic research in Canada seems to be mainly a consequence of US firms taking advantage of tax incentives to Canadian affiliates (see chapter 8).

Among the industries, pharmaceuticals is notable for its emphasis on basic research. The results show that this emphasis on overseas basic research is coupled with a significant bias

Table 7.1 Location, ownership and industry factors influencing the nature of overseas R&D

Regression number	1.1	1.2	1.3	1.4	1.5
Dependent variable	Basic research	Product development	Process development	Diversification	Technical support
Intercept	1.72***	2.16***	2.51***	1.68***	2.34***
	(5.03)	(6.23)	(10.73)	(5.42)	(5.76)
Location					
US	0.24	0.72**	0.37*	0.12	0.08
	(0.76)	(2.27)	(1.72)	(0.44)	(0.21)
Japan	-0.04	0.13	-0.29	-0.02	0.17
	(0.07)	(0.22)	(0.72)	(0.04)	(0.25)
EC	0.32	0.63*	0.43*	-0.07	0.14
	(0.99)	(1.93)	(1.93)	(0.24)	(0.36)
UK	0.02	0.45	0.66***	0.08	-0.21
	(0.07)	(1.41)	(3.10)	(0.28)	(0.58)
Canada	1.26**	1.02*	0.73**	0.02	0.15
	(2.42)	(1.93)	(2.02)	(0.05)	(0.24)
Other Europe	-0.06	-0.09	0.29	-0.63	-0.51
	(0.15)	(0.22)	(1.01)	(1.54)	(0.95)
Ownership					
US	-0.35	0.27	-0.24	0.36	0.12
	(1.46)	(1.12)	(1.47)	(1.58)	(0.42)
Japan	-0.24	-0.55	-0.11	-0.26	-0.37
	(0.60)	(1.38)	(0.42)	(0.73)	(0.80)
EC	-0.31	-0.11	-0.27*	0.39*	0.06
	(1.40)	(0.49)	(1.73)	(1.83)	(0.22)

UK	-0.40*	0.08	0.07	0.32	0.37
	(1.74)	(0.34)	(0.44)	(1.49)	(1.36)
Scandinavia	-0.68	-1.08**	-0.14	0.56	-0.68
	(1.50)	(2.36)	(0.43)	(1.36)	(1.27)
Canada	-0.47	0.30	-0.07	1.22***	-0.22
	(1.02)	(0.63)	(0.23)	(2.90)	(0.40)
Industry					
Pharmaceuticals	0.52**	-0.83***	-0.26*	0.18	-0.69***
	(2.51)	(3.82)	(1.83)	(0.95)	(2.81)
Office equipment	0.05	-0.68**	0.01	-0.11	-0.91**
	(0.18)	(2.26)	(0.04)	(0.40)	(2.49)
Motor vehicles	0.12	-0.59	-0.01	0.16	0.56
	(0.32)	(1.46)	(0.03)	(0.47)	(1.22)
Professional and scientific equipment	0.62	0.34	-0.60	-0.59	0.65
	(1.17)	(0.63)	(1.64)	(1.23)	(1.03)
Chemicals etc.	0.17	-0.41**	0.06	0.56***	-0.24
	(0.93)	(2.12)	(0.48)	(3.27)	(1.08)
Engineering	0.09	-0.70***	-0.12	0.44**	-0.10
	(0.23)	(2.90)	(0.79)	(2.09)	(0.37)
F-location	1.80	2.02*	2.55**	0.89	0.74
F-ownership	0.77	1.84*	1.38	2.19**	1.09
F-industry	1.43	3.25***	1.68	3.05***	3.22***
F-total	1.37	2.83***	1.89**	2.39***	1.84***
Number of observations	131	126	131	126	131
R^2	0.18	0.32	0.23	0.29	0.23
Mean	1.80	2.30	2.77	2.32	2.14

against overseas research in product and process development and technical support. The sample means show that overseas product and process development are much more common, but although pharmaceutical firms carry out such activities overseas they do so to a significantly lesser extent than firms in the control group.

Both the US and EC are biased towards product and process development, while the UK is biased toward process development only. Canada is biased towards product and process development as well as basic research, which leads to an impressive overall performance in terms of foreign-owned R&D.

So far as ownership is concerned, UK firms are biased against conducting basic research overseas. Scandinavian firms are biased against carrying out product development overseas, and EC firms against overseas process development.

Office equipment, like pharmaceuticals, is biased against overseas product development and overseas technical support. Chemicals and engineering are also biased against overseas product development. Overall, it is interesting that the propensity to undertake product development overseas is lower than the propensity to undertake new process development. When product development is undertaken overseas, there is a strong tendency for it to be based in North America. Access to a large market seems to be an important factor here. The results are also compatible with the view that product development is a more secret and sensitive area than process development, and is consequently carried out closer to home.

Location and ownership effects are totally insignificant in respect of technical support. This is perhaps not surprising, given that technical support activities tend to be based close to production sites, but have few other strategic implications.

In process industries such as chemicals there is a strong propensity for overseas R&D to be concerned with diversification. Such diversification may simply reflect the derivation of new products within an existing area of competence. Research in process industries tends to be geared to exploiting the potential of a particular type of raw material, although if supplies are approaching exhaustion it may be geared to the discovery of substitutes as

well. The link between raw materials and diversification is corroborated by the importance of Canadian ownership in diversification – Canadian multinationals are well known for their
technological leadership in the resources sector (Rugman, 1987).

It is, however, difficult to explain why engineering research and
EC-ownership should promote diversification too. A more general
explanation is that diversification is a major motive in mature
industries using well-proven technologies – such as chemicals and
engineering – and in countries such as Canada and the EC where
mature industries tend to dominate.

To corroborate these interpretations it is necessary to check
that the results for overseas laboratories do not merely reflect
results for all laboratories, including those at home. It is not,
unfortunately, possible in most cases to tie up individual overseas
laboratories with their parents because a complete set of responses
from all of a firm's laboratories was a relatively rare event. It is,
however, possible to compare the regressions for overseas laboratories as a whole with regressions for the parent laboratories as
a whole. The parent results contain another industry – other
manufacturing – which was not represented among respondents
to the subsidiary questionnaire.

The results for parent laboratories are shown in table 7.2. It
can be seen that the concentration on basic research is a general
feature of the pharmaceutical industry. On the other hand, an
emphasis on basic research is unique to foreign-owned laboratories in Canada; it is not shared by Canadian parents. The conjecture that product development tends to be done at home and
process development abroad is confirmed by columns 2 and 3 of
the table. The sample mean for product development is higher for
parents than for overseas subsidiaries, but the sample mean for
process development is lower. Product development is significantly weak in the Rest of the World control group, which
contains the most peripheral of the world's major markets.
Process development, on the other hand, does not differ significantly between any of the country groups so far as parent firms
are concerned.

Turning to diversification, the industry effects in chemicals and

Table 7.2 Location/ownership and industry factors influencing the nature of parent R&D

Regression number	2.1	2.2	2.3	2.4
Dependent variable	Basic research	Product development	Process development	Diversification
Intercept	1.78***	1.88***	2.87***	0.93**
	(3.27)	(6.41)	(7.11)	(2.07)
Locations/ownership				
US	0.16	0.88***	−0.21	1.45***
	(0.30)	(3.05)	(0.54)	(3.30)
Japan	0.55	0.84***	−0.09	1.57***
	(0.99)	(2.78)	(0.21)	(3.41)
EC	0.39	0.99***	−0.01	1.64***
	(0.70)	(3.26)	(0.03)	(3.51)
UK	0.27	0.97***	−0.30	1.56***
	(0.49)	(3.30)	(0.75)	(3.45)
Scandinavia	−0.40	0.75**	−0.44	1.14**
	(0.70)	(2.40)	(1.03)	(2.36)
Canada	−0.82	0.71**	−0.29	0.73
	(1.33)	(2.13)	(0.63)	(1.43)
Other Europe	−0.15	0.85**	−0.18	1.18**
	(0.24)	(2.50)	(0.38)	(2.28)

Industry

Pharmaceuticals	0.56**	0.22	−0.13	0.23
	(2.24)	(1.64)	(0.70)	(1.12)
Office equipment	0.31	−0.01	−0.16	0.37
	(0.80)	(0.03)	(0.55)	(1.13)
Motor vehicles	−0.29	0.01	−0.15	−0.22
	(1.06)	(0.08)	(0.76)	(0.96)
Aircraft	0.06	0.10	−0.23	0.19
	(0.20)	(0.60)	(1.00)	(0.73)
Professional and scientific equipment	0.32	−0.09	−0.37	0.37
	(0.97)	(0.49)	(1.54)	(1.38)
Chemicals etc.	0.22	0.12	0.13	0.07
	(1.36)	(1.35)	(1.05)	(0.52)
Engineering	0.16	0.06	−0.17	0.10
	(0.89)	(0.65)	(1.26)	(0.68)
Other manufacturing	1.05*	0.33	0.38	0.98**
	(1.92)	(1.10)	(0.93)	(2.16)
F-location	3.42***	2.09**	0.84	3.59***
F-industry	1.70	0.69	1.29	1.25
F-total	2.24***	1.28	1.00	2.28***
Number of observations	163	162	163	162
R^2	0.19	0.12	0.09	0.19
Mean	2.07	2.82	2.63	2.45

engineering are clearly specific to overseas laboratories. This could be due to the fact that when diversification research is needed the parent laboratory maintains a product development focus and the diversification research is established elsewhere. It could be part of a management strategy to prevent new lines of research being discouraged by vested interests in established technology within the parent laboratory. If so, the policy is only used selectively in certain industries because, as noted in the previous chapter, parent laboratories on the whole have a dominant role in diversification research (or at least their managers like to think they do).

7.3   LOCATION FACTORS

It is possible to analyse the attractiveness of locations by examining how responses to questions about the importance of environmental factors vary between locations. As indicated in chapter 6, R&D managers were asked to rate on a scale from one (irrelevant) to three (a major factor) the following influences on the development of the laboratory:

1 a distinctive local scientific, educational or technological tradition conducive to certain types of research project;
2 the presence of a helpful local scientific environment and adequate technological infrastructure;
3 the availability of research professionals; and
4 favourable wage rates for research professionals.

The results in table 7.3 are somewhat surprising. To begin with, no location emerges as particularly favourable. Canada scores highly on the availability of research professionals – as do Switzerland and Austria to a slightly lesser extent. The US comes out as a somewhat unhelpful environment – an explanation for this is suggested in chapter 8.

One way to interpret these results is in terms of a 'selection and survival' principle. Firms differ in their requirements according to the nature of the research they do. Firms that do not perceive a location to be attractive will not go there, and if they do and find later that they have made a mistake then they will leave. Most of the firms found at a given location, at a given time, will therefore be the ones that find the conditions tolerable there. But equally, it seems that few firms find their locations ideal – just no worse than the alternatives.

The influence of the nature of the research on the evaluation of a location can be discerned from the industry-specific factors. Thus pharmaceuticals – which is more heavily oriented to basic research than most – is the only industry to attach greater weight than the control group to all the characteristics identified in the table. Professional and scientific equipment, and chemicals, also weight local traditions and the availability of research professionals higher than the control group. This suggests that it may not be basic research *per se* which makes these factors important, but rather the demand for highly specialized professionals, such as chemists, biochemists and electronic engineers. The important thing in these industries, it may be suggested, is not so much the general scientific background of researchers but the existence of highly specific competences produced by a high level of specialization in education and training.

It is interesting to note that the wages of research professionals are of much less concern than their availability. This is consistent with the view expressed in chapter 3, that wages of scientists may be too low relative to market levels because of cultural constraints, and that shortage problems therefore persist because wages are not raised to encourage additional supply. In a well-functioning market wages would be perceived as more of a constraint than availability because availability problems would be solved by raising the wage.

The emphasis on availability rather than the wage is also consistent with the view that it is the availability of highly specialized personnel that is the problem, and that in the short run firms cannot find such personnel at any price. In this case market imperfection arises from the 'thinness' of the market – that is, from the small number of participants involved.

Table 7.3 Location and ownership and industry factors influencing the importance of environment to the overseas laboratory

Regression number	3.1	3.2	3.3	3.4
Dependent variable	Local traditions	Helpful environment	Availability of professionals	Diversification
Intercept	1.96***	2.15***	1.53***	1.58***
	(5.05)	(6.04)	(4.25)	(5.42)
Location				
US	-0.22	-0.58*	0.30	0.01
	(0.62)	(1.77)	(0.90)	(0.03)
Japan	0.09	-0.08	0.57	-0.78
	(0.13)	(0.14)	(0.93)	(1.58)
EC	-0.28	-0.51	0.21	-0.20
	(0.76)	(1.51)	(0.62)	(0.73)
UK	-0.10	-0.38	0.50	0.29
	(0.29)	(1.17)	(1.55)	(1.10)
Canada	-0.15	0.52	1.46***	0.60
	(0.26)	(0.94)	(2.63)	(1.35)
Other Europe	-0.21	-0.28	0.85*	-0.08
	(0.43)	(0.64)	(1.93)	(0.23)
Ownership				
US	-0.50*	-0.48*	-0.29	-0.39*
	(1.85)	(1.94)	(1.19)	(1.95)
Japan	-0.56	-0.35	-0.80*	-0.47
	(1.25)	(0.85)	(1.93)	(1.39)
EC	-0.38	0.02	-0.29	-0.59***
	(1.52)	(0.08)	(1.27)	(3.16)

UK	−0.41	−0.33	−0.32	−0.20
	(1.58)	(1.40)	(1.32)	(1.03)
Scandinavia	−0.34	−0.47	−0.71	−0.74*
	(0.66)	(0.99)	(1.48)	(1.93)
Canada	−0.48	−0.38	0.04	−0.11
	(0.92)	(0.78)	(0.07)	(0.27)
Industry				
Pharmaceuticals	0.66***	0.59***	0.56**	0.30*
	(2.72)	(2.71)	(2.56)	(1.72)
Office equipment	0.53	0.21	−0.04	−0.18
	(1.45)	(0.64)	(0.11)	(0.69)
Motor vehicles	−0.34	−0.13	0.20	0.69**
	(0.76)	(0.34)	(0.52)	(2.28)
Professional and scientific equipment	1.09*	1.01*	1.52***	0.17
	(1.80)	(1.81)	(2.70)	(0.38)
Chemicals etc.	0.43*	0.22	0.52**	0.19
	(1.95)	(1.14)	(2.60)	(1.18)
Engineering	0.40	0.34	0.33	0.24
	(1.47)	(1.40)	(1.34)	(1.22)
F-location	0.21	1.42	1.93*	2.29**
F-ownership	0.75	1.29	0.97	2.21**
F-industry	2.17*	1.92*	2.57**	1.46
F-total	1.25	1.66*	1.68*	1.58*
Number of observations	124	131	131	130
R^2	0.18	0.21	0.21	0.20
Mean	1.78	1.73	1.99	1.44

7.4   MARKET GROWTH AND TECHNOLOGICAL POTENTIAL

If the quality of the environment is not the overriding factor then perhaps the growth of the market is. It is to be expected that large and wealthy markets will encourage R&D – particularly with an emphasis on product development. The first column of table 7.4 confirms this is the case of the US, and to a lesser extent for Japan, but it does not seem to apply to EC countries.

An obvious reason why it may not apply to the EC countries is that the 'host market' is not the EC itself but the individual country. By focusing on the entire market served by the overseas subsidiary with which the laboratory is affiliated, a different answer may be obtained. But in fact the answer is the same – the

Table 7.4   Market growth and technological progress as factors influencing the strategies of overseas laboratories

Regression number	4.1	4.2	4.3
Dependent variable	Growth of host markets	Growth of other markets	Technological progress
Intercept	1.57^{***}	2.03^{***}	1.87^{***}
	(4.12)	(5.70)	(5.23)
Location			
US	1.05^{***}	-0.27	0.36
	(3.01)	(0.83)	(1.10)
Japan	1.11^{*}	-0.26	1.31^{**}
	(1.71)	(0.42)	(2.16)
EC	0.19	-0.23	0.32
	(0.53)	(0.68)	(0.94)
UK	0.24	0.09	0.44
	(0.70)	(0.28)	(1.36)
Canada	-0.23	0.32	0.59
	(0.38)	(0.57)	(1.06)
Other Europe	-0.21	0.26	0.24
	(0.45)	(0.59)	(0.56)

Table 7.4 (continued)

Regression number	4.1	4.2	4.3
Dependent variable	Growth of host markets	Growth of other markets	Technological progress
Ownership			
US	0.30	−0.04	0.13
	(1.12)	(0.18)	(0.25)
Japan	0.31	−0.84**	−0.25
	(0.70)	(2.03)	(0.60)
EC	−0.06	−0.38	0.15
	(0.24)	(1.60)	(0.63)
UK	−0.32	−0.21	0.22
	(1.25)	(0.88)	(0.89)
Scandinavia	−1.28**	−0.63	0.79*
	(2.54)	(1.31)	(1.66)
Canada	−0.41	0.45	0.72
	(0.79)	(0.93)	(1.49)
Industry			
Pharmaceuticals	−0.02	0.33	−0.28
	(0.09)	(1.52)	(1.30)
Office equipment	−0.46	0.49	0.12
	(1.27)	(1.53)	(0.35)
Motor vehicles	−0.18	0.01	0.32
	(0.44)	(0.03)	(0.86)
Professional and scientific equipment	0.01	0.06	−0.22
	(0.03)	(0.10)	(0.39)
Chemicals etc.	−0.22	0.25	0.12
	(1.07)	(1.29)	(0.62)
Engineering	−0.01	0.30	−0.02
	(0.53)	(1.24)	(0.10)
F-location	3.83***	0.53	0.92
F-ownership	2.33**	1.36	0.98
F-industry	0.54	0.71	1.01
F-total	2.02**	1.19	0.99
Number of observations	131	130	129
R^2	0.25	0.16	0.13
Mean	2.05	1.91	2.37

results in the second column show that overseas R&D in Europe is not oriented to the European market in the same way that overseas R&D in the US is. The European market *per se* does not seem to attract overseas R&D significantly more than does the control group. Part of the explanation may be that the control group contains markets with considerable growth potential – notably Brazil. But even so the results are not encouraging from the European point of view.

The sample means for the growth of markets are not all that high compared to the environmental factors, in any case. The dominant factor seems to be the rate of change of technology in the industry. This scores a relatively high sample mean of 2.37, with few significant differences between countries. The most striking point is that overseas R&D in Japan is significantly more technology-driven than overseas R&D in other countries – including the US. Interview evidence (chapter 8) suggests that it is the potential rather than the present reality of Japanese technological leadership that draws most overseas R&D to Japan. But notwithstanding this, it is disturbing from a Western point of view that a well-informed group of laboratory managers should perceive keeping up with technology as potentially more important than the growth of the market as a reason for investing in Japan.

One of the oldest debates about R&D is whether innovation is demand led or supply led – in other words, whether market growth or technology is the driving force. The results from this study on the whole support the supply-side view. Laboratory managers tend to perceive R&D as technology driven – although it is quite possible that this simply reflects their role within the firm, and that marketing managers, for example may take an opposite view.

7.5   BUSINESS STRATEGIES

A number of questions were asked about whether particular strategic considerations had governed the establishment of the overseas laboratory – such as the belief that local competitors

were weak, that the entry of another foreign firm could be fore-
stalled, and so on – but the evidence clearly indicates that these
considerations are very weak indeed. Only a small number of
firms admitted that they were of some importance and even fewer
that they were of major importance.

The only strategy to be widely used was that of matching the
local R&D of rival firms. This turns out to be particularly important in the establishment of laboratories in Japan (see table 7.5,
column 1). This supports the earlier conjecture that Japanese
investment in R&D is worrying Western rivals, who are investing
in Japan in order not to be left behind. The general strategy of
matching rivals is particularly favoured by EC-headquartered
firms and also by firms in the motor industry. UK firms tend to
use it more than do firms in the control group, but not to a significant extent. The second column of the table shows, however, that

Table 7.5 Patterns of business strategy motivating the establishment of
overseas laboratories

Regression number	5.1	5.2
Dependent variable	Match rivals' R&D	Forestall entry
Intercept	1.41***	0.98***
	(4.75)	(5.20)
Location		
US	– 0.05	– 0.04
	(0.19)	(0.26)
Japan	1.11**	0.44
	(2.18)	(1.39)
EC	– 0.08	0.15
	(0.29)	(0.83)
UK	– 0.18	0.04
	(0.68)	(0.26)
Canada	– 0.39	0.00
	(0.85)	(0.01)
Other Europe	0.02	– 0.04
	(0.04)	(0.25)

(continued)

Table 7.5 (continued)

Regression number	5.1	5.2
Dependent variable	Match rivals' R&D	Forestall entry

Ownership		
US	− 0.06	0.08
	(0.28)	(0.60)
Japan	− 0.35	0.01
	(0.90)	(0.04)
EC	0.33*	0.06
	(1.67)	(0.48)
UK	0.27	0.36***
	(1.34)	(2.75)
Scandinavia	0.21	0.06
	(0.53)	(0.23)
Canada	− 0.27	0.01
	(0.67)	(0.04)

Industry		
Pharmaceuticals	− 0.16	− 0.10
	(0.86)	(0.85)
Office equipment	0.05	0.09
	(0.20)	(0.52)
Motor vehicles	0.63*	0.09
	(1.87)	(0.41)
Professional and scientific equipment	− 0.26	0.42
	(0.56)	(1.44)
Chemicals, etc.	− 0.04	0.09
	(0.27)	(0.84)
Engineering	0.14	0.02
	(0.68)	(0.14)

F-location	1.36	0.76
F-ownership	1.27	1.74
F-industry	1.23	1.05
F-total	1.82**	1.14
Number of observations	127	127
R^2	0.23	0.16
Mean	1.41	1.11

UK firms are significantly more disposed to entry-forestalling strategies than other firms. This could be part of a wider phenomenon – namely that UK firms are more disposed to defensive rather than aggressive business strategies – but such a proposition could only be supported on the basis of much more extensive research.

7.6 THE ORGANIZATION OF INTERNATIONAL R&D

One of the major questions raised by the globalization of R&D is whether there are significant differences in the way that overseas laboratories are coordinated with the rest of the group according to where they are located, and according to the nationality of the parent firm. It is conceivable that differences in local or corporate culture, and differences in managerial competences, could cause systematic differences to emerge.

The results in table 7.6 show that, apart from the US, no such differences can be found. Laboratories in the US, and those owned by US firms, are less likely to belong to an internationally interdependent network of the kind describe in chapter 6. This is consistent with the results in chapter 5, which suggest that the internationalization of R&D is relatively less advanced among US firms, and with results in chapter 8 which suggest that foreign-owned laboratories in the US operate in a relatively autonomous manner. It may be that US laboratories like to dominate other laboratories in the group; parent laboratories can do so by formal subordination of overseas laboratories, while foreign-owned laboratories in the US react against foreign ownership by cultivating a high degree of independence.

Another possible explanation of the lack of international integration in US laboratories is that they are geared mainly to product development. It may be that laboratories geared instead to basic research or to diversification lend themselves more to interdependence and that overseas laboratories of this kind are less common in the US, or within US firms.

Table 7.6 Patterns in the type of overseas laboratory

Regression number	6.1	6.2	6.3
Dependent variable	Internationally interdependent	Locally integrated	Support
Intercept	2.00***	2.52***	1.84***
	(4.97)	(4.29)	(5.64)
Location			
US	− 0.62*	0.17	0.03
	(1.68)	(0.52)	(0.10)
Japan	0.03	0.39	0.12
	(0.05)	(0.68)	(0.19)
EC	− 0.12	− 0.03	0.34
	(0.31)	(0.07)	(0.92)
UK	0.08	− 0.17	0.09
	(0.23)	(0.54)	(0.25)
Canada	0.09	− 0.27	− 0.42
	(0.13)	(0.46)	(0.66)
Other Europe	0.09	− 0.45	0.83*
	(0.16)	(0.94)	(1.68)
Ownership			
US	− 0.30*	0.24	− 0.18
	(1.72)	(0.94)	(0.63)
Japan	0.67	0.32	− 0.22
	(1.30)	(0.72)	(0.50)
EC	0.09	− 0.06	− 0.04
	(0.36)	(0.26)	(0.14)
UK	− 0.26	0.23	0.01
	(0.93)	(0.95)	(0.03)
Scandinavia	0.16	0.45	0.30
	(0.30)	(0.97)	(0.61)
Canada	0.15	0.46	− 0.24
	(0.27)	(0.99)	(0.48)
Industry			
Pharmaceuticals	1.09***	− 1.02***	− 0.46**
	(4.42)	(4.75)	(2.00)
Office equipment	0.84**	− 0.97***	− 0.48
	(2.41)	(3.26)	(1.48)
Motor vehicles	0.27	− 0.18	− 0.56
	(0.60)	(0.45)	(1.34)

Table 7.6   (*continued*)

Regression number	6.1	6.2	6.3
Dependent variable	Internationally interdependent	Locally integrated	Support
Professional and scientific equipment	0.96 (1.56)	−0.67 (1.27)	0.25 (0.32)
Chemicals etc.	0.65*** (2.93)	−0.65*** (3.29)	0.17 (0.82)
Engineering	0.18 (0.66)	−0.35 (1.46)	0.24 (0.93)
F-location	1.35	0.64	1.02
F-ownership	1.48	1.12	0.23
F-industry	4.20***	4.76***	2.66**
F-total	0.31***	2.29***	1.51*
Number of observations	124	119	121
R^2	0.31	0.29	0.21
Mean	2.10	2.05	1.80

This conjecture is supported by the pattern of industry differences that is observed. The results indicate, loud and clear, that industry and not location or ownership is the major influence on the propensity for international integration. Industries such as pharmaceuticals and office equipment, which involve significant basic research, are disposed to international integration. So too is chemicals which, as noted earlier, is prominent in diversification-oriented research. It is also clear that industries which are disposed to international integration are biased against local integration. In other words it is the trade-off between international integration and local integration, rather than between international integration and technical support, that is crucial for the organization of R&D.

The results indicate that while many laboratories undertake technical support of some kind, relatively few respondents classified their laboratories as being primarily of this type. Technical support seems to be a fairly ubiquitous activity, in the sense that there are no significant location or ownership differences in the incidence of support laboratories and indeed, even among industries, it is only the pharmaceutical industry that is significantly biased against activity of this type.

7.7   INFORMATION FLOWS

A series of questions were asked about the use of libraries, the organization of seminars, publication policy and involvement in external consulting work.

1 What is the extent of reliance on local libraries, libraries of local research institutions/laboratories, personal collections of scientists, etc?
2 Are seminars relating to ongoing research held either on their own or in collaboration with other research institutions?
3 Are research findings published in journals?
4 Does the laboratory undertake consultancy work/contract jobs for public research institutions, universities, or other firms?

The sample mean responses (on the scale from 1 to 4) were 2.26, 2.05, 1.99 and 1.27 respectively. This indicates that in the average firm significant use was made of local libraries, seminars were organized whenever required (though not on a regular basis), research findings were sometimes published (though with key data often withheld) and that external contract work was only rarely undertaken.

The regression results are not shown because they are not particularly informative. On the whole, they confirm the null hypothesis that location, ownership and industry effects are insignificant. So far as the use of libraries is concerned, they show that only location effects are significant at the 10 per cent level. It turns out that overseas laboratories in Canada are significantly less likely (at the 5 per cent level) to use libraries than are laboratories in the control group, while Canadian-owned subsidiaries abroad are significantly more likely (at the 10 per cent level) to use them. It is, however, difficult to believe the obvious inference that

Canadian libraries are so poor that Canadian parents get their overseas affiliates to access libraries on their behalf. This inference is even less plausible when it is remembered that the control group includes countries such as India and Brazil in which the quality of scientific libraries is fairly modest by Western standards. A more plausible explanation is that Canadian laboratories are closely integrated with the firm's US laboratories from which much of their information is received.

Pharmaceutical firms are significantly more disposed to hold seminars at the 10 per cent level, but the F-tests indicate that overall industry effects, as well as location and ownership effects, are insignificant in this case. Industry effects, though, are significant at the 5 per cent level in respect of publication. Pharmaceutical firms are significantly more disposed to publish at the 1 per cent level, and office equipment and engineering firms are too at the 5 per cent level. Canadian-owned laboratories are significantly more inclined to publish at the 10 per cent level.

Location effects are significant at the 5 per cent level in respect of external contract work, though no individual country is significantly different from the control group at the 10 per cent level. It is perhaps worth noting, however, that the most significant result (at 11 per cent) is that external contract work is least common in the UK.

Another set of questions concerned the contracting out of work by the laboratory. The most interesting results here relate to Japan. Table 7.7 shows that in Japan, foreign firms are significantly prone to contract out to other corporate laboratories, whereas Japanese firms overseas are significantly disinclined to contract out with independent laboratories. One reason for overseas linkages in Japan may be to access Japanese technology, along the lines suggested earlier. Japanese technology is reputedly stronger within the corporate sector than within the university sector, and this may be why linkages with other firms rather than with universities are particularly desired. Another factor may be that contracting out is desired in order to simplify procedures for getting products approved for launch on the Japanese market. It has been alleged, for example, that it is easier to gain approval

Table 7.7 Patterns of contracting out to other laboratories

Regression number	7.1	7.2	7.3
Dependent variable	Independent laboratories	Universities	Other corporate laboratories
Intercept	1.72***	1.83***	0.94***
	(5.06)	(5.90)	(2.88)
Location			
US	0.09	0.17	0.18
	(0.31)	(0.62)	(0.66)
Japan	0.26	0.47	1.00**
	(0.49)	(0.97)	(2.32)
EC	0.12	0.27	0.03
	(0.38)	(0.96)	(0.13)
UK	0.06	0.17	−0.10
	(0.29)	(0.64)	(0.41)
Canada	0.20	0.45	−0.15
	(0.42)	(1.03)	(0.39)
Other Europe	0.29	0.12	0.07
	(0.75)	(0.34)	(0.21)
Ownership			
US	0.30	−0.13	0.37*
	(1.28)	(0.63)	(1.80)
Japan	−0.81**	−0.57*	−0.06
	(2.24)	(1.75)	(0.21)
EC	0.17	−0.08	0.35*
	(0.77)	(0.42)	(1.92)
UK	0.04	−0.34*	0.29
	(0.18)	(1.71)	(1.46)
Scandinavia	−0.18	−0.05	0.58*
	(0.37)	(0.13)	(1.75)
Canada	0.53	0.33	0.73**
	(1.26)	(0.85)	(2.15)
Industry			
Pharmaceuticals	−0.00	0.36**	−0.09
	(0.01)	(2.10)	(0.53)
Office equipment	−0.34	0.27	−0.24
	(1.29)	(1.12)	(1.18)
Motor vehicles	−0.09	0.53*	0.46*
	(0.27)	(1.80)	(1.77)

Table 7.7   (*continued*)

Regression number	7.1	7.2	7.3
Dependent variable	Independent laboratories	Universities	Other corporate laboratories
Professional and scientific equipment	-0.56 (1.18)	-0.29 (0.65)	0.24 (0.63)
Chemicals etc.	0.02 (0.13)	0.13 (0.82)	-0.04 (0.29)
Engineering	-0.28 (1.26)	0.07 (0.35)	-0.04 (0.25)
F-location	0.15	0.34	1.57
F-ownership	1.96*	1.28	1.54
F-industry	0.88	1.40	1.20
F-total	1.12	1.21	1.56*
Number of observations	120	124	106
R^2	0.17	0.17	0.24
Mean	1.92	2.06	1.29

for new pharmaceutical products if clinical trials in Japan have been delegated to a Japanese firm, and if plans are in hand to subcontract production to Japanese firms as well.

Japanese reluctance to contract out overseas could be due to a variety of factors: excessive secrecy, lack of confidence in the quality of independent work, or simply unfamiliarity with the environment which makes it difficult to find a suitable subcontractor.

Compared with the Rest of the World, contracting out is significantly favoured by US, EC, Scandinavian and Canadian-owned firms. It is disappointing to note, however, that while UK-owned laboratories are disposed to subcontract to local research institutions, they are significantly biased away from subcontracting work to universities. This result confirms the suspicion that university-business links are particularly weak in the UK.

Overseas laboratory managers were also asked about general liaison (rather than just subcontracting) and it is interesting that in one respect very different responses were obtained. Although Japanese laboratories are not disposed to subcontract, they are significantly more inclined than others to 'liaise' with local research institutions. It seems that Japanese investors aim to learn of Wesiern technology through liaison rather than formal contracting – which in turn may reflect a culturally-specific view of how relations with research institutions should be managed.

7.8 BUDGETING AND PERSONNEL

Firms were asked a series of questions about internal management, which emphasized finance and personnel matters. In a majority of laboratories the R&D budget is decided annually on the basis of a complex planing cycle. In a minority of firms other principles – or a combination of other principles – is used. Table 7.8 shows the ratings for five main principles mentioned in the questionnaire. The mean figure quoted shows the proportion of respondents who indicated that the principle in question was used. Canadian-owned laboratories were significantly inclined to report that no standard procedure was used, while UK-owned firms were more inclined to favour setting the budget as a fixed percentage of sales. Japanese firms were inclined to favour discretionary methods and EC-owned firms the allocation of a lump sum.

Table 7.8   Patterns of R&D budgeting

Procedure	Mean	Significant deviations
Fixed percentage of sales	0.14	UK parent[**](+), Pharmaceuticals[**](+), Office equipment[***](+)
Lump sum	0.11	EC parent[*](+)
Complex planning cycle	0.60	
Discretionary	0.12	Japan parent[*](+)
No standard procedure	0.17	Canada parent[*](+), Pharmaceuticals[*](−)

It is interesting to note that two very high-technology industries – pharmaceuticals and office equipment – were both inclined to favour a fixed percentage of sales (though some pharmaceutical firms were also inclined to avoid any standard procedure altogether). It is not at all obvious that a fixed percentage of sales is an appropriate budgeting procedure for an industry like pharmaceuticals in which long lead times are involved in product development and where profits are very sensitive to the sales of drugs that may have been developed several years ago. It also implies an element of inflexibility if the firms were to become caught up in a patent race.

The overall impression conveyed by these results is that R&D budgeting has received insufficient attention from management in many firms. While the complex planning cycle reported by a majority of firms may well be quite sophisticated, there are quite a lot of firms in which rather arbitrary procedures are employed, or even no standard procedure at all.

So far as personnel policy is concerned, it seems natural to begin by examining turnover rates. Several interesting conclusions emerge from the results in the first column of table 7.9. The first is that turnover in foreign-owned laboratories in Japan is significantly below that for the control group, but that the turnover in Japanese-owned laboratories abroad is not. This suggests that Japanese research workers can transfer their concept of loyalty and long-term attachment to Western laboratories in Japan. The Japanese cannot, apparently, export their concept of loyalty to Western employees employed in their laboratories abroad. This provides – admittedly tentative – support for the view that loyalty to the company may be a non-transferable element of Japanese culture – at least so far as research workers are concerned. More precisely, the loyalty inculcated in Japan is transferable to Western employers in Japan, but the inculcation of loyalty is not a Japanese management skill that can be made to work on non-Japanese employees outside Japan.

Long-term research can be easily disrupted by high turnover and it is therefore particularly worrying that turnover is significantly high in UK-owned laboratories. One factor promoting such turnover might be the high degree of internationalization in

Table 7.9 Patterns in personnel policy

Regression number	9.1	9.2	9.3
Dependent variable	Turnover	Movement between laboratories	Exchange programmes
Intercept	1.99***	2.46***	0.92***
	(5.96)	(5.33)	(4.05)
Location			
US	−0.14	0.26	0.39*
	(0.45)	(0.62)	(1.77)
Japan	−1.16**	1.34*	0.50
	(2.08)	(1.71)	(1.33)
EC	−0.44	0.15	0.41*
	(1.38)	(0.34)	(1.94)
UK	0.06	−0.03	0.29
	(0.22)	(0.07)	(1.40)
Canada	0.50	−1.05	0.60*
	(1.00)	(1.49)	(1.80)
Other Europe	−0.41	0.77	0.73***
	(1.01)	(1.36)	(2.66)
Ownership			
US	0.03	0.06	−0.26*
	(0.14)	(0.19)	(1.71)
Japan	0.32	−1.17**	−0.46*
	(0.85)	(2.20)	(1.84)
EC	0.18	−0.46	−0.09
	(0.83)	(1.55)	(0.63)
UK	0.44*	−0.93***	−0.21
	(1.96)	(3.01)	(1.41)
Scandinavia	−0.52	0.24	−0.40
	(1.18)	(0.39)	(1.40)
Canada	−0.32	−0.53	0.09
	(0.71)	(0.84)	(0.32)
Industry			
Pharmaceuticals	−0.04	−0.33	0.19
	(0.21)	(1.18)	(1.46)
Office equipment	−0.79***	0.30	0.61***
	(2.78)	(0.76)	(3.29)
Motor vehicles	−0.50	−0.54	0.51**
	(1.43)	(1.12)	(2.26)

Table 7.9 (*continued*)

Regression number	9.1	9.2	9.3
Dependent variable	Turnover	Movement between laboratories	Exchange programmes
Professional and scientific equipment	− 0.55 (1.08)	− 0.00 (0.01)	0.70** (2.07)
Chemicals etc.	− 0.47** (2.53)	0.12 (0.47)	0.07 (0.55)
Engineering	− 0.50** (2.16)	0.07 (0.22)	0.14 (0.99)
F-location	2.15**	1.54	1.56
F-ownership	1.58	2.97***	1.38
F-industry	2.70**	0.99	2.91**
F-total	1.84**	1.63*	1.88**
Number of observations	127	131	130
R^2	0.24	0.21	0.23
Mean	1.66	2.31	1.26

UK-owned research (noted in chapter 5), which inflicts a high degree of intra-firm mobility on employees. But in fact the opposite seems to be the case. Column 2 of table 7.9 indicates that mobility between laboratories is significantly lower in UK-owned firms than in the control group. It looks as though, for some reason, UK firms are bad employers. One possible reason is that they pay too low wages, dictated by traditional status-based differentials between managers and scientists, of the kind alluded to in chapter 3.

It might be expected that a high level of movement between laboratories would be associated with a high level of exchange activity with other local research institutions, but this does not appear to be the case. Exchange programmes tend to occur where intra-firm movement is merely average, as in office equipment, motor vehicles, and professional and scientific equipment. A characteristic of these three industries is close long-term links with key suppliers and major customers, and it may be that the

Table 7.10 Correlations between residuals relating to environmental factors, etc., and the nature of research

	Basic research	Product development	Process development	Diversification	Technical support
Type of research					
Basic research	1.00	−0.10	0.05	−0.01	−0.32***
Product development		1.00	0.23**	0.21**	0.30***
Process development			1.00	0.25***	0.04
Diversification				1.00	0.01
Technical support					1.00
Quality of environment					
Local traditions	0.11	−0.04	0.29***	0.02	−0.17*
Helpful environment	0.19**	0.07	0.22**	0.13	−0.26***
Availability of professionals	0.21**	0.08	0.14	−0.02	−0.26***
Wage of professionals	0.02	0.07	−0.10	−0.04	0.16*
Potentialities					
Growth of host market	−0.13	0.05	0.41***	0.23**	0.11
Growth of other markets	0.15	0.02	0.23**	0.04	−0.16*
Technological progress	−0.02	0.14	0.07	0.13	−0.01
Strategies					
Match rivals	−0.02	0.04	0.10	0.28***	0.10
Forestall entry	−0.07	0.16*	0.15*	0.10	0.12

exchange of personnel takes place across this particular kind of interface.

As with budgeting policy, the overall impression is a patchy one. It seems that internal strategies respond to a wide range of different factors, which may have much more to do with the idiosyncrasies of the corporate culture than with systematic factors of the kind which were important earlier.

7.9   RESIDUALS ANALYSIS

The interplay between systematic and idiosyncratic factors can be elucidated by further statistical analysis. The idea is to identify the nature of the research as a laboratory-specific factor, and to explain laboratory-specific variation from the overall pattern in terms of the nature of the research. For this purpose it is appropriate to eliminate the location, ownership and industry effects from the nature of research itself. Statistically, the procedure involves correlating the residuals from table 7.1 with the residuals from the regressions in table 7.3–7.7 and 7.9. The correlation coefficients reported in table 7.10 are zero-order Pearson coefficients, and the asterisks denote levels of significance in the normal way.

The first point to note, from the first line of the table, is that the conduct of basic research is a characteristic quite independent of involvement in product or process development, or diversification. The only systematic pattern involving basic research is its dissociation from technical support, which is, of course, at the other end of the spectrum so far as academic skill and time horizon are concerned. The second point to note, from lines 2 and 3, is that the distinction between process and product development is, in practice, rather unclear. Product development is more closely associated with technical support than is process development – which certainly conflicts with conventional wisdom. The ambiguity becomes even greater when it is observed from lines 10 and 11 of the table that process development is more closely associated with the growth of the market, and less associated with the need to keep up in technology, than is product development.

Table 7.11 Correlations between residuals relating to external linkages, etc., and the nature of research

	Basic research	Product development	Process development	Diversification	Technical support
Type of laboratory					
Internationally interdependent	0.17*	−0.07	−0.01	−0.04	−0.24***
Locally integrated	−0.12	0.08	0.23**	0.20**	0.21**
Support	−0.19**	0.07	−0.09	−0.04	0.31***
External linkages					
Seminars	0.31***	0.04	0.09	0.12	−0.05
Libraries	−0.10	−0.15*	−0.28***	−0.07	0.06
Publication	0.31***	−0.08	0.16*	0.07	−0.28***
External consultancy work	0.19**	0.01	−0.08	0.06	0.06
Contracting out to					
Independent laboratories	0.05	0.06	0.11	0.04	−0.02
Universities	0.26***	−0.01	0.04	0.11	−0.18*
Other corporate laboratories	−0.04	−0.10	0.05	0.23**	0.20

There is evidence that both basic research and process development are particularly sensitive to the quality of the environment. The highly specialized skills required for basic research explain why the availability of professionals appears important in this case. The emphasis on local traditions in respect of process development probably reflect the economies of agglomeration emphasized in chapter 4 – the availability of sophisticated local component suppliers who can help to engineer new types of capital equipment. Note also that the wage of professionals is deemed important only in respect of technical support. This confirms the earlier suggestions that wages are important when there is an efficient market for fairly general skills, but the availability dominates in inefficient markets for highly specialized skills.

It should be observed, in passing, that research into diversification possibilities is closely associated with both product and process research, as might be expected since both are clearly relevant to the appraisal procedure. The main strategic motive for diversification research seems to be to match rivals – which is plausible given the oligopolistic nature of many high-technology industries.

Table 7.11 suggests that the internationally interdependent laboratory is typically engaged in basic research. Locally integrated laboratories are engaged mainly in process development, product development and technical support. The growth of international interdependence, it seems clear, has much to do with an international division of labour within the firm between related areas of basic research. These results confirm the point made earlier, that the key distinctions between basic research and other forms and that the distinctions among the other forms are fairly vague. Another way of putting this is to say that specialization in basic research – and nothing else – is more common than specialization in, say, product development, which is typically associated with a mix of other activities too. The reason for lack of specialization outside basic research may be that laboratories engaged in applied research need to be extremely versatile in order to respond quickly to changing conditions. To maintain this versatility they retain a wider range of competencies than a laboratory allocated to a particular programme of long-term research.

Table 7.12 Correlations between residuals relating to budgeting and personnel strategies and the nature of research

	Basic research	Product development	Process development	Diversification	Technical support
Budgeting					
Fixed percentage of sales	-0.01	0.15*	0.02	0.10	-0.17
Lump sum	0.15*	-0.08	-0.01	-0.14	0.03
Complex planning cycle	-0.04	-0.12	0.01	-0.03	0.02
Discretionary	-0.13	-0.07	0.04	0.09	-0.01
No standard procedure	-0.09	0.04	-0.14	0.02	0.07
Personnel					
Turnover	0.13	-0.04	0.06	-0.07	-0.03
Movement between laboratories	0.06	-0.04	0.06	0.04	-0.09
Exchange programmes	0.24***	0.15*	0.06	0.03	-0.12

As expected, laboratories oriented to basic research have a strong propensity to organize and participate in seminars, and to contract out work to universities. It is also interesting to note that laboratories geared to diversification tend to subcontract research to other corporate laboratories. This is presumably because they lack relevant skills in the areas they are planning to enter, and so rely on external consultants for guidance.

Table 7.12 confirms that the nature of research has little influence on budgeting methods and personnel policies. The only significant correlation above the 10 per cent level indicates that exchange programmes are most common in basic research, which is hardly a surprising result. Thus while many aspects of laboratory behaviour are tuned to the nature of the research, the internal administration is apparently not. One explanation could be that differences are too subtle to be captured by a questionnaire. Another is that all R&D management is essentially just the management of human relations among creative individuals, and no fine-tuning of methods is required. But there must remain the suspicion that R&D management is very much an art rather than a science, and that fine-tuning would improve performance if only the principles were better understood.

7.10   SUMMARY

The location-ownership and industry-specific factors examined in this chapter have only a limited influence on the R&D strategies of overseas laboratories. The managers of most overseas laboratories were broadly satisfied with their host country location, although some reservations were expressed by respondents located in the US. UK-owned laboratories seemed to experience significantly higher turnover than others, suggesting that a culture-specific tendency to underpay researchers (relative to market rates) may be at work.

Most parent laboratories expressed similar attitudes towards overseas laboratories whatever their nationality, although US-owned parents tended to emphasize authority relations more and cooperation among equals less than did their European counterparts. This may reflect the fact that overseas R&D is less important for US firms than it is for European ones. Many European firms carry out product development in the US (due to the size of the market, and the strictness of consumer and environmental protection regulations there) and they seem to find that US laboratories tend to behave in a relatively autonomous manner anyway.

This autonomy is only partly a US-specific factor, however. In general product development is closely linked into local production and marketing, and fairly loosely linked to basic research at headquarters. On the other hand, basic research at different laboratories is closely linked, so that tight research coordination is most characteristic of firms that do basic R&D rather than just development work overseas.

Overseas basic research by US MNEs is heavily biased towards Canada. It seems to be attracted there both by the ready availability of research professionals and by fiscal incentives, which until recently were quite generous. Basic research by US firms in Canada appears to be very tightly integrated in the sense that foreign-owned laboratories in Canada make little use of local sources of information. They appear to be internal subcontractors, receiving information from, and supplying processed information back to, the US parent.

Perhaps the most interesting ownership difference concerns the Japanese – although these results need to be treated with caution because of the relatively small number of respondents involved (as indicated in chapter 6). Japanese firms appear to invest in R&D laboratories in the West in order to 'liaise' with 'research institutions' whereas Western investors in Japan appear to 'contract' with indigenous firms instead. Each appears to be motivated by a desire to retain (or regain) technological leadership, but the Japanese perceive informal links with research institutions as the appropriate way to access technology, whereas Western firms rely on corporate partners instead. This may partly reflect cultural attitudes to learning, and also an objective assessment of the kinds of institution where basic research strengths lie. Another factor may be that Western firms are obliged to find Japanese partners to access the Japanese market, and find it easiest to remain with these partners so far as access to new technology is concerned.

So far as cultural differences are concerned, it seems that Japanese 'loyalty to the firm' is location-specific rather than ownership-specific, in the sense that Western investors in Japan can benefit from the loyalty of their scientific employees whereas Japanese investors have so far failed to elicit similar loyalty from scientists in the West.

Overall, the relative insignificance of location and ownership factors means that the results obtained using simple cross-tabulations, which were reported in chapter 6, stand unchanged. The regression analysis identifies only a few refinements to the picture presented earlier. This conclusion also applies to industry factors. Although industry factors are sometimes quite significant, it is the same fundamental distinctions – between high-technology industries and low-technology industries and, within the high-technology sector, between pharmaceuticals and the rest – that emerge as important.

When location-, ownership- and industry-specific factors are stripped away, it is just the laboratory-specific factors that remain. Residuals analysis indicates that the key laboratory-specific factor is whether basic research is carried out or not. Laboratories undertaking basic research have been located with the *quality* of local personnel in mind, and are tightly integrated with others, whereas those oriented to technical support are located more with the *cost* of local personnel in mind, and are integrated into local production and marketing instead. But while the distinction between basic and applied research is important, the distinction between product and process development seems to be of little significance in connection with overseas laboratories.

8

A Review of Recent Trends

8.1 INTRODUCTION

This chapter examines current trends in R&D from the perspective of both the parent and the subsidiary. It is based on the analysis of the responses to open-ended questions about recent and anticipated changes in the direction and organization of research within the firm. Several questions of this nature were included in both the parent and subsidiary questionnaires. Only a minority of respondents bothered to answer these questions. Those that did so either amplified their answers to earlier questions, or directed attention to additional topics they believed should have been covered. Some of the responses were clearly designed to persuade rather than inform, but most respondents seemed quite genuinely to strive for a degree of objectivity.

Because of the modest number of responses it cannot be claimed that the results are representative. But the fact that the respondents took the trouble to write – occasionally at length – about these issues indicates that they were perceived as crucial by at least a subset of firms. Most of the responses fall into clearly defined categories, and these categories form the basis for the tabulations below. The results are reported separately for headquarters and overseas laboratories. They are also classified by laboratory location – the four-way classification includes UK, US, Europe (including Scandinavia, Switzerland and Austria) and elsewhere (principally Japan, Australia and Brazil). The results for headquarters and subsidiaries are broadly consistent. But whereas headquarters respondents tended to concentrate on questions of changing corporate philosophy, the subsidiaries focused on frustrations about host government policies.

The interpretation of the written responses has been facilitated by 27 interviews with a subset of the respondents. Interviews were concentrated on firms which appeared to have relatively sophisticated strategies, provided intriguing written responses, or were statistical 'outliers'. Their views, though probably unrepresentative, were nevertheless extremely helpful in clarifying what lay behind some of the general concerns and anxieties expressed by other firms.

8.2 THE CHANGING SCOPE OF CORPORATE R&D

Tables 8.1 and 8.2 indicate a significant trend for corporate R&D to become more applied – there is less 'R' and more 'D', as many respondents put it. This trend is stronger in some cases than in others.

Headquarters laboratories in the US have undergone major changes in this respect. Post-war, some of these laboratories became major institutions for fundamental research. In the 1980s their roles have often been redefined to encourage more active support of product development in the companies' operating divisions.

The same trend is apparent in the headquarters laboratories of UK and European firms. But in some other countries – notably Japan and Brazil – the movement has been the other way. There is now a greater emphasis on fundamental research and less on applied. Leading Japanese firms are now establishing corporate research institutes on the US model to complement the factory-based development work on which they have traditionally relied. There seems, therefore, to be a convergence of R&D practice: the fundamentally-oriented Western firms are becoming more applied, and the applied-oriented Japanese firms more fundamental. This is consistent with the result noted in chapter 7, that Western firms are investing in Japan to gain access to Japanese *corporate* know-how, while Japanese firms are investing in the West to gain access to institutions of fundamental research. Firms in newly industrializing countries such as Brazil are following a similar path to the Japanese, but have not yet reached the stage of establishing foreign subsidiaries in the West. Most of the upgrading of work in these countries so far is concerned with the work of foreign-owned subsidiaries there.

So far as respondents to the questionnaire were concerned,

Table 8.1 Current trends in R&D reported by headquarters respondents

	Location of laboratory				
	Total	UK	US	Europe	Other
Scope of R&D					
To fundamental from applied	12	2	5	1	4
To applied from fundamental	20	5	13	2	0
To applied from technical support	3	0	3	0	0
To technical support from applied	2	0	1	1	0
More diversified	14	5	7	2	0
More focused	6	1	2	2	1
Closer to customer	12	3	7	2	0
Closer to producer	3	0	2	1	0
More emphasis on quality	0	0	0	0	0
More 'full length'	1	0	0	0	1
External relations					
More university links	2	0	1	1	0
Fewer university links	0	0	0	0	0
More use of external contractors	0	0	0	0	0
Expansion of external contract work	1	0	1	0	0
More 'turnkey' work	1	0	0	1	0
Nature of work					
More multi-disciplinary projects	3	1	1	1	0
New techniques in R&D itself	3	1	2	0	0
Shorter development cycles	2	0	2	0	0

there were no statistically significant differences between US and Japanese parent firms in the propensity to undertake basic or applied research, or to focus on product as opposed to process development (see table 7.2). This contrasts with other studies (Mansfield, 1988; Rosenberg and Steinmueller, 1988) which suggest that Japanese firms are more inclined than their US counterparts to emphasize 'D' rather than 'R', and to focus 'D' on process- rather than product-related work. Since these studies are

Table 8.2 Current trends in R&D reported by foreign subsidiary respondents

| | Total | Location of laboratory | | | |
		UK	US	Europe	Other
Scope of R&D					
To fundamental from applied	14	3	8	2	1
To applied from fundamental	22	8	8	4	2
To applied from technical support	2	1	0	1	0
To technical support from applied	2	1	0	1	0
More diversified	13	3	8	0	2
More focused	5	1	2	1	1
Closer to customer	10	5	4	1	0
Closer to producer	5	2	1	2	0
More emphasis on quality	4	1	2	1	0
More 'full length'	3	0	3	0	0
External relations					
More university links	3	0	2	1	0
Fewer university links	1	0	1	0	0
More use of external contractors	1	1	0	0	0
Expansion of external contract work	5	1	3	0	1
More 'turnkey' work	0	0	0	0	0
Nature of work					
More multi-disciplinary projects	0	0	0	0	0
New techniques in R&D itself	7	2	3	2	0
Shorter development cycles	2	1	1	0	0

retrospective views of the 1970s and 1980s, comparison with the questionnaire results for 1989 suggests that the process of convergence may well now be complete. It is probable, though, that this is true of only the very largest firms, of the kind included in our study. The legacy of the past may still be significant in small and medium-sized parent firms.

While differences between parents may be limited, however, the traditional strength of the US in fundamental corporate research is reflected in the response of foreign subsidiaries. Although US overseas affiliates are becoming increasingly applications-oriented, like their headquarters, foreign subsidiaries in the US are not. In the 1980s European and Japanese investors attracted to the US by the size of the market and the advantages of local product development appear to have reoriented some of their acquisitions to do more fundamental research for the group as a whole. In doing so they have made good use of the US science base, which offers a wide range of specialized skills (albeit at relatively high wage rates). Thus while the transition to applied research remains valid at the corporate level, within some European and Japanese corporations there is a trend to locate certain fundamental aspects of research in the US.

There is a trend for R&D to become more diversified – especially in laboratories located in the US and UK. On the face of it this is somewhat surprising. Current thinking in corporate strategy suggests that firms would have become more focused instead. But only a small number of respondents indicated that such was the case.

Part of the answer seems to lie in the new cross-disciplinary linkages being invoked to solve research problems – for example, the synthesis of biochemistry and advanced computing in molecular modelling. The fact that *line of business* is becoming increasingly focused is perfectly compatible with the fact that *research competence* is becoming more broadly based. This trend to broader research competence is also linked to the emergence of more loosely coordinated teams within the 'network firm' (Chesnais, 1988, 1990).

Another part of the explanation for the diversification of research competence may be the need to redeploy researchers in mature industries such as steel and heavy chemicals. In some industries there is also a need to integrate backwards into new sources of supply – for example, to investigate the use of wood in place of oil within the energy sector.

Finally, part of the explanation may lie in the difference between growing and declining firms. Growth-oriented firms are concerned to explore the full commercial potential of their core technology. They have a new method or technique which is in search of problems to solve, and this leads them to a diversified programme of research. Research becomes diversified because they are following the logic of the 'scope economies' inherent in general scientific knowledge. While they are focused in terms of scientific thought, therefore, they are diversified in terms of applications.

Declining firms, on the other hand, have typically abandoned fundamental research as too costly, too high risk and too long term. They lack secure funding and cannot cope with the difficult managerial judgements involved. They are 'sticking to the knitting' in terms of a narrow range of applications for which they know a market already exists. It seems to be the minority of declining firms that report that they have become more focused. (One reason that they may appear as only a small minority is that responses are somewhat biased towards the more successful firms.)

Another characteristic of the successful firms with diversified R&D seems to be a trend towards strengthening university links. This is hardly surprising, given the more fundamental nature of their research and the difficulty of managing a diversified programme without external assistance. Several Japanese firms have recently set up basic research laboratories in UK university science parks, for example. One UK-based laboratory reported increased use of external contractors generally.

It is interesting to note, though, that few managers referred to universities as a source of imaginative new ideas. They were perceived rather as a source of highly specific technical competencies, which could be used to break bottlenecks or overcome particular stumbling blocks. This applied not just to basic research, moreover, but often to process research as well. There is evidence that many corporate R&D managers preferred to do long-range speculative thinking for themselves.

A characteristic of declining firms is the expansion of work as an external contractor. While several successful firms indicated that they achieved fuller ultilization of expensive facilities (such as engine test-beds) by renting them out to other firms, the future of these laboratories clearly did not rest on selling their general scientific expertise on the open market. In an expanding firm there are plenty of internal demands for new product development to keep the research staff fully occupied. The renting out of equipment is simply a reflection of the high cost of operating (and depreciating) the most sophisticated equipment available. But in a declining firm the laboratory may well lose internal custom for product development and so be forced to sell its services outside if it is to survive. One manager in this position expressed the view that offering to consult for more sophisticated firms in related areas was a good way of getting ideas and finding out what potential rivals were up to. What benefit his customers derived from his company's advice is difficult to say!

Across the board there was a strong feeling that researchers needed to 'get closer to the customer'. In practice this seems to mean better liaison with the marketing department, greater participation in pre-market testing, and more involvement with the launch and post-launch warranty problems. When the firm has a small number of major customers it can also mean more involvement in customized design, and closer liaison with researchers and production managers in the customer institution.

There was much less enthusiasm for getting closer to the producer. Many of the R&D managers interviewed feared day-to-day involvement with fire-fighting production problems. Only five per cent or so of such incidents raised any serious issue about plant design, claimed one manager – the inference being that the usual cause was inadequate training of production workers. It should be added that the comment came from a UK-based laboratory; it is rather doubtful whether a similar comment would be made in Japan. It was also suggested that close involvement with production encouraged the static and unimaginative attitude that the *status quo* in production technology was the natural state of affairs. In several cases the laboratory had recently moved to get away from the local production site. Other plants were often suspicious that the laboratory gave superior technical support to its local plant, and this soured relations within the firm. Removing the laboratory from a plant site could therefore help the laboratory to 'get closer' to other plants in the group.

Several laboratories reported that they had undergone considerable changes in methods of research. The main factor was advances in computing. These included the use of computer models in place of physical simulations, a related change from analogue to digital computing, and the coordination of researchers through networked work-stations accessing a common core of data. In the pharmaceutical industry genetic engineering techniques had become very important too.

Other trends reported include a greater emphasis on the quality of research (presumably a spin-off from current trends in general management thinking) and greater use of multi-disciplinary research teams. Some firms noted that they now took 'full-length' responsibility for research projects, seeing things through from start (initial concept) to finish (post-innovation performance), rather than concentrating on just product development. Firms in the electronics industry reported a striking shortening of product development cycles from 18 months or more to a mere 12 months. This reflected an accelerating pace of innovation, with a high frequency of incremental product up-grading. Pharmaceutical firms, on the other hand, were concerned that if their development cycles grew any longer there would be insufficient time to appropriate monopoly rents before their patents expired.

8.3 TRENDS IN ORGANIZATIONAL STRUCTURE

There is a continuing debate in the organization of R&D between those who favour putting all R&D into the operating divisions to ensure its practical relevance, and those who favour a separate central facility which is detached from operational pressures and can take a long-term strategic view. This debate surfaced in the

US chemical conglomerate Du Pont as early as 1902 (Hounshell and Smith, 1988).

The argument in favour of a central laboratory is strengthened if it can be linked to other central services which provide complementary strategic inputs in marketing and finance. In one reported case, the central laboratory itself was involved in business and economic forecasting, while in another the director of the laboratory advised the main board on acquisitions.

The disadvantage of the central laboratory is that it can be 'hijacked' by an academically oriented scientific élite. The danger is mitigated in some laboratories by giving scientists up to 10 per cent 'playtime' during which they can carry on their own private projects. Many central laboratories also encourage publication, though crucial measurements (such as the temperature of chemical processes) are usually withheld. The existence of a central laboratory also creates a problem of multiple allegiance in the division laboratories, whose heads need to report both to the head of the central laboratory and the head of their own division. Such problems can arise even in the absence of a central laboratory, but they can be more difficult to resolve if the senior R&D director is the head of a central laboratory which he regards as his 'home constituency'.

The 1980s was a difficult decade for managers who wished to defend the central laboratory's prerogative to conduct pure research. They had to rebuff both the threat of closure, and the threat of 'capture' by the divisions, who would redeploy them to development work.

In practice, though, compromise solutions were possible. In many growing firms fundamental research was distributed among all the major laboratories in the group on the basis of merit. The central facility then became just another facility within an international network of laboratories of equal status. The only distinguishing feature of the central laboratory that remains is that it handles particularly difficult scientific problems referred to it by the other laboratories. Its staff are typically better qualified, and represent a greater diversity of professional specialisms than others.

In a very large firm only a proportion of the laboratories may be members of the network. The formation of a network is sometimes associated with the downgrading of certain laboratories to carry out only local production or marketing support. This top-down rationalization of research was quite prominent in the 1960s and 1970s, but seems to have become less common recently, though. Modern research methods frequently allow sub-problems – such as the writing of special software – to be subcontracted to almost any laboratory where capable scientists are employed. Thus research laboratories in developing countries can still do important work even though they may be short of sophisticated hardware. Laboratories in India and Brazil, which employ highly educated scientists, need no longer be peripheral to global research. The trend seems to be for networks to be extended to include many more of the laboratories within a group.

In several companies there were two dominant laboratories – one in Europe and one in the US. The most interesting case is where the US laboratory has been recently acquired by a European firm. There is anecdotal evidence that some European managers have difficulty influencing their US counterparts. It is claimed (rightly or wrongly) that they behave as if they were superior to, rather than formally subordinate to, the European management.

A more extreme form of network is to constitute the central laboratory as a profit centre rather than a cost centre, and relegate it formally to a consulting role. The laboratory receives only a proportion of funds from the group as a whole – say 25 per cent – and relies on 'internal sponsorship' for the rest. This 'customer-contractor' principle requires the laboratory managers to go out and sell their services within the group. In a declining group, internal sales may be unsuccessful, and the laboratory may then move to external contracts to maintain its viability (see earlier). In some instances the development of a large external customer base has led to consideration of a management buy-out by the scientific staff.

The network principle may also extend to laboratories that are not wholly owned by the group. The networking of joint venture partnerships has become quite fashionable in the 1980s (Contractor and Lorange, 1988). Joint ventures allow a firm with limited capital and managerial capacity to extend the scope of its influence very markedly provided it is willing to sacrifice formal control. When the individual partners are much smaller than the core firm then loss of control need cause little concern, however. The joint venture approach is sufficiently flexible that it can be extended to include non-profit research associations as well as ordinary private firms.

Table 8.3 indicates that while networking is very much the dominant trend, many headquarters managers retain the view that some degree of hierarchy between central and divisional laboratories is essential. The reorganization of the central laboratory as a consultancy involves some firms in the UK and Europe but very few, it would seem, in the US. The evolution of headquarters into a nexus of joint venture partnerships is even more of a minority trend, it would seem. Our sample is, however, too small to draw any firm conclusions. But interview evidence suggests that inter-firm collaboration in R&D is still viewed with suspicion in many firms.

The foreign subsidiaries' perspective on organizational change is shown in table 8.4. The trend towards networking is confirmed by the strong movement towards greater interdependence within group research. The interdependence applies to interactions with both headquarters and other subsidiary laboratories. The trend towards more formal mandating of subsidiaries for global or

Table 8.3 Trends in organization structure perceived by headquarters respondents

		Location of laboratory		
	Total	UK	US	Europe	Other
Maintenance of hierarchy	18	7	5	4	2
Development of network	24	8	10	5	1
Reorganization as consultancy	6	2	0	3	1
Nexus of partnerships	2	0	1	1	0

Table 8.4 Trends in organization structure perceived by subsidiary respondents

	Location of laboratory				
	Total	*UK*	*US*	*Europe*	*Other*
Greater interdependence with other laboratories					
Without special mandate	16	1	10	1	4
With special mandate	7	4	2	1	0
Greater independence	4	2	1	1	0
Greater subordination	0	0	0	0	0

regional product development is more limited. One Canadian subsidiary of a US firm specifically complained that mandating was inflexible. Because of government pressures, products developed in Canada had to be first produced in Canada, even though Canada was not a good production site. The linking of research to production in government-imposed mandating may actually work against the interests of a laboratory, it was claimed. Research that the laboratory is well qualified to do may be done elsewhere because the parent firm does not wish to be tied to subsequent production in the country concerned.

A few managers said they expected their laboratories to achieve greater independence. These laboratories seemed to belong to firms where hierarchical coordination was still in use. Independence was seen as a way of achieving self-sufficiency in fundamental research, so that headquarters would simply leave them to get on with their projects alone.

8.4 THE PRACTICE OF R&D MANAGEMENT – EVIDENCE FROM INTERVIEWS

R&D strategies seem to be in a continual state of flux. Several respondents referred to cycles in which the emphasis of research shifted from pure to applied, from upstream problems of supply shortage to downstream problems of product innovation, and so on. Some reported that their laboratories had seen 'massive' changes – surviving only because of the flexibility of their employees.

An increasing impact of social concerns was evident. Tobacco firms were preoccupied with researching into the links between smoking and health, cement firms were investigating ways of extracting gravel with minimal environmental damage, food laboratories were working on the reduction of fat content and the elimination of additives, while information technology specialists were researching the impact of computer networks on the social organization of groups. Other problems that engaged researchers included combating food poisoning in supermarkets, preventing sabotage in chemical plants and developing protocols for dealing with HIV infection among production line workers in the food and pharmaceutical industries. In some cases the research on these issues was perceived negatively – as an additional cost and as a distraction from more interesting lines of work. In other cases they were seen as providing profitable opportunities for the innovation of safer or 'friendlier' products.

A number of laboratories had been bought and sold several times, as a result of mergers, acquisitions, divestments and buyouts. One manager indicated that his laboratory had been sold four times since he had worked there, and that it was currently up for sale again. Subsequently, it was bought and then resold again within a month.

The immediate cause of many of these changes was the financial position of the company. A minority of managers felt reasonably secure. Hitachi R&D in the US, for example, is governed by the philosophy that 'though we cannot live one hundred years, we should be concerned about one thousand years hence'. At least, that is the company's official line, and it is one that is corroborated by the evidence on the stability of Japanese R&D expenditure growth reported in chapter 1. Managers of US- and UK-owned laboratories do not seem so assured. 'R&D is the first to be cut back – it's a soft target' was a common complaint. Cutbacks were expected not only in times of exigency, however, but whenever a bid for the company was in the offing. Laboratory managers clearly believe that short-termism in equity markets makes general management nervous about over-investing in prestigious long-term R&D.

In the pharmaceutical industry funding can be particularly volatile. Even large companies often derive a substantial proportion of their profits from a single product – and the profit flow can dry up completely once the patent expires. The funding of R&D as a fixed percentage of sales, noted in chapter 7, can only increase anxieties in such a case. Following the Beecham-Smith Kline merger, a further wave of mergers was confidently predicted – not all of which, it was suggested, would succeed. A shake-out of the less successful laboratories seems to be anticipated in the industry.

Notwithstanding these difficulties, morale in many of the laboratories we visited seemed quite high. Some subsidiary managers were keen to explain the devices they used to hide away reserves. New equipment was ordered in advance of requirements when profits were high, and budget restrictions were consequently lax, and replacements deferred when times were hard. Most R&D managers, like their counterparts in general management, had invested considerable effort in learning how to 'play the system'.

Short-termism is not confined to capital markets, according to our interviewees. Marketing executives too have short time horizons, and these are difficult to reconcile with the planning cycle in R&D. Because they lack scientific training, marketing executives are inclined to ask for the impossible – and to want delivery by the end of the week. One company has attempted to solve this problem by a promotional spiral, in which managers alternate between posts in marketing and research. Managers following one another up this spiral normally face an opposite number who has had experience doing their sort of job.

A consequence of putting researchers onto a general management track, however, is that they are removed completely from the laboratory bench. The majority of managers interviewed were scientists who had begun their career at the bench (often with the same company) and had then moved onto the management track. It was fairly unusual to find a non-scientist managing R&D. Some interviewees claimed that a non-scientist could not do their job at all because he could not win peer group respect.

Scientists who do not move onto the management track often

face a dead end so far as pay, prestige and power are concerned. There seems to be a widespread view among senior managers – at least in the UK – that scientists are motivated by the enjoyment of work and involvement in the local community, rather than by pay. They are seen as risk-averse individuals who like to remain close to the major agglomerations of laboratories, so that if they need to change jobs to advance their career they can do so without moving far. They are also believed to be relatively immobile, so far as overseas secondment is concerned, once they enter early middle age. According to this stereotype, mobility is characteristic only of junior scientific staff.

To improve the career prospects of the dedicated scientist, one UK firm had instituted a competitive scheme for high-profile research fellowships tenable at any of the company's laboratories. This can take respected research professionals outside the conventional hierarchy of pay and authority. Another company had turned down a similar scheme, and the manager concerned believed that some of his key scientists would leave to take up university professorships as a result.

Most of the R&D managers we interviewed clearly belonged to the 'human relations' school of personnel management. Researchers had to be trusted to get the best out of them, it was claimed, and anyone who could not be trusted should not be employed at all. One manager likened his job to that of managing a football team (he was referring to the Liverpool team, it should be noted). Most managers were also familiar with business strategy concepts such as first-mover advantage, niche marketing and fit (see chapter 2). The only striking weakness was that few had a clear strategy regarding technology licensing. 'Never license your technology unless you have something better in the pipeline' was the only coherent strategy we were told about. The main impression was that licences are often *ad hoc* agreements negotiated at board level, with limited consultation with R&D. On the whole it would seem that licences, joint ventures and other formal kinds of external collaboration are top down initiatives which are disliked by practitioners of R&D.

Overall, though, the research managers we met were extremely self-confident individuals who seemed to combine the roles of technologist and intrapreneur quite successfully. They claimed to have a good awareness of what research rival firms were engaged in. Indeed, they seemed to share information with their opposite numbers fairly freely, in terms of the kind of work going on. While patent races were a recognized feature of certain industries, everyone seemed to have a good idea of who was in the race and whether it was going to be a tight finish or not.

Despite this strong competitive element, though, there was a widespread view that it was unethical to poach staff, either to disrupt a rival's project or to learn secrets from him or her. Indeed, it was claimed that new recruits would not expect to be systematically debriefed on their former employer's operations. Conversely, people who were about to leave would not be ostracized or have their security clearance reduced. This is very different from the way that professional staff are handled in, for instance, international banking.

Underlying this ethical view was, apparently, a view that 'tit for tat' response was likely. A firm that head-hunted key personnel to disrupt a rival's research would find its own staff poached in return. It is even possible that the leading firms might conspire to punish a deviant firm by excluding it from the informal information network. Objective evidence for the existence of a strong informal network within the UK comes from the coherence of collective lobbying over issues such as patent lifetime and government funding of basic R&D, and the existence of some quite lively inter-firm cooperative research programmes.

Research managers do not customarily enjoy a high profile so far as the financial press is concerned. Nevertheless, our interviews suggest that the decisions these managers make are often crucial for the long-run profitability of the firm. These decisions are subtle and complex, and often involve technical matters on which laypeople cannot easily judge. But what can be judged is the way that the most successful managers combine their scientific knowledge with a grasp of financial issues and an intuitive feeling for personnel management. However competent the manager, though, it is always possible for him or her to be marginalized because of prejudices against technology or long-term thinking at the highest levels of the firm. Firms which tend to marginalize

Table 8.5 Changes in government policy desired by foreign subsidiary respondents

	Total	UK	US	Europe	Other
		Location of laboratory			
Reduced regulation					
General reduction	6	0	5	1	0
Faster decision making	3	2	0	1	0
In social matters: relaxed reporting requirements in					
Product safety and premarket testing	3	0	2	0	1
Occupational safety	2	0	2	0	0
Animal experiments	2	1	0	0	1
Environment	3	0	1	1	1
In industrial policy					
Fewer antitrust restrictions on collaborative R&D	1	0	1	0	0
Less pressure for global mandating of subsidiaries	1	0	0	0	1
Less restriction on commercial-ization of spin-offs from government funded R&D	1	0	1	0	0
Less restriction on export of key technologies	2	0	2	0	0
In marketing policy					
More flexibility over pricing	1	0	0	1	0
Abolish 'limited list' for prescriptions	2	2	0	0	0
Improvement of education and science base					
Increased support for university centres of excellence	3	2	0	0	1
More joint fellowships, studentships, etc.	3	2	0	0	1
More science graduates	2	2	0	0	0
Improve social status of engineering	1	1	0	0	0
Improved labour mobility through easier immigration of research professionals	2	0	1	1	0

Source: Questionnaire.

R&D in this way will find it difficult to retain the most able staff, and so they will finish up with the quality of R&D management they deserve. Conceivably the performance of R&D management is one of the 'hidden factors' which can explain – perhaps better than competitive strategy – the comparative long-run growth and profitability of high-technology firms.

An important point that emerged from the comparison of the UK and overseas interviews was that it was more common to find the 'R&D culture' permeating the whole firm in the US and EC than in the UK. It was in North America that we met the president of the company rather than the R&D manager because the president considered himself the executive in charge of R&D. Senior management in his company was dominated by engineers, who sold the products to other engineers who managed procurement in the client companies. Other evidence suggests that this engineering culture is fairly common among US, German and Scandinavian parent firms. We encountered no instance of it in parents or subsidiaries in the UK.

8.5 GOVERNMENT POLICY

Headquarters respondents had relatively little to say about government policy – perhaps because their concerns were global rather than national, or perhaps because they were simply out of touch with the frustrations of managing a foreign-owned subsidiary in an alien environment. Subsidiary respondents, on the other hand, had quite a lot to say. Their views are summarized in table 8.5.

The popular view of the US as a deregulated economy takes a sharp knock. Foreign investors complain about the amount of form-filling involved in US operations, particularly in dealing with social matters. It is the Federal agencies which are most to blame. The Food and Drug Administration, for example, is considered unnecessarily stringent in its requirements for pre-market testing. The cost of drug trials, for example, can be up to ten times the cost of drug discovery and development. Bureaucratic demands absorb resources that could better be employed elsewhere. Occupational safety reporting requirements are also perceived as relatively stringent in the US.

Industrial policy too is problematic in the US. Antitrust measures are claimed to deter cooperative R&D with other firms. The commercialization of spin-off from government contracts is unduly inhibited, it is claimed; enforced delays in patenting inventions, and restrictions on the intra-firm export of technology should be eliminated.

Both Switzerland and the US are perceived as inflexible over the immigration of foreign research workers.

The UK is believed by some to have a too-strict policy on animal experiments but is perceived as fairly liberal over environmental issues. (Whether this policy stance is regarded as satisfactory or problematic will not be considered here.)

Two pharmaceutical subsidiaries in the UK expressed concern about the 'limited list' – the reduction in the number of proprietary medicines which doctors are able to prescribe to National Health Service patients, and the consequent switch of government-funded demand to generic products. A related concern over pricing restrictions was expressed by a pharmaceutical subsidiary in Belgium.

Managers of subsidiaries expressed concern over the future of the education system in the UK, and the erosion of the science base. It is worth noting that no complaints of a similar nature were made in the US or elsewhere in Europe. Two firms called for increased support for university centres of excellence, and two for more joint research posts – and in particular the expansion of CASE (Collaborative Awards in Science and Engineering) scholarships. There was also a call for increased output of graduate scientists and an improvement in the social status of engineers (from a firm in the office equipment industry). It is also worth noting that in interviews, and at our preliminary conference, several research managers were emphatic on these points. Clearly the respondents were aware that they were telling academic researchers what they wanted to hear. But it is evident that they have been making the same points, quite independently, to government too.

8.6 GOVERNMENT FUNDING

Strong views were also expressed on funding issues, as indicated in table 8.6. Unlike the previous responses, these were expressions of hopes and fears, rather than reports on actual developments. As might be expected, respondents were generally in favour of more government funding for R&D, though there were differences of opinion as to how this should be done.

There was a widespread view – particularly in continental Europe – that government should increase its funding for fundamental and high-risk research in the corporate sector. This would effectively subsidize long-term projects whose returns were difficult to quantify. The precise rationale for this view was not clear, however. It could reflect a belief that private returns from such projects are difficult to appropriate compared to the social

Table 8.6   Fiscal changes desired by foreign subsidiary respondents

	Location of laboratory				
	Total	UK	US	Europe	Other
More grants					
for fundamental or highly innovative research	12	3	3	6	0
for private research generally	11	4	1	4	2
for cooperative research	6	3	2	0	1
More funding for specific projects					
defined by company	2	0	1	0	1
competitive bidding for projects defined by government	4	1	3	0	0
Tax incentives					
tax credits for R&D	10	2	5	0	3
lower corporate income tax	1	0	0	1	0
soft loans	1	0	0	1	0

Source: Questionnaire.

benefits conferred (an externality argument) or that the government's obligation to future generations implied a lower rate of discount than management's obligations to its shareholders.

Some respondents sought more funding for corporate research of all kinds, while others suggested that existing schemes to promote cooperative research (within the European community, for example) should be expanded. On the other hand, one UK respondent claimed that government discrimination in favour of cooperative research meant that his laboratory could no longer use government funding because of the threat to secrecy.

Several US-based laboratories favoured an expansion of Federal projects put out to competitive bidding. Another respondent complained, however, that such projects were always awarded to 'Beltway Bandits' – politically-networked firms that specialized in winning contracts but had no coherent research strategy of their own. This sceptical view was shared by several interviewees, who were adamant that government was a very poor judge of the kind of fundamental research that needed to be done. Instead of special projects, they favoured general incentives such as tax credits.

Tax credits on R&D expenditure seem very popular – they are a familiar fiscal instrument which subsidizes R&D but leaves the corporation free to decide what research to do. Foreign subsidiaries in Australia seemed very impressed with the commonwealth government's use of tax credits (though they were less impressed by the tight environmental restrictions imposed by some state legislatures). If the case for R&D subsidies is accepted by government, then tax credits seem to provide a simple and acceptable mechanism for implementing them.

8.7   SUMMARY

R&D management is one of the most difficult and sophisticated areas of management, yet it is one that has until recently received only limited attention from academics – a rather paradoxical situation, given that many academics are themselves intimately involved in the management of (not-for-profit) research. This deficiency is now being remedied though (Gomes-Mejia and Lawless, 1988; Khalil and Bayraktar, 1990; Loveridge, 1990).

R&D management involves very long-term imaginative thinking, since technologies not only take a long time to implement but in the case of fundamental research their very feasibility is often uncertain. The teaming up of highly individualistic creative thinkers with different professional backgrounds, which is important in the most ambitious research, is an extremely difficult task. The coordination of such activity on a global basis is thus one of the most challenging tasks in modern management.

Some corporate cultures are clearly better adapted to supporting R&D management than others. In particular short-term preoccupation with the firm's equity valuation – reflecting continuing anxiety about takeovers – is believed by many research managers to induce instability in research funding and a lack of commitment to long-term goals such as steady corporate growth.

Over the past decade research managers have faced a number of important challenges – the questioning of the commercial viability of corporate funding of basic research, and the consequent undermining of the authority of the central laboratory, the changing nature of the technology of R&D itself – in particular the building of group research around networked computer systems rather than face-to-face contact – and increasing accountability to a public worried about some of the health and environmental hazards caused by the commercial exploitation of science. Research managers have responded to the concerns of the stock market by getting closer to the customer and accepting greater responsibility for seeing an innovation right through from the drawing board into the customer's hands. They are responding to new technological opportunities by using information technology to establish closer working relationships between distant research teams, and to public opinion by reorienting some of their research to produce more environmentally friendly products.

Research managers believe that government should support fundamental research through university funding and inter-firm cooperation, but leave the technological experts to decide exactly which are the most promising lines of inquiry. R&D is best supported financially through a system of tax credits, they believe.

9

Summary and Conclusions

9.1 THE ROLE OF R&D IN CORPORATE INNOVATION: AN OVERVIEW

Overall, the story of globalized R&D is the story of a fairly small number of very large firms carrying out research in a small number of leading industrialized countries. Few of these firms are UK-owned, although UK ownership of overseas laboratories is quite significant in relation to the size of the UK economy as a whole. A very significant number of large multinationals have laboratories in the UK, however. One industry – pharmaceuticals – dominates global R&D in terms of a combination of the length of R&D projects, the ratio of R&D expenditure to sales and the decentralization of research, although other industries, such as office equipment, scientific instruments and aircraft are also significant in some of these respects.

R&D is much more technology-driven than the business strategy literature suggests. The quality of R&D is probably the key determinant of long-run performance in high-technology industries. As such, it has received less attention than it deserves from academic specialists.

On close examination, R&D is a collection of interdependent activities. Just as R&D interacts with other major functional areas, such as marketing and production, so R&D itself comprises a set of subsidiary areas which interact with each other. These range from basic research at one extreme to technical support on the other. Between these limits lie the development of new products and processes and their adaptation to local environments.

The initial stage of development often produces a generic concept which has a number of different applications. Each generic can therefore lead to a number of variants, each of which is particularly suited to some subset of local markets or production locations.

A distinctive generic, which has applications outside the firm's traditional fields of operation, can stimulate diversification. A chance discovery can also pull a firm into diversification as it follows up the spin-off involved. A firm may also be pushed into diversification because of stagnation in its major markets, or because the entry of new low-cost producers has intensified competition in them.

Some of the constituent activities can, in principle, be subcontracted to independent institutions. Economies of internalizing information flow normally discourage this, but certain activities such as basic research or diversification research are more readily separable than others, it would seem. Basic research is sometimes carried out in liaison with universities or independent research institutions, while both basic research and diversification research sometimes involve joint venture collaboration.

On the whole, inter-firm collaboration is not popular with laboratory managers, though. In practice, it would seem, collaboration is often promoted by a top down board-level initiative. The idea of 'strategic alliances' with technologically sophisticated partners is much more popular at board level than it is with laboratory managers. Laboratory managers have their own informal networks, and their own methods of evaluating prospective partners based on peer group status. There seems to be a good deal of informal collaboration, in terms of collective lobbying and avoidance of duplicated effort, which goes entirely unrecorded. It is quite possible that this bottom-up informal collaboration is potentially much more effective than the formal top down variety.

Laboratory managers also take only a limited interest in licensing strategy. On the whole, they prefer to license out a technology only when there is a better one in the pipeline. They are not particularly keen to license other firms' technologies either, except when there is a serious problem to be overcome. This is a variant of the well-known 'not invented here' syndrome.

The greatest interest in inter-firm collaboration relates to the improvement of vertical linkages. Developing innovative capabilities in subcontractors through joint R&D is one of the possibilities raised. At the other end of the chain, intermediate product suppliers and capital goods suppliers are prepared to contemplate joint R&D with their major business customers. There is little evidence, however, of enthusiasm for collaboration with firms operating at a similar stage of production in a related field, even though, in theory, this would help to broaden the firm's core competencies and avoid duplication of effort.

9.2 THE RESTRUCTURING OF R&D

R&D management has witnessed major upheavals in many firms in recent years. Much of this stems – either directly or indirectly – from their declining competitiveness. While in the long run R&D strategies determine performance, in the short run corporate profitability dictates the size of the R&D budget and the speed with which pay-offs are required by the board.

Western firms have undergone a good deal of self-examination by management – and external examination by institutional shareholders – over the last decade. Corporate self-diagnosis has mainly concentrated on the problem of poor value for money in basic research. Many research managers seem reluctant to admit that they do any basic research, even in technologically sophisticated industries. The key points that emerge are:

1 Basic research is easily hijacked by scientists who are more concerned with academic approval than with financial returns. By striving to please their academic peers, they duplicate the kind of work that is best left to universities, and neglect the kind of work that industry requires. Central laboratories, divorced from operating divisions, are particularly prone to 'pure' research of this kind.

2 A related problem is that basic research too easily gets stuck on

the drawing board because of an interest in technical perfection for its own sake. Basic researchers are too interested in quantum leaps in the state of the art, and too little concerned with continuous incremental improvement within existing paradigms. Senior managers often lack the technical expertise to determine which high-risk projects need to be killed off before they reach the very expensive development stage.

3 Many post-war growth industries have now matured technologically, and basic research is no longer as financially rewarding as it used to be.

Resources saved on basic research are now devoted to getting closer to the customer instead. The customer is perceived as increasingly sophisticated and demanding. In some consumer goods industries these demands express themselves directly in the market place, through increased awareness of the brands that offer high performance and reliability. In other cases they are mediated by governments through safety regulations, user pollution standards, and so on. Customers in capital goods industries such as engineering, or intermediate product industries such as aircraft or office equipment, are in any case more sophisticated, but because they too are subject to new competitive pressures they have passed these pressures onto their suppliers through the procurement process.

These tougher quality requirements mean that development costs at the final pre-market stage have increased considerably. Because development is more expensive than basic research, savings on basic research are insufficient to finance this extra expense. The net increase in costs has forced innovative firms to think in terms of larger markets. The idea that new innovations can trickle down from a small high-income market to a mass market as the product matures is no longer acceptable. Sophisticated modern customers are not prepared to help producers 'debug' expensive new products, for a start. The firm must concentrate its efforts on obtaining a quick return by launching on all major markets simultaneously. Because of the continuing need for information feedback from the market, firms are increasingly drawn to the major market places to complete their development work. The most important of these markets is the US. The European market will become increasingly attractive if economic integration maintains its momentum and the EC continues to enlarge, but cultural heterogeneity remains an obstacle to the development of truly European products (Stopford and Baden-Fuller, 1988).

While product development is drawn to major markets, basic research may remain attached to traditional centres of excellence. New centres of excellence may also emerge. Although a great deal of basic research remains concentrated on parent laboratories – particularly in US and Japanese firms – a significant amount is quite widely dispersed. Although the vast majority of overseas laboratories are geared mainly to adapting products and processes, and providing technical support for local plants, a number of them quite clearly have a strong orientation to basic research. Some of them are quite small – contrary to conventional academic opinion, economies of scale do not require the concentration of basic research on a single large laboratory except in one or two industries.

A basic research-oriented laboratory is quite likely to make a point of minimizing its links with local production and marketing units in order to concentrate on its research. Fire-fighting production problems is not, claimed several laboratory managers, a good source of ideas for basic research (though Japan is an exception – see below). The desire to eliminate technical support clearly indicates that research-oriented laboratories of efficient scale do not need to take on other activities in order to keep their specialists fully employed. Such aversion to technical support is also part of a more general phenomenon – even in firms that were very anxious to get closer to the customer, there was little enthusiasm for getting closer to the producer too.

Certain types of diversification and process development can also be conducted quite successfully at laboratories away from a major market, our evidence suggests. Although the managers of parent laboratories express a desire to control diversification research, the statistics suggest a significant tendency to carry it out overseas in certain industries. There is also evidence that process development benefits, like basic research, from university links, and also from access to local capital goods producers. The role of university links in process research seems to reflect the use of academics, not as fundamental thinkers, but as highly specialized consultants who can be called upon as and when desired.

9.3   THE ROLE OF JAPAN

Any discussion of the changing environment of R&D must recognize the importance of Japanese competition over the last two decades. As already noted, Japanese competition has reduced profitability in many Western industries and so dried up internal corporate funding for R&D. So at a time when Japanese firms are investing a steadily increasing proportion of their resources in R&D, their Western rivals are doing less – certainly at the basic level, though in some countries more is being done in product development than before.

The effects of this are all too clear from the patent statistics, which show that the Japanese have wrested technological leadership from the West in engines and motor vehicles, and now pose a serious challenge in office equipment and scientific instruments too.

The Japanese are noted for their incremental approach to innovation, in which successive small improvements are made as a result of bottom-up suggestions from the factory floor. The Japanese have overthrown conventional Western ideas of the product life cycle by tooling up for mass production at the outset and using 'learning by doing' to improve the product in the course of production. As indicated above, this has encouraged Western imitators to shorten their own product life cycles and invest in continuous product and process improvement.

Part of the price paid for this has been the downgrading of basic research. There is evidence, however, that the Japanese are now moving strongly towards basic long-term research and are establishing laboratories in the West not only to support product and process adaptation but to carry out more fundamental research as well. Although apparently averse to formal contracting out of research, the Japanese appear to be developing informal links with Western universities and independent research institutions. By contrast, Western firms in Japan are more inclined to seek out Japanese corporate partners. Partly this is because that is where much Japanese technology resides. By repute, corporate partnerships also help in getting official approval for new products and in locating suitable production premises. The cross-flows of R&D investments are therefore slightly different, but the net effect is to produce a convergence of R&D practice in Japan and the West, at least so far as the balance between basic research and development work is concerned.

9.4　COMPETITIVENESS OF THE UK ECONOMY

The overall competitiveness of the UK economy has aroused a good deal of controversy. Much of this has centred on the mismatch between productivity and real wages in the manufacturing sector as a cause of deindustrialization. A deindustrialized economy can, however, still be a wealthy one if there is a buoyant service sector, and if there are substantial profit remittances from abroad. R&D can contribute in both of these respects.

If R&D is considered, for the moment, as an activity quite distinct from the manufacturing activities with which it is associated then it is apparent that R&D is a service activity, rather like private education or entertainment, in the sense that highly skilled labour is used to generate an intangible output of considerable commercial value. If R&D were to expand at the expense of manufacturing then the country's command of technology might increase rather than decrease. There might also be substantial environmental benefits if manufacturing were carried out at less congested sites abroad. Whether or not the R&D was UK-owned, it would provide skilled employment in the UK. If it were UK-owned as well, its international exploitation would generate profit remittances from overseas production too.

The UK service sector appears, in general, to be more competitive than its manufacturing counterpart – statistics on exports of tourism and financial services certainly support this view. One reason may be a relatively low incidence of labour-management conflict, as reflected in strikes, etc. R&D too is generally immune from industrial relations problems – even though craft technicians are quite widely employed (see below). Concentration of employment on R&D can therefore be seen as part of a general strategy of strengthening an existing comparative advantage in service activity.

The idea that R&D can be divorced from manufacturing is, of course, contrived, but it is not entirely implausible. Basic research, as we have seen, may actually benefit from being geographically remote from manufacturing, and some diversification research may fall into this category too. Process research requires support from sophisticated equipment manufacturers, but not necessarily from proximity to a plant in the user industry itself. On this view, it is only selected high-technology capital goods industries that are important in supporting R&D. Deindustrialization in other industries may not be so important as it might seem. Thus the loss of indigenous capability in mechanical engineering might be a serious problem, but the loss of chemical plants or petroleum refineries may not be.

The major problem, it can be argued, is not in divorcing basic research from manufacturing but rather in divorcing product development from the mass market. In the past, the UK has been seen by US firms as a gateway to European (and some Middle Eastern and African) markets. Production subsidiaries have been established for this purpose, and in some cases technical support units were established which have subsequently evolved to undertake adaptive R&D. In other cases a new R&D facility has been built – sometimes on the same site as the production plant, and sometimes not – specifically to do major development work.

The European market is relatively segmented compared to the US market, however. This means, firstly, that the mass market for European products is considerably smaller than the analogous market in the US. Secondly, it makes it important for the firm to select the most appropriate European country for pre-market testing. Where the European market is heavily segmented, product development may be focused on just one or two of the wealthiest markets, with the remaining ones being treated as purely peripheral. Given their population and living standards, this criterion favours West Germany and France rather than the UK.

West Germany, in particular, represents a large sophisticated market which may well become a natural centre of European product development in certain industries. In motor oils, for example, West German motorists drive sophisticated vehicles harder and longer than other people and are more discriminating in the quality of lubricants used. It is thus in West Germany, rather than in the UK, that researchers can get 'closest to the customer'.

The unification of Germany will further enlarge its domestic market and consequently damage the prospects for attracting product development to the UK. Liberalization of the Eastern European economies in general also gives West Germany a more 'geocentric' position in Europe, and makes the UK more peripheral still.

There is, however, an alternative to focusing product development on just one leading European market. This is to synthesize European market intelligence by pooling information from different national markets. Product development is then carried out close to the European marketing headquarters rather than close to the leading market itself. This strategy is much more favourable to the UK. So long as the UK remains a good centre for the location of European marketing activities, product development may continue to be attracted to the UK.

This approach links the fortunes of R&D in the UK very much to the future of the UK as an international service centre in general. In particular, the continued role of the UK as a transport hub and information centre, linking the US and Japan to the EC, is crucial. Also important is an adequate supply of indigenous business services such as advertising agencies, office automation consultants, and so on. One implication of this is that the training of more specialists in these complementary professions may help rather than hinder the long-term expansion of R&D.

9.5   THE SUPPLY OF SCIENTISTS AND ENGINEERS

The availability of research professionals remains a strong point in the UK's favour, though by no means as strong as it was. Cutbacks in university funding may have encouraged university administrations to promote contract research for industry, but at the same time the amount and quality of doctoral training has declined, due to the academic brain drain and to competing claims on academic time.

A potential weakness of the university system is an élitist bias towards pure research. Spokesmen for British industrialists are certainly prone to complain about a dislike of applied and heavily empirical research, which they claim is imparted at university. No direct evidence for this was found in the present study, although some interviewees gave the impression that managers who shared this belief could be found within their own company.

One of the traditional strengths of the UK educational system is in the training of specialists – in contrast to the US, where a more general training is provided at school and undergraduate level. The early specialization of scientific training in the UK has two distinct consequences – one is that scientists obtain skills which may be difficult to redeploy elsewhere, and the second is that non-scientists lack even a rudimentary knowledge of certain areas of science.

The first means that when research in a particular area goes into decline, scientists may find it difficult to transfer to another area. Instead of being redeployed within the UK they emigrate to carry on with their specialism instead. The enormous internationalization of English as the language of science (and ordinary life) makes it increasingly easy to do this. The second factor means that senior managers in the UK may have much less understanding than their counterparts elsewhere of where the technological potential in their industry lies and how their own R&D department can best exploit it. This may be one of the reasons why so few UK-owned firms occupy leading positions in high-technology industries.

Although excessive specialism has its drawbacks, the wide range of established specialisms available in UK education is undoubtedly one of its strengths. Foreign-owned firms have not been slow to exploit it. In the photographic industry, for example, four major foreign MNEs successfully carry out research in the UK even though there has never been any major UK competition in this field. A somewhat similar story could be told in other high-technology industries. Under these conditions, it is difficult to sustain the argument that foreign firms crowd out UK firms in the scientific labour market. It seems most likely, indeed, that as the major employers, the foreign firms are responsible for maintaining job opportunities in many specialized disciplines.

9.6   CORPORATE CULTURE IN THE UK

The real issue is not crowding out, but why UK firms perform so badly in the high-technology field. This is true not only of their domestic operations but their international operations too. Patent statistics show that the main areas of UK corporate strength are in low-technology industries such as food, drink and tobacco, construction equipment and textiles. They are also successful in services: banking, hotels, retailing and so on.

The strongest UK manufacturing industries are, in any case, industries in which patent origination is highly dispersed, so that the UK has done no more than maintain its position among the leading countries. In industries where the pattern of patent origination has shown greatest mobility in recent years – such as industrial engines, motor vehicles and nuclear power – the strongest UK firms of twenty years ago have invariably lost out. In industrial engines and motor vehicles they have lost out to Japan. This is, perhaps, excusable, on the grounds that others too have lost out – such as West Germany, which has even lost out to Japan in other key sectors such as office equipment. In nuclear power, however, the UK has lost out to France and Germany as well as Japan.

Even in low-technology industries there is a question mark

about the overall efficiency of research. Although UK firms are highly internationalized in their research, this does not seem to imply any great degree of sophistication. It certainly cannot be claimed, on the basis of UK experience, that the globalization of R&D is *ipso facto* a successful strategy that can be recommended to other firms. The high degree of UK internationalization is not the result of any special plans that will weaken the UK research base, either. Rather, it seems to be a consequence of the nature of the industries in which UK MNEs operate. Food, drink and tobacco, for example, requires considerable adaptive R&D to match technology and products to quality of local inputs and to local consumer tastes, and this is best carried out on the spot in an overseas laboratory.

This heavy involvement in adaptive R&D may also explain why UK firms have been relatively slow to network their international laboratories. UK firms are more disposed than most to maintain the traditional distinction between the headquarters and the subsidiary laboratories. Networking, by contrast, is most often found in high-technology industries where the basic research, once done only by the parent laboratory, has been decentralized. It is this kind of decentralization that partly accounts for the presence of so many foreign-owned laboratories in the UK. Thus laboratories based in the UK are often networked – reducing the hierarchical dominance of the parent – even though UK laboratories overseas are not.

Further evidence on UK backwardness is that UK-owned firms report higher turnover rates among their scientific personnel, which is usually taken as an indication of poor management. One reason for this, suggested by the interviews, is the limited career prospects for scientists in UK firms. Table 9.1 shows that UK firms paid less than their foreign rivals within the UK in 1981 (the last date for which directly comparable data are available).

Part of the explanation may be a cultural one. Some of the laboratory managers we interviewed felt that the board regarded science as a vocation, and expected the scientists who were employed to be biased towards pure research. The attitude was that people who were interested in pay would instead choose management as a career, or at any rate join the firm as a scientist

Table 9.1 Average wages and salaries of R&D employees in UK manufacturing industry, 1981

Industry	Foreign firms £	All firms £
All products	10,115	8,429
Chemicals	9,956	9,942
Mechanical engineering	9,389	8,195
Electrical engineering (including electronics)	10,539	7,023
Vehicles (including aerospace)	9,218	9,220
Other products	11,228	9,083

Source: Pearce (1987), table 8, derived from *Business Monitor M014*, 1981, table 16.

and convert from the laboratory bench to the management ladder later on.

There is independent evidence (CEST, 1990) to suggest that UK employers believe that UK scientists are underpaid by European (let alone US) standards and expect to have to raise salaries after 1992, to combat greater mobility. But apparently, while they complain about skill shortages, they are not prepared to raise salaries in the short run.

Cultural attitudes may be of wider significance than scientific pay.

The status of engineers is also an important issue. A study of engineering and management in West German firms found not only that engineering graduates enjoy relatively higher status than in the UK (Hutton and Lawrence, 1981; Lawrence, 1980) but are also more pervasive in senior management positions. Line managers in Germany typically have more specialized engineering expertise than their UK counterparts, and hence have less need to rely on 'backroom specialists' for advice. When experts are employed in specialist roles – notably in industrial design – their influence is much wider than in Britain because the managers they report to share their professional allegiance and esteem their expertise.

Two major waves of German scientific emigration – before

each of the two world wars – transmitted some of these cultural values to the US. It is not surprising, therefore, that a comparison of interview experiences in UK- and US-owned laboratories suggests that in US firms technology is much more a part of the general business culture. R&D is sometimes little more than a specialized functional area in UK firms, while it serves as the recruitment base for top management in some of their US rivals. This suggests, in turn, that UK firms may suffer from a social division between arts and science specialists, in which the former dominate general management and the latter R&D. While this can only be conjecture, it is certainly consistent with the main results reported in this book (see also Hutton and Lawrence, 1981; Lawrence 1980). It suggests that UK firms in marketing-oriented industries and in the service sector may be more successful because there is greater cultural homogeneity within the management team, centred on an arts-based education. Conversely, US, Japanese and German firms may be more successful in high-technology industries because in these firms the technological culture pervades almost the whole of the management.

9.7 AGGLOMERATION AND STRATEGIC FISCAL POLICIES

During the 1970s and early 1980s there was a modest tendency for R&D to agglomerate in major centres. In some cases this was the result of established centres consolidating their strength, but in others it was caused by the emergence of Japan as a technological power. Agglomeration in several industries increased because Japan opened up a more significant gap between itself and other non-US rivals than had previously existed between these rivals and Japan. The UK was the country that suffered most from this. It can hardly be deemed accidental, since R&D spending in the UK fell well behind the trend growth path for OECD countries over this period.

The tendency for R&D to agglomerate can be explained by the existence of critical mass. Because R&D requires complementary expertise from many specialist sources, and much of this expertise must be delivered tacitly, as face-to-face advice, it is advantageous to have a large and varied pool of specialists in a particular location. Critical mass also helps to provide a wider choice of jobs for any given specialist, and so provides income security. Critical mass may also improve competitive conditions in the labour market, helping to prevent the salaries of scientists and engineers from being held down by tacit collusion between employers committed to maintaining traditional differentials. Because of the high degree of specialization in UK scientific training, and the cultural importance of traditional differentials, the critical mass required for efficient R&D may be particularly high in the UK. This means that the UK economy could be particularly vulnerable to a marginal reduction in the level of scientific activity.

Critical mass is associated with an economy of scale. Strategic trade theorists (Brander, 1986; Helpman and Krugman, 1989) have argued that when economies of scale are present it may be advantageous for a nation to subsidize local activities. By lowering the marginal cost of local operations the subsidy raises the level of domestic activity and thus induces, through oligopolistic reaction, a compensating reduction in activity by unsubsidized rivals elsewhere. If the effect on rivals is large then their loss of scale economies may be so great that they are put out of business altogether.

It is alleged – particularly in the US – that strategies of this kind have been used by Japan against the West in selected industries where there are manufacturing economies of scale – semiconductors, motor vehicles, and so on. The Japanese response is that their competitiveness in manufacturing stems from a genuine productivity advantage and that no subsidies are involved. By and large, the West's response has been to accept this argument, but with the qualification that because many Western exports are effectively excluded from Japanese markets, Western firms are denied the scale economies available to Japanese exporters. It is then argued that while subsidies may not be warranted, protection of the domestic market is.

A similar line of argument in favour of subsidies can be applied to R&D. The subsidization of R&D employment at one location may not only benefit R&D at that location through domestic substitution in the labour market, but also attract researchers from other locations. The loss of employment elsewhere will raise the costs of R&D at these locations and so generate a virtuous circle so far as the subsidized location is concerned.

Indeed, even in the absence of foreign reactions, subsidization of R&D will be beneficial so long as domestic scale economies are available. At any rate, this is true in theory. For with scale economies, competitive markets will normally lead to under-investment, and a subsidy can serve to compensate for this. If the subsidy can be financed through lump-sum taxation then it is unambiguously beneficial: it fine-tunes the incentive to employ researchers without distorting incentives elsewhere in the economy. Even in the absence of non-distortionary lump-sum taxation the subsidy may still be beneficial, though the requirements are more stringent in this case.

The objection to such a strategy is two-fold. First, the benefit to any given nation of pursuing this strategy when others do not considerably exceeds the benefit to the world as a whole. If other nations also pursue a subsidy strategy then the additional benefits to the subsidizing location due to the international redistribution of research activity will be lost. Subsidy-matching by rival governments can be anticipated in the long run, since they are likely to learn from their mistake and imitate the successful policy. Of course, in some cases they may be too late – having lost critical mass there may be substantial costs involved in regaining it. But, overall, the probability that at least some rivals will match the strategy qualifies the case for using subsidies as an offensive strategy.

The second objection is practical. It is difficult to define R&D precisely, and so subsidies directed at R&D are likely to spill over onto other non-innovative activities. The fact that the UK government already manipulates its interpretation of R&D for strategic reasons suggests that corporate accountants are likely to use just as much creativity in their own interpretation if subsidies are offered on R&D. This is part of a wider problem of the incentive for manipulation associated with all selective fiscal schemes. Once selective subsidies are given, it encourages the beneficiaries to lobby for more. The beneficiaries may even organize themselves into a group and employ public relations experts to put a misleading case for still higher subsidies. In the context of Western democracies, where lobbying is an established feature of political life, this is a powerful argument for avoiding selective subsidies even though, if administered fairly, they would prove effective.

9.8 GOVERNMENT SUPPORT FOR BASIC RESEARCH

One of the key questions in technology policy is 'Who should fund basic R&D?' Economic theorists tend to argue that the state should fund basic R&D. This is because the knowledge generated by basic R&D has 'public good' properties which make it difficult to exclude potential users from access, and hence make it impractical to charge for use. The output of basic R&D is, moreover, both heterogeneous and versatile, so that the administration of user charges through, say, a licensing system, would be extremely complex. Finally, since the results of different types of basic R&D are often synthesized in applications, it is often difficult to attribute applications to specific basic research projects.

There are two main problems with this policy stance, however. The first is that it exaggerates the difficulty of exclusion. In certain cases potential users may be able to form a club to exclude others. The club members can then fund the basic R&D and share the results. It is important, however, that the members either have non-competing applications in mind, or that they collude over competing applications in order that potential rents are not dissipated.

The second difficulty arises because knowledge is truly international. When the state funds basic R&D it cannot necessarily exclude other states from benefiting too. The problem of benefits accruing to other states is exacerbated by the globalization of corporate R&D, as described in this book. It is no longer possible (if it ever was) for basic research funded by the UK government, for example, to be exploited commercially only by UK-owned firms operating only in the UK. Foreign firms with UK laboratories are quite likely to exploit the results instead, so that the profits ultimately accrue overseas. Even if UK-owned firms exploit the basic research results, they may do so at an overseas facility.

In the light of this, the state funding of basic R&D really needs to be carried out on a supranational basis. Ideally, the funding should be global, with each state contributing in proportion to its benefits and everyone having the right of access. In practice collaboration is organized on a more restrictive basis – the European Community, for example, has developed a number of collaborative research programmes which are designed to benefit European companies in their competition with the US and Japan.

In the 1950s and 1960s the case for state funding of basic research was widely accepted, particularly in countries such as the US, France and UK, where research was 'mission-oriented'. However, the relatively disappointing commercial spin-offs from mission-oriented research into space exploration and nuclear energy, together with the growing 'fiscal crisis' of rising state expenditure financed from a relatively narrow tax base, has led to a reduction of state funding in the 1970s and 1980s. The amount of basic research carried on defence budgets has been reduced as well.

The 'diffusion-oriented' technology policies of West Germany and Switzerland – with their emphasis on state-private partnerships in technical education, product standardization and university-industry research links – appear to have performed better than the mission-oriented ones. These policies are increasingly imitated by countries who are abandoning the mission-oriented approach.

Nevertheless, many Western firms appear to believe that they cannot even afford to participate in collaborative programmes of basic research, because the short-term pressure from the stock market to maximize the value of the firm means that they must distribute dividends rather than retain them for apparently nebulous purposes. For example, managers of some UK firms alleged that German and Japanese firms could afford to invest more heavily in long-term research programmes because their owners were less preoccupied with short-term gains.

If this is correct then it seems that, in the UK at least, no one really wants to fund basic research any more. There is increasing emphasis on acquiring basic research results from wealthier countries, whose governments have sufficient tax revenue to subsidize R&D, and whose shareholders have longer-term horizons. Whereas in the past Japanese firms successfully imitated and adapted Western technologies, so now UK firms are encouraged to copy US and Japanese technology. The emphasis is no longer on fundamental discoveries, but on the commercial exploitation of customer-oriented innovations of a more incremental nature.

The danger with this strategy is that US and Japanese governments *will* find a way of excluding 'foreign' firms from the benefits of their basic research – for example, through increasingly strict policies on international technology licensing and prohibitions on the export of sophisticated producer goods. The fact that in Japan much basic research is carried out within the corporate sector, rather than within the universities, makes the exclusion of foreign uses much easier anyway, compared to the UK where universities do much of the basic research. If exclusion is effective, then UK firms will fall further behind in their command of new industrial technologies. This risk is even greater if UK firms decide not to 'buy in' to European collaborative research projects either.

9.9   ATTRACTING FOREIGN LABORATORIES

The weakness of UK firms in R&D means that R&D activity tends to be highly concentrated on just a few UK firms that are world class. Even when the UK activities of foreign firms are included, UK R&D is highly concentrated at the firm level. Table 9.2 shows that the top five R&D spenders account for 32 per cent of corporate expenditure and 29 per cent of employment in R&D.

One of the most successful UK industries in attracting foreign R&D is the pharmaceutical industry. This is a high-technology industry *par excellence*, and also another case – like photographic equipment, but not so extreme – where foreign firms have prospered even though indigenous firms are relatively weak. There are successful UK firms in the industry, of course – Glaxo,

Table 9.2   Concentration of R&D activity in UK
by size of firm, 1985

| Size group | Percentage of total | |
	Self-financed expenditure	Employment
Top 5	32	29
Top 10	48	43
Top 15	57	50
Top 20	64	60
Top 50	80	75
Top 100	89	84
All	100	100

Source: UK Department of Trade and Industry (1988),
table 8.

ICI, Wellcome, for example – but in terms of patenting foreign
firms still dominate. More generally, the pharmaceutical industry
is one in which research expertise is fairly well diversified world
wide, and although the UK has improved its relative position as
a research base it is by no means dominant in global terms.

Viewed from this perspective, it is disappointing that recent
policy changes by the UK government appear to have undermined
the confidence of some of the foreign-owned firms in the UK.
Restrictions on drug prescription within the National Health
Service, and the associated reduction in standards of hospital
care, mean that UK medicine is no longer, on the whole, state of
the art. Moreover, the UK's role as a research base depends a
great deal on the international reputation of certain centres of
academic excellence in biochemistry and medicine, notably in
Cambridge and London, and it is claimed by some of these institutions that academic work is now impaired by financial exi-
gencies.

Clearly the financing of health care and education raise wider
issues than the attraction of foreign R&D. Nevertheless, their
importance in this context demonstrates the more general point

that there are few aspects of government policy that are not relevant to R&D.

It was suggested above that the UK's underlying comparative advantage is in basic research rather than, say, global product development. In this case policy should be directed towards enhancing those natural advantages which relate to basic research. It must be accepted that successful basic research may lead to the later stages of product development being switched to the US. Development work for the European market may, however, be retained in the UK – especially when the European marketing headquarters is already based there.

One of the key features of basic research is that specialists as well as generalists are required (Webster, 1990). Reform of education in Britain has plenty of scope to expand the supply of generalists through wider access without diverting resources away from established specialisms. R&D depends increasingly on highly-qualified people (see table 9.3) and so cutbacks in specialist training, particularly at doctoral level, need to be reversed as quickly as possible.

Basic research in an overseas subsidiary requires regular interaction with personnel from the parent and from other overseas laboratories in the network. It is not unusual for over 20 per cent of employees in an overseas basic research facility to be foreign nationals. A streamlined procedure for handling work permits

Table 9.3 Occupational mixture of UK R&D employment, 1975–1985

	1975		1985	
Occupation	*Number (000s)*	*Percentage*	*Number (000s)*	*Percentage*
Scientists and engineers	62	34	81	47
Technicians, laboratory assistants and draughtsmen	61	34	50	29
Administrative, clerical, industrial and other staff	58	32	42	24
Total	181	100	173	100

Source: UK Department of Trade and Industry (1988), table 12.

quickly is a great advantage here. One of the potential dangers of the 'Fortress Europe' mentality is that because of greater mobility within Europe, the European Community may become increasingly strict over procedures to admit people into Europe in the first place.

It is not only the secondment of employees that is important in basic research, but short visits too. A good infrastructure of communications is essential. This is evident from the way that major laboratories in the UK have agglomerated in two main areas – the South East, with access to London's Heathrow and Gatwick airports, and the North West, with access to Manchester's Ringway airport. Table 9.4 shows, moreover, that compared to UK firms, foreign firms tend to avoid the Midlands and South West and so are even more highly concentrated than the UK firms. This suggests that the up-grading of provincial airports to handle more scheduled international flights – for example, at Glasgow and Newcastle – might assist the decentralization of R&D.

Table 9.4 Regional distribution of principal corporate R&D laboratories in UK, 1989

Region	UK-owned	Foreign-owned
South-east England	28	36
East Anglia	2	3
Midlands	9	2
North-east England	5	4
North-west England	5	5
South-west England	5	3
Wales, Scotland, Ireland	1	2
Total	55	55

Note: The regions are defined as follows (counties having no R&D facility are not listed); *South-east England* – Bedfordshire, Buckinghamshire, Essex, Hampshire, Kent, Middlesex, Northamptonshire, Oxfordshire, Surrey, Sussex, Greater London; *East Anglia* – Cambridgeshire, Huntingdonshire, Suffolk; *Midlands* – Derbyshire, Leicestershire, Lincolnshire, West Midlands, Staffordshire, Worcestershire; *North-east England* – Humberside, Yorkshire, Tyne and Wear; *North-west England* – Cheshire, Lancashire, Merseyside, Greater Manchester; *South-west England* – Avon, Glocestershire, Somerset, Wiltshire.

Another advantage of the South East is that it provides a market of considerable depth for scientists and engineers. Not only are labour markets thinner elsewhere, but the regional disparities in house price inflation have, until recently, been a major factor discouraging scientists from moving North. It seems that it is not so much a lower quality of life that people fear, but the difficulty of re-entering the South East housing market later, should career progression dictate a move back.

More recently, house prices have begun to rise in parts of the North as well. While solving one problem it has tended to raise another – namely the general level of scientific pay in relation to local housing costs. This is an issue on which the government's efforts to reduce the overall level of income taxation have been helpful, although the limitation of mortgage tax relief, and the high-interest rate macroeconomic policy have tended to exacerbate the problem.

One factor encouraging regional decentralization in the UK is the increasing problems of traffic congestion and very high housing densities in the South East. The lack of any clear strategy for improving the transport infrastructure in Greater London is reducing the attractiveness of the South East generally as a location for R&D. Capitals such as Paris (and perhaps Berlin) are seeking to strengthen their competitiveness as international service centres, and so have the potential to divert R&D activity away from the UK altogether. The English language is no longer a UK monopoly, even within Europe, and neither is a reputation for integrity, confidentiality and political stability. It seems likely, therefore, that the UK government needs to take a range of interrelated measures if it is to maintain the competitiveness of the UK as a location for R&D.

9.10   A POLICY AGENDA

The advocacy of policy cannot be based on facts alone: an analytical framework is needed to interpret the facts and, more importantly still, some basic moral judgements must be made about the kind of world (or at least the kind of country) in which we wish to live. Accepting, though, that all policy advice is value laden, it can be said that the evidence presented in the book points clearly to the danger of a deterioration of the R&D potential of the UK economy unless certain aspects of government policy are reversed.

If it is true that the strengths of the UK economy lie in training specialists to undertake basic research then the current emphasis on more breadth and less depth in education may be partly misplaced. Sufficient breadth to ensure that all school-leavers achieve a reasonable understanding of science may be commended, but without endorsing the view that fewer scientific specialists should be trained as a result.

Moreover, if these scientists are to concentrate on basic research then a clear allocation of responsibilities for funding basic research needs to be established. At the moment no one appears willing to take responsibility, and the government is using this as a pretext for passively tolerating an erosion of the 'science base'.

A major step towards the resolution of this difficulty would be for the UK government to take a more active role in promoting European-wide collaborative R&D programmes – and perhaps seek to extend these programmes to embrace full-scale international collaboration too. If full-scale international collaborative projects were to be developed, there would be a strong case for locating some of the activities in the UK, because of the UK's position as a transport and communications hub. A simple way of financing UK contributions to collaborative research would be to provide tax credits to participating firms, and to fund academic participation through grants awarded on the basis of peer-group review.

The role of the UK as a transport hub leads to a further point. The UK government is currently failing to invest in the infrastructure improvements which appear to be necessary to maintain and enhance this role. In particular, delays over the Channel tunnel rail link, poor coordination of regional and international airports with respect to trunk and feeder routes (allied to inadequate investment in air traffic control) and the failure to invest in urban rapid transit systems to alleviate road congestion (especially in the South East) are all symptoms of this problem. As with basic research, disagreement and confusion over who is responsible for funding such investments appear to be impeding progress. Ideological differences over funding should not be allowed to delay projects which are essential to maintaining the long-run viability of the UK as a location for R&D.

References

Acs, Z.J. and Audretsch, D.B. 1989: Patents as a measure of innovative activity. *Wissenschaftszentrum Berlin für Sozialforschung Discussion Paper*, FS IV 89–5.

Ahlström, G. 1982: *Engineers and Industrial Growth: Higher Technical Education and the Engineering Profession during the Nineteenth and Early Twentieth Centuries: France, Germany, Sweden and England*. London: Croom Helm.

Archibugi, D. and Pianta, M. 1989: *The Technological Specialization of Advanced Countries*. Report to the Commission of the European Communities, Technical Report of the National Research Council, Rome.

Arrow, K.J. 1962: Economic Welfare and the Allocation of Resources for Invention. In R.R. Nelson (ed.) *The Rate and Direction of Inventive Activity: Economic and Social Factors*. Princeton, N.J.: Princeton University Press for National Bureau of Economic Research, 609–26.

Arthur, W.B. 1989: Competing technologies, increasing returns, and lock in by historical events. *Economic Journal*, 99, 116–31.

Bacon, R.W. and Eltis, W.A. 1976: *Britain's Economic Problem*. London: Macmillan.

Bairoch, P. 1988: *Cities and Economic Development*. Chicago: University of Chicago Press.

Balassa, B. 1965: Trade Liberalization and 'Revealed' Comparative Advantage. *Manchester School of Economic and Social Studies*, 33, 99–123.

Bank of Japan Research and Statistics Department, *Corporate Management under an Expanding Economy*. Special Paper No. 184, January 1990, table 16.

Bartlett, C.A. and Ghoshal, S. 1990: Managing Innovation in the Transnational Corporation. In C.A. Bartlett, Y. Doz and G. Hedlund (eds) *Managing the Global Firm*. London: Routledge, 215–55.

Baumol, W.J. and McLennan, K. (eds) 1985: *Productivity Growth and US Competitiveness*. New York: Oxford University Press.

Behrman, J.N. and Fischer, W.A. 1980: *Overseas R&D Activities of Transnational Companies*. Cambridge, Mass.: Oelgeschlager, Gunn and Hain.

Bowker 1987: *Directory of American Research and Technology 1988*, 22nd edn. New York: R.R. Bowker.

Brander, J.A. 1986: Rationales for Strategic Trade and Industrial Policy. In P.R. Krugman (ed.) *Strategic Trade Policy and the New International Economics*. Cambridge, Mass.: MIT Press, 23–46.

Brooke, M.Z. 1984: *Centralization and Autonomy: A Study in Organization Behaviour*. London: Holt, Rinehart and Winston.

Buckley, P.J. and Casson, M.C. 1976: *The Future of the Multinational Enterprise*. London: Macmillan.

Buckley, P.J. and Casson, M.C. 1985: *Economic Theory of the Multinational Enterprise: Selected Papers*. London: Macmillan.

Buckley, P.J. and Casson, M.C. 1988: A Theory of Cooperation in International Business. In F.J. Contractor and P. Lorange (eds) *Cooperative Strategies in International Business*. Lexington, Mass.: Lexington Books, 31–53.

Buckley, P.J., Pass, C.L. and Prescott, K. 1988: Measures of International Competitiveness: A Critical Survey. *Journal of Marketing Management*, 4, 175–200.

Bud, R.F. and Roberts, G.K. 1984: *Science versus Practice: Chemistry in Victorian Britain*. Manchester: Manchester University Press.

Cantwell, J.A. 1987a: Technological Advantage as a Determinant of the International Economic Activity of Firms. *University of Reading Discussion Papers in International Investment and Business Studies*, No. 105.

Cantwell, J.A. 1987b: The reorganisation of European industries after integration: selected evidence on the role of multinational enterprise activities. *Journal of Common Market Studies*, 26, 127–51.

Cantwell, J.A. 1989: *Technological Innovation and Multinational Corporations*. Oxford: Basil Blackwell.

Cantwell, J.A. 1990a: Trends in international patterns of technological innovation, 1890–1914 and 1963–86. In J. Foreman-Peck (ed.) *New Perspectives on the Late Victorian Economy: Quantitative Essays on British Economic History*. Cambridge: Cambridge University Press.

Cantwell, J.A. 1990b: The effects of integration of the structure of transnational corporation activity in the EC. In J.H. Dunning (ed.) *The Implications of the Completion of the Single Internal Market of the EC for Transnational Corporation Activity*. New York: United Nations.

Cantwell, J.A. and Sanna Randaccio, F. 1990: Catching up amongst the world's largest multinationals. *Economic Notes*, 19, 1–23.

Casson, M.C. 1990: *Enterprise and Competitiveness: A Systems View of International Business*. Oxford: Clarendon Press.

Casson, M.C. 1991: *Economics of Business Culture: Game Theory, Transaction Costs and Economic Performance*. Oxford: Clarendon Press.

Casson, M.C. and Jones, G.G. 1989: The Development of International Service

Centres: Economic, Geographical and Cultural Interactions. Paper presented to the ESRC Development Economics Studies Group Annual Conference, Leicester, July.

CEST 1990: *Attitudes to the Exploitation of Science and Technology: Final Report.* Manchester: Centre for Exploitation of Science and Technology.

Chandler, A.D., Jr. 1977: *The Visible Hand: The Managerial Revolution in American Business.* Cambridge, Mass: Belknap Press of Harvard University Press.

Chesnais, F. 1986: Science, Technology and Competitiveness. *STI Review No. 1*, Paris: OECD, 85–129.

Chesnais, F. 1988: Technical Cooperation Agreements between Firms. *STI Review No. 4*, Paris: OECD, 51–119.

Chesnais, F. 1990: The Network Firm. Paris: OECD, *mimeo*.

Cohen, J.M. 1956: *The Life of Ludwig Mond.* London: Methuen.

Contractor, F.J. and Lorange, P. (eds) 1988: *Cooperative Strategies in International Business.* Lexington, Mass.: Lexington Books.

Creedy, J. 1975: *Careers in Chemistry: Report of a New Survey.* London: Royal Institute of Chemistry.

Dertouzos, M.L., Lester, R.K. and Solow, R.M. 1989: *Made in America: Regaining the Productive Edge.* Cambridge, Mass.: MIT Press.

Divall, C. 1990a: A Measure of Agreement: Employers and Engineering Studies in the Universities of England and Wales, 1897–1939. *Social Studies of Science*, 20, 65–112.

Divall, C. 1990b: Engineer or Scientist? Educating Engineers in Britain's Universities 1945–80. Paper presented to the Science Museum/EASST/SPSG Conference on Policies and Publics for Science and Technology, London.

Dosi, G. 1989: Institutions and markets in a dynamic world. *Manchester School of Economic and Social Studies*, 56, 119–46.

Dunning, J.H. 1977: Trade, Location of Economic Activity and the Multinational Enterprise: A Search for an Eclectic Approach. In B. Ohlin, P.O. Hesselborn and P.M. Wykman (ed.) *The International Allocation of Economic Activity.* London: Macmillan.

Dunning, J.H. 1988: *Explaining International Production.* London: Unwin Hyman.

Dunning, J.H. and Pearce, R.D. 1985: *The World's Largest Industrial Enterprises, 1962–1983.* Farnborough: Gower.

Edgerton, D.E.H. 1988: Industrial Research in the British Photographic Industry, 1879–1939. In J. Liebenau (ed.), *The Challenge of New Technology: Innovation in British Business since 1850*, Aldershot: Gower, 106–34.

Ergas, H. 1987: Does Technology Policy Matter? In B.R. Guile and H. Brooks (eds) *Technology and Global Industry: Companies and Nations in the World Economy.* Washington, D.C.: National Academy Press, 191–245.

Evan, W.M. and Olk, P. 1990: R&D Consortia: A New US Organizational Form. *Sloan Management Review*, 31(3), 37–46.

Export–Import Bank of Japan 1990: Global Management and Overseas Direct Investment. *Research Institute of Overseas Investment Monthly Bulletin*, January.

Fagerberg, J. 1987: A Technology Gap approach to why growth rates differ. *Research Policy*, 16, 87–99.

Fagerberg, J. 1988: International Competitiveness. *Economic Journal*, 98, 355–74.

Falvey, R.E. 1981: Commercial Policy and Intra-industry Trade. *Journal of International Economics*, 11, 495–512.

Fieldhouse, D.K. 1978: *Unilever Overseas: The Anatomy of a Multinational 1895–1965*. London: Croom Helm.

Findlay, R. and Kierzkowski, H. 1983: International Trade and Human Capital: A Simple General Equilibrium Model. *Journal of Political Economy*, 91.

Fröhlich, H-P. 1989: International Competitiveness: Alternative Macroeconomic Strategies and Changing Perceptions in Recent Years. In A. Francis and P.K.M. Tharakan (eds) *The Competitiveness of European Industry*, London: Routledge, 21–40.

Gomes-Mejia, L.R. and Lawless, M.W. (eds) 1988: *Managing the High Technology Firm: Conference Proceedings*. Boulder: University of Colorado.

Griliches, Z., Pakes, A. and Hall, B.H. 1987: The value of patents as indicators of inventive activity. In P. Dasgupta, and P. Stoneman (eds) *Economic Policy and Technological Performance*. Cambridge: Cambridge University Press, 97–124.

Håkanson, L. 1990: International Decentralisation of R&D – the Organizational Challenges. In C.A. Bartlett, Y. Doz and G. Hedlund (eds) *Managing the Global Firm*. London: Routledge, 256–78.

Hannah, L. 1989: Anti-business Culture and the Changing Business Environment. *Warwick Economic Research Papers*, No. 341.

Hart, P.E. 1990: Skill Shortages in the UK. *National Institute of Economic and Social Research Discussion Paper*. No. 169.

Helpman, E. and Krugman, P.R. 1989: *Trade Policy and Market Structure*. Cambridge, Mass.: MIT Press.

Hewitt, G. 1980: Research and Development performed Abroad by US Manufacturing Multinationals. *Kyklos*, 33, 308–26.

Hewitt, G. 1983: Research Development performed in Canada by American Manufacturing Multinationals. In A.M. Rugman (ed.) *Multinationals and Technological Transfer – the Canadian Experience*, New York: Prager, 36–41.

Hirschey, R.C. and Caves, R.E. 1981: Internationalisation of Research and Transfer of Technology by Multinational Enterprises. *Oxford Bulletin of Economics and Statistics*, 42(2), 115–30.

Hounshell, D.A. and Smith, J.K. Jr., 1988: *Science and Corporate Strategy; Du Pont R&D, 1902–1980*. Cambridge: Cambridge University Press.

House of Lords 1985: *Report of the Select Committee on Overseas Trade* (Aldington Report). London: HMSO.

Hutton, S. and Lawrence, P. 1981: *German Engineers: The Anatomy of a Profession*. Oxford: Clarendon Press.

James, F.A.J.L. (ed.) 1989: *The Development of the Laboratory: Essays on the Place of Experiment in Industrial Civilization*. London: Macmillan.

Kaldor, M., Sharp, M. and Walker, W. 1986: Industrial Competitiveness and Britain's Defence. *Lloyds Bank Review*, October 31–49.

Kaku, S. 1980: The Development and Structure of the German Coal-Tar Dyestuffs Firms. In A. Okochi and H. Uchida (eds) *Development and Diffusion of Technology: Electrical and Chemical Industries*. Tokyo: University of Tokyo Press, 77–94.

Kennedy, G. 1989: Defence R&D: Not Guilty. *mimeo*, Heriot-Watt University, Edinburgh.

Khalil, T.M. and Bayraktar, B.A. 1990: *Management of Technology II: The Key to Global Competitiveness*. Proceedings of the Second International Conference on Management of Technology, Miami, Florida, Norcross, Georgia: Industrial Engineering and Management Press.

Lawrence, P. 1980: *Managers and Management in West Germany*. London: Croom Helm.

Lawrence, R.Z. 1984: *Can America Compete?* Washington, D.C: Brookings Institute.

Lazonick, W. 1986: Strategy, Structure, and Management Development in the United States and Britain. In K. Kobayashi and H. Morikawa (eds) *Development of Managerial Enterprise*, Tokyo: University of Tokyo Press, 101–46.

Liebenau, J. 1987: *Medical Science and Medical Industry: The Formation of the American Pharmaceutical Industry*: London: Macmillan.

Liebenau, J. 1988: Corporate Structure and Research and Development. In J. Liebenau (ed.) *The Challenge of New Technology: Innovation in British Business since 1850*, Aldershot: Gower, 30–42.

Longman 1987: *Industrial Research in the United Kingdom: A Guide to Organizations and Programmes*, 12th edn. Harlow, Essex: Longman.

Longman 1988a: *European Research Centres: A Directory of Scientific, Technological, Agricultural and Medical Laboratories*, 7th edn. Harlow, Essex: Longman.

Longman 1988b: *Pacific Research Centres: A Directory of Organizations in Science, Technology, Agriculture and Medicine.*, 2nd edn. Harlow, Essex: Longman.

Loveridge, R. 1990: Footfalls of the Future: The Emergence of Strategic Frames and Formulae. In R. Loveridge and M. Pitt (eds) *The Strategic Management of Technological Innovation*. Chichester: John Wiley, 95–124.

Lundvall, B.A. 1988: Innovation as an interactive process: from user-producer interaction to the national system of innovation. In G. Dosi, C. Freeman, R. Nelson, G. Silverberg, and L.L.G. Soete (eds) *Technical Change and Economic Theory*. London: Frances Pinter, 349–369.

Mansfield, E.S. 1988: Industrial R&D in Japan and the United States: A Comparative Study. *American Economic Review*, 78(2), 223–8.

Maxcy, G. and Silberston, Z.A. 1959: *The Motor Industry*. London: Allen and Unwin.

Mowery, D.C. 1986: Industrial Research, 1900–1950. In B. Elbaum and W. Lazonick (eds) *The Decline of the British Economy*, Oxford: Clarendon Press, 189–222.

Neary, J.P. and van Wijnbergen, S. 1986: Natural Resources and the Macroeconomy: A Theoretical Framework. In J.P. Neary and S. van Wijnbergen (eds) *Natural Resources and the Macroeconomy*, Oxford: Blackwell, 1–45.

Neumeyer, F. and Stedman, J.C. 1971: *The Employed Inventor in the United States*. Cambridge, Mass: MIT Press.

OECD 1989: *Science and Technology Indicators, Report No. 3, R&D, Production and Diffusion of Technology*. Paris: OECD.

Parkinson, S.T. 1984: *New Product Development in Engineering: A Comparison of the British and German Machine Tool Industries*. Cambridge: Cambridge University Press.

Patel, P. and Pavitt, K. 1988: Large firms in Western Europe's technological competitiveness. Paper presented at the Prince Bertil Symposium on Corporate and Industrial Strategies for Europe, Stockholm, November.

Patel, P. and Pavitt, K. 1989: Do Large Firms Control the World Technology? *University of Sussex Science Policy Research Unit Discussion Paper*, 66, January.

Pavitt, K. 1987a: International patterns of technological accumulation. In Hood, N. and J.E. Vahlne (eds) *Strategies in Global Competition*. London: Croom Helm.

Pavitt, K. 1987b: Uses and abuses of patent statistics. *University of Sussex Science Policy Research Unit DRC Occasional Paper*, No. 41.

Pearce, R.D. 1986: The internationalisation of research and development by leading enterprises: an empirical study. *University of Reading Discussion Papers in International Investment and Business Studies*, No. 99.

Pearce, R.D. 1987: Host countries and the R&D of multinational: issues and evidence. *University of Reading Discussion Papers in Investment and Business Studies*. no. 101.

Pearce, R.D. 1988: The Determinants of overseas R&D by US MNEs; an analysis of industry level data. *University of Reading Discussion Papers in International Investment and Business Studies*, No. 119.

Pearce, R.D. 1989: *Internationalisation of Research and Development by Multinational Enterprises*. London: Macmillan.

Porter, M.E. 1990: *The Competitive Advantage of Nations*. London: Macmillan.

Reader, W.J. 1975: *Imperial Chemical Industries: A History, Vol. II*. Oxford: Oxford University Press.

Reich, L.S. 1985: *The Making of American Industrial Research: Science and Business at GE and Bell*. Cambridge: Cambridge University Press.

Robson, M. 1988: The British Pharmaceutical Industry and the First World

War. In J. Leibenau (ed.) *The Challenge of New Technology: Innovation in British Business since 1850*, Aldershot: Gower, 83–105.

Roderick, R.W. and Stephens, M.D. 1972: *Scientific and Technical Education in Nineteenth-Century England*. Newton Abbot: David and Charles.

Ronstadt, R.C. 1977: *Research and Development Abroad by US Multinationals*. New York: Praeger.

Rosenberg, N. 1982: *Inside the Black Box: Technology and Economics*. Cambridge: Cambridge University Press.

Rosenberg, N. and Steinmueller W.E. 1988: Why are Americans such Poor Imitators? *American Economic Review*, 78(2), 229–34.

Rugman, A.M. 1987: The Firm-specific Advantages of Canadian Multinationals. *Journal of International Economic Studies*, 2, 1–14.

Scherer, F.M. 1983: The propensity to patents. *International Journal of Industrial Organisation*, 1, 107–28.

Scott, J.D. 1962: *Vickers: A History*. London: Weidenfeld and Nicolson.

Soete, L.L.G. 1987: The Impact of Technological Innovation on International Trade Patterns. The Evidence Reconsidered. *Research Policy*, 16, No. 1.

Soete, L.L. G. and Wyatt, S.M.E. 1983: The Use of Foreign Patenting as an Internationally Comparable Science and Technology Output Indicator. *Scientometrics*, 5, No. 2.

Sterlacchini, A. 1989: R&D, Innovations and Total Factor Productivity Growth in British Manufacturing. *Applied Economics*, 21, 1549–60.

Stoneman, P. 1989: Overseas Financing for Industrial R&D in the UK. Paper presented to Section F of the British Association for the Advancement of Science, Sheffield, September.

Stopford, J.M. and Baden-Fuller, C. 1988: Regional-Level Competition in a Mature Industry: the Case of European Domestic Appliances. in J.H. Dunning and P. Robson (eds): *Multinationals and the European Community*. Oxford: Blackwell, 71–90.

Trebilcock, C. 1977: *The Vickers Brothers: Armaments and Enterprise 1854–1914*. London: Europa.

Tweedale, G. 1988: Science, Innovation and the 'Rule of Thumb': The Development of British Metallurgy to 1945. In J. Leibenau (ed.) *The Challenge of New Technology: Innovation in British Business since 1850*. Aldershot: Gower, 58–82.

UK Department of Trade and Industry 1988: *Industrial Research and Development Expenditure and Employment*. MO 14, 1985, London: HMSO.

Ulph, D. and Winters, A. 1989: Strategic Manpower Policy and International Trade. Paper presented at the NBER/CPER Conference on Empirical Studies of Strategic Trade Policy, October.

UNIDO 1986: *International Comparative Advantage in Manufacturing: Changing Profiles of Resources and Trade*. Vienna: United Nations Industrial Development Organization.

US Department of Commerce, 1981: *US Direct Investment Abroad: 1977 Benchmark Survey Data*. Washington DC, Bureau of Economic Analysis.

US Department of Commerce 1985: *US Direct Investment Abroad: 1982 Benchmark Survey Data*. Washington, DC: Bureau of Economic Analysis.

US Department of Commerce 1990: *Survey of Current Business 1986*. Washington, DC.

US Tariff Commission, 1973: *Report on the implications of Multinational Firms for World Trade and Investment and for US Trade and Labor*. Washington DC.

Usher, A.P. 1954: *A History of Mechanical Inventions*. Cambridge, Mass.: Harvard University Press.

Vernon, R. 1966: International Investment and International Trade in the Product Cycle. *Quarterly Journal of Economics*, 80, 190–207.

Vernon, R. 1979: The Product Cycle Hypothesis in a New International Environment. *Oxford Bulletin of Economics and Statistics*, 41, 255–67.

von Weiher, S. 1980: The Rise and Development of Electrical Engineering and Industry in Germany in the Nineteenth Century: A Case Study – Siemens & Halske. In A. Okochi and H. Uchida (eds) *Development and Diffusion of Technology: Electrical and Chemical Industries*. Tokyo: University of Tokyo Press, 23–44.

Webster, A.D. 1987: Human Capital Subsidies as a Strategic Trade Policy. *University of Reading Discussion Papers in Economics*, No. 197.

Webster, A.D. 1990: Educational Specialisation as a Source of International Trade and Specialisation in Final Goods. University of Reading, *mimeo*.

Weinberg, A.M. 1967: *Reflections on Big Science*. Oxford: Pergamon Press.

Westney, D.E. 1990: Internal and External Linkages in the MNC: the Case of R&D Subsidiaries in Japan. In C.A. Bartlett, Y. Doz and G. Hedlund (eds) *Managing the Global Firm*. London: Routledge, 279–300.

Wilkins, M. 1974: *The Maturing of Multinational Enterprise*. Cambridge, Mass.: Harvard University Press.

Wilkins, M. 1989: *The History of Foreign Investment in the United States to 1914*. Cambridge, Mass.: Harvard University Press.

Williams, M. 1988: Technical Innovation: Examples from the Scientific Instruments Industry. In J. Liebenau (ed.) *The Challenge of New Technology: Innovation in British Business since 1850*. Aldershot: Gower, 8–29.

Wilson, C. 1954: *The History of Unilever: A Study in Economic Growth and Social Change*. 2 vols. London: Cassell.

Wilson, C. 1968: *Unilever 1945–1965: Challenge and Response in the Post-war Industrial Revolution*. London: Cassell.

Wrigley, J. 1986: Technical Education and Industry in the Nineteenth Century. In B. Elbaum and W. Lazonick (eds) *The Decline of the British Economy*. Oxford: Clarendon Press, 162–88.

Index